Noel Cazenave's book provides a d~~~~~~ful analysis of racial repression in 2~~~ ~~~~~~ ~~~~~~~. The book is well grounded in academic literature and the history of racial violence, but without losing focus on the current era in which media and political leaders, including the president of the United States, contribute to a racist culture that infects our criminal justice system and other institutions. *Killing African Americans* is a must read for anyone interested in understanding how this culture dehumanizes and criminalizes young black males and enables, encourages, and normalizes both vigilante and police violence.

Carter A. Wilson, Ph.D., Professor and Department Head of Political
Science and Public Administration, Northern Michigan University

This is the book so many and I have been looking for in the social sciences for going on three decades! The "right to bear arms" should not entail a license to bully, hunt, and kill black and brown peoples. Yet such has been its practice. *Killing African Americans* brings together data and social theory on police and white vigilante killing of African Americans with breathtaking clarity. Its thesis of violence often being used to push back moments of progress against systems of racial stratification is supported by that undercurrent of counter-hegemonic history—namely, evidence. Read this book! Learn from it! And in so doing, join those fighting to bring intelligence to bear against this social malediction.

Lewis R. Gordon, author of Fear of a Black Consciousness,
and Honorary President of the Global Center for Advanced Studies

Noel Cazenave has done it again! A theoretically and empirically grounded book for this crisis era in white racism's long history. Republican Trumpism has again intensified racial conflict for white racial and political gain. Savaging African American boys and men is as old as slave patrols and Jim Crow lynchings, and as new as today's many police killings and mass incarceration. Violence-buttressed racial control is not temporary, but foundational and systemic in U.S. society. Pressing progressives to truly make "black lives matter," Cazenave concludes with perceptive plans to end police violence and bring fundamental social change.

Joe R. Feagin, Distinguished Professor, Texas A&M University,
and author of How Blacks Built America *and* Racist America

Killing African Americans

Killing African Americans examines the pervasive, disproportionate, and persistent police and vigilante killings of African Americans in the United States as a racial control *mechanism* that sustains the racial control *system* of systemic racism. Noel A. Cazenave's well researched and conceptualized historical sociological study is one of the first books to focus exclusively on those killings and to treat them as political violence. Few issues have received as much conventional and social media attention in the United States over the past few years, or have, for decades now, sparked so many protests and so often strained race relations to near breaking point. Because of both its timely and its enduring relevance, *Killing African Americans* can reach a large audience composed not only of students and scholars, but also of Movement for Black Lives activists, politicians, public policy analysts, concerned police officers and other criminal justice professionals, and anyone else eager to better understand this American nightmare and its solutions from a progressive and informed African American perspective.

Noel A. Cazenave is Professor of Sociology at the University of Connecticut (UConn). He is also on the faculty of the Urban and Community Studies program of UConn's Hartford campus and is a faculty affiliate with UConn's Africana Studies Institute and its American Studies Program. His recent and current work is in the areas of: racism theory, U.S. poverty policy, political sociology, urban sociology, criminal justice, and the sociology of emotions. In addition to numerous journal articles, book chapters, and other publications, Professor Cazenave co-authored *Welfare Racism: Playing the Race Card against America's Poor*, which won five book awards, and has since then published *Impossible Democracy: The Unlikely Success of the War on Poverty Community Action Programs*, *The Urban Racial State: Managing Race Relations in American Cities*, and *Conceptualizing Racism: Breaking the Chains of Racially Accommodative Language*. His current book project is tentatively titled *The Courage to Be Kind*.

New Critical Viewpoints on Society Series
Edited by Joe R. Feagin

For a full list of titles in this series, please visit www.routledge.com/
New-Critical-Viewpoints-on-Society/book-series/NCVS.

Killing African Americans

Police and Vigilante Violence as a Racial Control Mechanism

Noel A. Cazenave
Department of Sociology
The University of Connecticut

Routledge
Taylor & Francis Group
NEW YORK AND LONDON

First published 2018
by Routledge
711 Third Avenue, New York, NY 10017

and by Routledge
2 Park Square, Milton Park, Abingdon, Oxon, OX14 4RN

Routledge is an imprint of the Taylor & Francis Group, an informa business

© 2018 Taylor & Francis

Library of Congress Cataloging-in-Publication Data
Names: Cazenave, Noel A., 1948- author.
Title: Killing African Americans : police and vigilante violence as a racial
control mechanism / Noel A. Cazenave, Department of Sociology, The
University of Connecticut.
Description: New York : Routledge, Taylor & Francis Group, 2018. |
Series: New critical viewpoints on society series | Includes bibliographical
references and index.
Identifiers: LCCN 2017061306| ISBN 9781138549920 (hbk) | ISBN
9781138549937 (pbk) | ISBN 9780429507045 (ebk)
Subjects: LCSH: African Americans--Violence against. | African
Americans--Crimes against. | Violence--United States. |
Homicide--United States. | Police brutality--United States.
Classification: LCC E185.615 .C39 2018 | DDC 305.896/073--dc23
LC record available at https://lccn.loc.gov/2017061306

ISBN: 978-1-138-54992-0 (hbk)
ISBN: 978-1-138-54993-7 (pbk)
ISBN: 978-0-429-50704-5 (ebk)

Typeset in Adobe Caslon Pro
by Sunrise Setting Ltd, Brixham, UK

To Anita
Your love and kindness is an eternal flame
that will forever brighten and warm the hearts of
all who have known you

CONTENTS

PREFACE AND ACKNOWLEDGMENTS

There seems to be a war raging in America, with no end in sight. A war whose outcome may well determine whether many African American children will live to reach adulthood, and the state of American race relations for decades to come. More precisely, at times what is happening looks and feels like a race war that pits the right of African Americans to live with dignity against the right of often angry white policemen and vigilante-minded individuals with guns to kill them with impunity.

My decision to write this book was the result of the convergence of a number of forces that formed a perfect storm from which, despite some resistance, I ultimately realized I had no other escape. In the early spring of 2014, while eating some good Southern cooking and talking with three other racism scholars at Black Eyed Sally's in downtown Hartford, I heard myself saying words that were shocking to my own ears. At that moment, in the wake of a spate of vigilante-style killings (e.g., Trayvon Martin, Renisha McBride, Jordan Davis), I found myself articulating the need to conceptualize what increasingly seemed to be a sense of entitlement by many "whites" to kill "black" youth. That suspicion was further stoked not long afterwards when I read an internet posting about a gun-rights group composed of European American men, who planned to march through a low-income African American neighborhood in Houston, Texas brandishing assault rifles to demonstrate their right to bear such arms whenever and wherever they pleased.

I further crafted the ideas that served as the basis for this book in a talk I gave to a group of mothers in Hartford whose sons had been killed as a result of gun violence. That forum was held in the wake of the killings of Eric Garner, Michael Brown, and Ezell Ford by European American police officers on Staten Island, New York; in Ferguson, Missouri; and in Los Angeles, California, respectively. In my talk, I made the link between racism and poverty and both African American-on-African American gun violence and the usually European American police and vigilante-styled killings of African Americans. I stressed the need for an effective social movement challenge to bring about the systemic change required to better protect our youth from such dangers both within and outside of our communities. I also noted that as I continued to observe the killings by those from outside our communities I became increasingly convinced that they are acts of racial terrorism that the perpetrators see, in their own perverted way, as a form of morality enforcement that serves the same function as lynchings and the Ku Klux Klan during earlier periods of U.S. history, especially in the South. Building on Michelle Alexander's reference to the mass incarceration of African American men as "the new Jim Crow," I surmised, as other African Americans have, that we might best think of such lethal terrorism as the new, 21st-century version of lynchings. Like the old ones, these "new lynchings" send a message that it is so-called "white" people who are in control and that "black" people had better stay in our place and behave as "white" men with guns would have us behave. Finally, I concluded that the underlying premise behind these new lynchings is that we African Americans have no rights, and that "white" men, whether in uniform or not, have the right to kill "black" people as they please.

In time, I came to realize that what was really behind my questions was exhaustion; that old African American feeling of being "tired of being tired." It was the fatigue of having experienced what seemed like daily, often outrageous killings of unarmed people of African descent since the highly publicized killing of Amadou Diallo and the acquittals of the four policemen who shot him. With each new killing, I became increasingly convinced that there could be no act this nation's white power structure would deem so outrageous as to say: "Enough is

enough; there must be systemic change!" Finally, another likely influence, albeit one of which I did not become aware until later, was an
article I wrote some time ago with Margaret A. Zahn on women who
were murdered as they tried to escape often physically abusive relationships. In that study, we found that the men who killed them justified
their actions based on ownership norms which presumed that the penalty for attempting to leave such relationships was death. Because those
men thought and felt that they owned the women with whom they had
been intimately involved, they concluded that they were entitled to do
with them as they pleased if they violated certain rules; and the rights
they claimed included the right to kill. The same ownership and social
control norms seemed to be at work in the police and vigilante killings
of African Americans who were seen as deviating from the path of racial
accommodation.[1]

As I pondered the reasons for the disproportionate and common
killings of African Americans by police officers and vigilante types it
became clear that a lethal mix of racist stereotypes and emotions, hypermasculinity, and entitlement fueled their actions. For example, because
the victims were usually, but not always, boys or men, and the killers
were almost always men, I suspected that what was going on was in part
a highly racialized macho issue, an assertion of white male dominance.
I also realized that, because they are normative, such actions are not
only justified but protected by police and vigilante attitudes and culture.
Moreover, they are condoned by the larger society, not only because they
are deemed to be acceptable, but because they are actually thought to be
good, in that they serve some useful racial control functions.

It also became increasingly evident to me that, ironically, another factor that may be contributing to the police and vigilante-style killings
of African American youth is the progress we African Americans have
made toward securing our full citizen rights. This is consistent with, just
to give one quick example, the fact that in the United States, lynchings of
African Americans increased dramatically after the abolition of slavery.
The progress experienced by today's African American youth because of
the civil rights movement has resulted in their having a much greater
sense of entitlement as citizens than their parents and grandparents.

Most actually expect to be treated as first-class citizens and will accept nothing less. Or, to put it in very crude and racist Jim Crow-era terms, today's African American youth "don't know their place." There is all too often fatal conflict when that right to be treated with dignity collides with the highly racialized and gendered right of European American men with guns to kill when challenged.

The main argument I make in *Killing African Americans* is that the pervasive and disproportionate police and vigilante killings of African Americans exist and persist because, as a violence-centered mechanism of racial control, they serve important economic, social status, and political functions for European Americans. Such killings are justified by suppositions that certain moral codes have been violated by African Americans stereotyped as dangerous black criminals. Those infractions can be as trivial as a teenager having his music turned up too loud or his not reacting quickly and differentially enough to a rude, if not profane, command to clear the area.

In contrast to the stark black-and-white color contrast that epitomizes so much of American race relations, this book's title, *Killing African Americans*, may seem to be a rather understated way of characterizing such racially dramatic events. A title like *Killing Black Folk* or one containing some variation of the well-publicized slogan "Black Lives Matter" would certainly have been more racially colorful, bolder, and arguably more powerful. So why did I choose *Killing African Americans*? I did so because I believe that that subtler phrase has its own unique power—power which, while not as overtly dramatic, is in its own way quite subversive to the racial status quo. The three simple words "Killing African Americans" succinctly capture what I argue many of those killings are actually about. They highlight the fact that, in highly racialized nations like the United States, political violence is often used to contain racialized ethnic and pan-ethnic groups at precisely those moments when they try to break free of racial classification as an inherently inferior color/race. In brief, this book's title, *Killing African Americans*, reflects the basic racial control argument articulated in its subtitle, *Police and Vigilante Violence as a Racial Control Mechanism*. That is, both historically and today, when African Americans aspire to break free of the fetters of racial categorization and oppression by articulating their own positive notions of who they are and what and where they can be, the penalty is, all too often, death.

Although *Killing African Americans* examines a number of factors related to the pervasive, disproportionate, and persistent police and vigilante killings of African Americans, I make no apology for the fact that, as the subtitle suggests, *its main focus is systemic racism.* Here racism is examined directly and explicitly, although certainly not exclusively. As such, *Killing African Americans* is not a study that engages in what I refer to in my *Conceptualizing Racism* book as the conceptual colonialism and conflation of treating racism as if it is ancillary to other factors assumed to be larger and ultimately more important, such as the economic oppression that benefits largely economic elites. As you will see in this book's literature review, other studies have analyzed the treatment of African Americans by the criminal justice system through a class lens, as I do in a chapter of this book dedicated specifically to that task. Such analyses are essential. However, that is not the goal of this study. Instead, here I have chosen to give voice to what I consider to be a valuable and underexamined racism-centered perspective shared by tens of millions of African Americans, which I believe must be heard if we are to seriously address this problem and heal the many racial wounds it causes.[2]

At the same time, I have attempted to bring into my analysis numerous other relevant factors. Indeed, I have incorporated so much in this book that a valid criticism may well be that it tries to do too much and at times loses focus on its main racial control argument, which may not seem capable of fully explaining every police and vigilante killing that it examines. But providing a comprehensive model of the police and vigilante killings of African Americans is not my goal. If it were, then a valid criticism might be: "You are all over the place. What is your core argument?" Trying to keep the optimum balance between incorporating many important factors into a brief book that makes a cogent and simple argument has been my greatest challenge. I fully recognize that no single book on any topic can please all its potential readers and I willingly accept criticism for what it does not do. Hopefully such criticism will encourage others to undertake other work that remains to be done.

This was not the book I had planned to write. I had hoped to cap my career as a sociologist by moving away from misery-centered topics such as poverty, racism, and other forms of social oppression to a happy project like a study of kindness, joy, or some other positive emotion; or perhaps even something as different and awe-evoking as mysticism or awakening experiences. But instead, it was as if this study reached up its wretched hand from the grave to beckon me, once again, to enter a dark and foreboding place. I finally accepted that challenge as I experienced an epiphany that with my previous work on family violence, male gender roles, racism, poverty, African Americans and social protest, and political sociology; my development of the urban racial state-analytical frame-work; and my new interest in the sociology of emotions, I was uniquely prepared to write this book. Indeed, in my two most recently published books I found myself giving numerous case examples of racially charged police and vigilante killings. Another important part of that preparation was my decades of meditation and other spiritual practice, which I felt would allow me to once again descend deeply into what many others might find to be a far too depressing place. When I finally decided to do this study, I celebrated by placing a request to the library for about a dozen books on lynching and vigilantism in United States. At the point, I wasn't sure whether I should be singing "happy days are here again" because I had a new book project about which I cared deeply, or shouting for someone to bring me some Prozac. In any case, here it is.

There is little of who I am or what I do that does not reflect the spirit, essence, and struggles of my hometown, New Orleans. So it was no surprise that some of the earliest sources of encouragement and support for this project came from two long-time friends from that very special place. Thanks to historian Lenus Jack, Jr. for our many stimulating conversations about the historical context and functions of European American killings of African Americans and for a useful bibliography on political violence. Thanks also to my high-school classmate and retired New Orleans Police Department detective Larry Williams for his helpful insights and useful citations on implicit bias and police shootings.

I also appreciate the help I received from Marisol Ramos, UConn's sociology subject specialist librarian, in doing a word search of the *New York Times*. And thanks to my professional colleague and Connecticut friend, Johnny Williams, for his list of resources on the Black Lives Matter movement.

One day during the spring of 2017 I found myself writing a somewhat whimsical Facebook post titled "When Loves Knocks Unexpectedly at Your Door." Those who read it may have been surprised to find that the "love" I was referring to was not what they initially thought. Instead, it was the strong belief in this book project expressed by Routledge's Senior Editor for Sociology, Dean Birkenkamp, and its Series Editor, Joe Feagin. Those two men convinced me that that there would be a receptive audience for *Killing African Americans* at a time when my spirits needed that boost. Their enthusiasm, support, and guidance energized me and made the remaining work to be done a labor of love. Thanks also to the reviewer who provided me with a set of comments that made *Killing African Americans* better and to Routledge senior editorial assistant Tyler Bay and production editor Francesca Hearn, who made my work easier. Last but certainly not least, I wish to express my gratitude to the students in my Topics in Sociology and Human Rights course, who, through their inspiration and comments, helped me to flesh out its ideas.

Notes

1. Noel A. Cazenave and Margaret A. Zahn, "Women, Murder, and Male Domination: Police Reports of Domestic Violence in Chicago and Philadelphia," in Emilio C. Viano, ed., *Intimate Violence: Interdisciplinary Perspectives* (Washington, DC: Hemisphere, 1992), 83–97.
2. Noel A. Cazenave, *Conceptualizing Racism: Breaking the Chains of Racially Accommodative Language* (Lanham, MD: Rowman and Littlefield, 2016), 24.

1

THE POLICE AND VIGILANTE KILLINGS OF AFRICAN AMERICANS IN THE TWENTY-FIRST CENTURY

Around midnight on February 4, 1999, as the world contemplated the coming of a new millennium—one in which America might finally cross the "color line" that W.E.B. DuBois had warned would be its great challenge of the twentieth century—reality raised its ugly head for all to see. Amadou Diallo, a street vendor from Guinea, was shot nineteen times by four plainclothes New York City Police (NYPD) officers who, after mistaking him for a suspected rapist, fired a barrage of forty-one bullets as he stood in front of his apartment door in the Bronx holding a wallet in his hand, which they mistook for a gun. His killers were all "members of the NYPD's cocky Street Crime Unit, whose macho motto was 'We own the night.'" For African Americans in the nation's largest city, on that night and many others, they certainly did.[1]

Killing African Americans: Past, Present, and Future

That appalling slaughter of an unarmed and hardworking young immigrant who was here seeking the American dream, only to end up enveloped in its racial nightmare, shocked not only this nation but much of the world. There was a profound sense that something was fundamentally wrong in the way the police treated dark-skinned people in the United States and that surely things could not now simply return to normal. Unfortunately, that is exactly what happened as a verdict was read that cleared all four police officers of any wrongdoing, and an administrative review by the NYPD concluded that the officers had, in fact, acted consistently with departmental guidelines. Although the City of New York later settled a civil suit with Diallo's family for three million dollars, that criminal trial verdict and the administrative ruling did more than spare those officers any punishment for their reckless actions; they reaffirmed for all to see that American police officers could kill with impunity those they deemed to be "black" and "dangerous." The slaying of Amadou Diallo was but one of many racially charged acts of police violence that decade in the United States' premier city, during the racially intense era of the Rudolph Giuliani administration, against men such as Anthony Baez, Abner Louima, Antoine Reid, and Patrick Dorismond. Such violence was so pervasive and routine, not just in New York City but throughout the United States, that it supported historian Manning Marable's conclusion that "the central civil rights issue of the 1990s was racism within all aspects of the U.S. criminal justice system."[2]

From Outrageous to Routine

Unfortunately, for many African Americans, the public outrage over the killing of Amadou Diallo toward the end of that decade seemed to have been snuffed out by a much more powerful and enduring state-issued license to kill on the part of the police: one which makes little if any distinction between the will, the right, and the need to do so. That incident, and its business-as-usual outcome, confirmed that it was indeed possible that there could be no act of police violence so egregious and morally reprehensible that it would force politicians to reform the criminal justice system they build and maintain. Instead, they seemed to echo the ruling articulated by Supreme Court Chief Justice Roger B. Taney's determination in the 1857 Dred Scott case that African Americans "had no rights which the white man was bound to respect." The resilience of such violence and of such an apparent attitude was evident early into the twenty-first century, just two years later, in Cincinnati, Ohio.[3]

Timothy Thomas (2001): Racial Tensions Explode in Cincinnati

On April 7, 2001, a European American police officer killed an unarmed African American teenager in Cincinnati's impoverished Over-the-Rhine neighborhood as he fled arrest for various minor misdemeanors, like his failure to fasten his seat belt. Timothy Thomas was the fifteenth African American male who was shot to death by a Cincinnati police officer over the six-year period from 1995 to 2001. Most of those men were unarmed, and the problem appeared to be escalating. Indeed, Thomas was just the latest of five African Americans killed by the police since September of the previous year.[4]

That shooting did not go over well with the city's African American residents and their leaders. Peaceful protests were soon overshadowed by violence. During three nights of violent unrest, "dozens of people were injured and more than 800 were arrested before a citywide curfew was imposed" and more than two dozen windows were broken at City Hall—an obvious symbol of white power and aggression. Although, unlike in so many other cases, the officer who killed Thomas—Stephen Roach—was tried, as usual when there *is* a trial, he was acquitted. Long after the violent protests died down, local African American leaders continued their economic boycott against the city—a boycott they vowed not to end until Cincinnati's city government settled lawsuits brought against its police for their use of excessive force in handling the unrest that followed Thomas' killing. The city settled those lawsuits for four and a half million dollars.[5]

Back to the Future: America's Legacy of Police Killings and Racial Unrest

Such violent protests against what many African Americans see as state-sanctioned repression by the police should have come as no surprise. They were merely a repeat of much larger and more destructive racial rebellions such as those in Watts in 1965, in Newark and Detroit in 1967, in Miami in 1980, and in Los Angeles in 1992, as well as an omen of what was to come in places such as Ferguson, Missouri in 2014 and Baltimore the following year. In each case, the violent unrest was sparked by an incident of perceived police misconduct and fueled by a long history of unresolved grievances against the local police. They all fit the finding of the 1968 National Advisory Commission on Civil Disorders report that there was "a widespread belief among Negroes in the existence of police brutality and in a 'double standard' of justice and protection—one for Negroes and one for whites." That document, which came to be known as the Kerner report, included the results of a survey of a sample of the scores of cities that experienced civil unrest, in which African Americans ranked "police practices" first among their grievances. It concluded that as a nation, the United States was splitting into "two societies, one black, one white—separate and unequal." Fast forward to nearly a half-century later, when the author of a highly publicized book on racial inequality in the criminal justice system in the United States has asserted that the appropriate metaphor to describe current race relations in that country is "a colony in a nation," in which European American citizens of the "nation" receive all of the rights and protections of "law" while the African American residents of its occupied racial "colony" receive only the often violent imposition of its racially repressive "order."[6]

In the minds of many African Americans, such fatal police violence is closely related to recent vigilante killings that have sparked similar levels of outrage, and have thus become so central to what has evolved into the Movement for Black Lives. For that reason, I have included in this book, as appropriate, examinations of some of the most highly publicized and outrageous cases of vigilante killings of African Americans. I have, however, decided to keep my primary focus on the police killings, for the following reasons. First, there are many more highly publicized police killings as compared to vigilante killings. Second, it is those police killings that are carried out in the name of the state that are most likely to go unpunished. Finally, because they are state-sanctioned and happen with impunity, it is police killings that most effectively reinforce the racist ideology of "black criminality" used to justify still more violence and other forms of racial oppression. However, as the history of the Movement for Black Lives makes clear, African Americans see both police and vigilante violence as racially targeted acts of political violence, not as separate and unrelated phenomena. Let's take a closer look at a few of those vigilante killings that, like their cousin the police killings, continue to terrorize African Americans.

Trayvon Martin (February 2012): American Vigilantism and the New Emmett Till

The best known and most infamous of those vigilante killings, the fatal shooting of Trayvon Martin, has become as significant to the history of the African American struggle against racial violence in the twenty-first century as the lynching of Emmett Till was in the twentieth century. It is within this socio-historical context that we can best understand the dramatic impact that the killing of seventeen-year-old Martin by a Neighborhood Watch captain of European and Latino descent, George Zimmerman, had and continues to have on American race relations and the collective consciousness and memory of African Americans.[7]

Although vigilante killings in the United States are not officially sanctioned by the state, and the perpetrators are not afforded the same degree of protection as police officers, there is often a strong measure of governmental and popular support. In Florida, they are backed by the state's highly racialized "Stand Your Ground" law, which empowers gun owners to shoot those who they can then argue presented a threat— even when they have the option of simply removing themselves from harm's way. To many of them, that "threat" has a color, and that color is black. It was within this environment that—despite the many questions raised about Zimmerman's "self-defense" account of the shooting, including his need to follow and confront Martin, who wore a hoodie over his head that night to protect himself from the rain—no charges were initially brought. Indeed, it was not until after more than six weeks of both local and national protests that Zimmerman was indicted. Those protests included social media postings of photographs of prominent middle-class and middle-aged African Americans expressing solidarity with Martin by wearing hoodies—the stereotypical image, for many European Americans, of "black" youth criminality.[8]

Nationwide, African Americans found themselves in a state of shock, less than six months after President Obama was inaugurated for his second term as the nation's first African American president, when the jury—which included only one person of color, and which was given instructions on the state's racially charged Stand Your Ground law, which they discussed during their deliberation, even though Zimmerman did not actually use that defense—acquitted Zimmerman of all charges. No other act of violence had provoked as much outrage among African Americans since the savage and also unpunished murder of fourteen-year-old Emmett Till in Mississippi in 1955, nearly six decades earlier. One response by a frustrated, but determined, young African American woman by the name of Alicia Garza was the posting of a message of love for African American people that soon evolved into the twitter hashtag #blacklivesmatter. It is such collective consciousness and memory, and its periodic refueling by still more horrific images of violence against African Americans, that must be understood if we are to comprehend the growth, persistence, and intensity of what came to be known as the Black Lives Matter movement, and more recently the Movement for Black Lives.[9]

When acts of horrific violence go unpunished they have an impact that extends way beyond any particular incident. They create a climate of terror that has resulted in the all too often told story of an African American mother who tightly holds and kisses her teenage son before he leaves home each morning with the knowledge that due to the actions of the police, or today's lone vigilantes, she may never see him again. And there is yet another consequence of such violence happening with apparent impunity: it may encourage others to take similar actions.

Jordan Davis (November 2012) and Renisha McBride (November 2013): Two More Vigilante Killings, But with Different Endings

In that same state of Florida, nine months after Trayvon Martin was killed, Michael Dunn, a European American software developer, angrily confronted seventeen-year-old Jordan Davis and three other African American boys at a gas station for playing their music too loud. In the ensuing argument, Dunn shot Jordan three times. Standing behind Florida's Stand Your Ground law, which does not require proof that a perceived threat was real, Dunn pleaded self-defense based on his claim that Davis pulled a shotgun on him and threatened to kill him. A key part of Dunn's defense was the depiction of Davis and the other boys in the car as dangerous thugs. No shotgun was found by the police or seen by witnesses, and in the first trial Dunn was convicted on charges of attempted murder of the three surviving youngsters. However, the jury could not reach the required unanimous agreement on the first-degree murder charge, in part because of confusion over how they should interpret the state's Stand Your Ground law. In the second trial, "the jury found that Mr. Dunn intended to kill Mr. Davis and acted with premeditation as he reached into his glove compartment for his gun and fired 10 times at Mr. Davis and the Durango, even as it pulled away to evade the gunfire." Dunn was sentenced to life in prison with no chance of parole.[10]

Of course, such violence is not limited to African American males, and certainly not, more specifically, to seventeen-year-old African American boys in Florida. Less than a year after Jordan Davis was killed, Renisha McBride, a nineteen-year-old African American woman who had been drinking and using marijuana on the night of her murder, was shot in the face with a twelve-gauge shotgun through a locked screen door by Theodore Wafer, a European American, as she sought help on the front porch of his suburban Detroit home after hitting a parked car. Unlike Florida with its self-defense law, in Michigan the use of lethal force is permitted only in those cases when an individual has a credible reason to believe that his or her physical well-being or life is in imminent danger. Consistent with their reading of that law, the prosecutors in that case argued that Wafer's actions were not lawful because he failed to call the police and instead shot the unarmed McBride. He was charged with and convicted of second-degree murder and related crimes, and sentenced to a minimum of seventeen years in prison.[11]

The three vigilante killing cases briefly discussed here suggest that, although the state can provide a measure of protection for vigilantes, it is generally not as great as that which it gives those whom it authorizes to officially use lethal force, and that it is the nature of self-defense and other laws that vary from state to state that determine how much protection vigilantes are afforded.

Eric Garner (July 2014): "I Can't Breathe" Video Goes Viral

Approximately eight and a half months after Renisha McBride was killed, a police killing of an unarmed African American man was captured on a cellphone video that shocked the world and convinced many more Americans that, in their routine dealings with African Americans, the police were simply out of control. What made that video, which was watched by millions of people worldwide, so dramatic was that it did not capture the rapid fire of a police shooting, but the slow killing of Eric Garner, a forty-three-year-old husband and father of six who was held in a chokehold by a European American police officer as he pleaded "I can't breathe" eleven times. The incident began when the police approached Garner as he sold "loosies" (single untaxed cigarettes) on the street to help support his family. Apparently in reference to previous such incidents, which he viewed as police harassment, Garner asserted that "It stops today," asked why he was being arrested, and pulled back his hands from the officers as they tried to handcuff him; however, in no way did he react violently. As numerous officers held Garner down, one of them, Daniel Pantaleo, administered what proved to be the fatal, department-banned chokehold. And when officers summoned an ambulance they did so with the codeword "unknown," which called for a low-priority response.[12]

What appeared to be an irrefutable case of police misconduct to many, if not most, of those who viewed the video was made even more shocking when Garner's death was ruled a homicide by the New York City Medical Examiner. The significance of the Garner case was increased considerably three weeks later when the nation became embroiled in another intense racial conflict following the fatal police killing of an unarmed African American teenager named Michael Brown in Ferguson, Missouri, in what initially appeared to be an execution-style shooting. After grand juries in both cases declined to indict the officers involved, racial tension and protests swept the nation. As is often the case in NYPD misconduct cases, where families of victims are not uncommonly given large cash settlements from the city to avoid civil trials (in which the burden of proof is less onerous), a year after Garner was killed his family received a 5.9-million-dollar settlement.[13]

Michael Brown (August 2014): "Hands Up, Don't Shoot!" and the Crystallization of the Black Lives Matter Movement

It was that killing of Michael Brown, in a largely African American and economically struggling suburb of Missouri, and the yearlong Ferguson movement of social protests provoked by it that made the increasingly visible Black Lives Matter movement, as it would soon come to be known, a central and enduring feature of American life, politics, and culture.

On August 9, 2014, the unarmed eighteen-year-old was shot near his grandmother's home "at least six times, including twice in the head," following a confrontation with Darren Wilson, a European American police officer, who stopped Brown and a friend for walking in the road instead of on the sidewalk. Brown was killed in what to many appeared to be an execution-style shooting, from a distance of about thirty-five feet while he was, according to some witnesses, facing Wilson with his arms clearly raised where they could be seen—an account later challenged by conflicting forensic evidence and witness testimony. Then, as if to send a message of terror to other community members, Brown's bloody body was left in the street for several hours, with no family members allowed near it. That was followed by another slow response from Ferguson officials: not releasing Wilson's name until nearly a week after the shooting. Those and other actions, plus a long history of tension and distrust between the police, city officials, and the African American community, sparked weeks of sometimes violent protests and hundreds of arrests.[14]

After more than one hundred days of protest, a grand jury released its decision not to prosecute officer Wilson—who testified that he shot the teenager because he was charging toward him and that he had feared for his life—in a process many African Americans believed was rigged by an extremely pro-police district attorney with many years of bad relations with local African Americans. That decision was followed by a wave of sometimes violent protests, both locally and nationally, with what seemed like countless images of African Americans and other activists shouting "Hands Up, Don't Shoot!" as they thrust their hands into the air in a way that was reminiscent of the images of African Americans wearing hoodies during the waves of protest after the killing of

Trayvon Martin. As if now official, it was obvious to even the most casual observer that what was happening was not just a matter of periodic outbursts of anger but part of a national and sustainable movement against police and vigilante killings of African Americans, with both deep historical roots and a far-reaching future.[15]

Such protests, and the city administration's reaction to them, helped shine a bright light on what it meant to be an African American living in Ferguson, which was captured in the report on a U.S. Department of Justice investigation released seven months after Brown was killed. That report documented a pattern of racial bias by both the Ferguson Police Department and other town officials against African Americans, which included vehicle stops, arrests, the use of force, jail time, and the systematic violation of their constitutional rights. Among its findings was a fact that placed what happened that fateful day to Brown and his friend in its larger racial context: 95 percent of the people stopped for jaywalking in Ferguson were African American. That investigation—the type of Justice Department scrutiny unlikely to happen under the Trump administration—resulted in the forced resignation of the chief of police, the city manager, and the municipal court judge, and the city reaching an agreement with the Justice Department to reform the Ferguson Police Department under the watchful eye of a federal monitor. An interesting addendum to the story of the killing of Michael Brown after he was stopped for jaywalking, which illustrates Chris Hayes' distinction between living in a colony and a nation, is the latter's recounting of an interview he carried out with the mayor of Ferguson as they walked down the middle of the street in a nice, largely European American neighborhood, with, of course, no fear of being confronted by the police for jaywalking.[16]

Laquan McDonald (October 2014) and "Video Games": Shot Sixteen Times as He Walked Away

When a tree falls in a forest and there is no one there to hear it, does it make a sound? Despite growing concern about the issue, without a credible national data bank there is no solid evidence that the actual numbers of police and vigilante killings of African Americans are increasing. Again, it might just be that with new technology such as smartphone videos, social media, and twenty-four-hours-a-day/seven-days-a-week cable news coverage, such incidents are now more likely to be documented, and then disseminated worldwide. It is also important to keep in mind that such killings are often symptomatic of much larger systemic operations that go way beyond and much deeper than just the attitudes and actions of a few rogue individuals.

Both factors were clearly at play in Chicago in what to many African Americans appeared to be another execution-style killing: in this case that of Laquan McDonald, a seventeen-year-old African American. There was much that supported the widespread suspicion among African Americans in Chicago that different levels of city government and its criminal justice system played what might be characterized as various "video games" to suppress the evidence of what actually happened that day that was, or that should have been, recorded. Here are the facts that eventually surfaced. McDonald, who had taken the drug PCP and had a knife in his hand, had begun walking away from the police when he was shot sixteen times in fourteen seconds by Officer Jason Van Dyke, a European American, shortly after the latter arrived at the scene. Officer Van Dyke was in the process of reloading his—by then empty—gun when he was told to stop shooting by another officer on the scene. Finally, Van Dyke had had many complaints filed against him by local residents, "including allegations of using excessive force and racial slurs." Still, it was only shortly before Mayor Rahm Emanuel's administration released the video evidence under the order of a judge—a year after McDonald was killed—that Anita Alvarez, Cook County State's Attorney General, charged Van Dyke with first-degree murder.[17]

In response to the mayor's characterization of that and another controversial police killing as the acts of rogue police officers, a team of reporters for the *Chicago Tribune* concluded that "that City Hall narrative" did not fit the facts of "decades' worth of police torture and wrongful conviction cases, corruption and slapdash, ineffectual oversight practices in shootings and other excessive force actions," and noted that "time and again, the department has quickly cleared officers of allegations, only to have civil litigation later reveal video and other evidence that painted a much darker picture of police conduct."[18]

Mayor Emanuel's attempt to reduce McDonald's killing to the act of a rogue cop was also challenged by the fact that it was indeed the suppression of the video evidence that revealed what actually happened that night that kept the case out of the national spotlight for a year. That year included the mayor's hotly contested, but successful, re-election, which he—the former chief of staff for President Obama—won because of widespread African American support. As questions about what happened to numerous videos of the incident arose, the story of what appeared to many to be blatant attempts to keep buried the truth of what occurred that night became an issue as big and outrageous as the shooting itself. For example, of the five police dashboard-camera videos released of the shooting in response to the judge's order, only one had video of the incident, and none had audio clear enough to make out what the officers were saying. If that were not enough, there were suspicions of police tampering with videos shot by cameras at a local Burger King. While video cameras showed police officers walking into the restaurant and later provided images of an officer working on a laptop computer there, in between there was a mysterious eighty-minute gap instead of footage of what was happening outside over a period that included the McDonald shooting. The police dashboard-camera video that was released revealed that the Chicago Police Department (CPD) and city officials had good reason to be concerned, because it contradicted the critical facts of the CPD's reports based largely on the testimony of the police officers who were on the scene. While those reports presented Van Dyke's account of the shooting, which was collaborated by at least five other officers who witnessed the incident and indicated that McDonald turned toward the police in a threatening manner, the video clearly showed McDonald walking away, and that he was on the ground for all but one of the fourteen seconds during which he was being shot.[19]

Amid fear that the city would explode in violent unrest, within hours of the judge's ruling ordering the release of a police dashboard-camera video of the shooting, Mayor Emanuel condemned the shooting for the first time. Not long afterward, he fired his police superintendent, who, he said, had lost the trust of the city's residents. Months earlier, without waiting for the completion of the criminal investigation, the Chicago City Council had approved a five-million-dollar settlement to

McDonald's family. That settlement fit a pattern over the previous ten years, uncovered in an investigation by the Better Government Association, during which the city government of Chicago paid out a half-*billion* dollars in such settlements and related costs for police misconduct. Officer Van Dyke was charged with six counts of first-degree murder, one count of police misconduct, and sixteen counts of aggravated battery. Two officers who filed reports that proved to be radically different from what was shown by the dashcam video were placed on desk duty, and four officers were suspended for a week for failure to ensure that their dashboard cameras operated properly the night McDonald was killed.[20]

The reaction against what was widely seen as a corrupt and racist criminal justice system in Chicago was not limited to massive protests and pressure on the mayor to act. Anita Alvarez, the Cook County prosecutor upon whom much of the blame for the delayed prosecution of the case was placed, was soundly defeated in her bid for re-election by a highly energized African American electorate. But that did not deter the local police union, which seemed determined to send its own message by hiring former officer Van Dyke as a janitor. Finally, Mayor Emanuel, who was under intense social-protest pressure to resign, appointed a "Police Accountability Task Force" to make recommendations for reforming the CPD. In the executive summary of its report, the task force began addressing the question "How did we get to this point?" by stating: "We arrived at this point in part because of racism." And it started a section heading titled "RACISM" with this sentence:

> The Task Force heard over and over again from a range of voices, particularly from African-Americans, that some CPD officers are racist, have no respect for the lives and experiences of people of color and approach every encounter with people of color as if the person, regardless of age, gender or circumstance, is a criminal.

Even that bold acknowledgement did little to assure many Chicago citizens that meaningful change in the Chicago Police Department would be forthcoming. A *Chicago Tribune* editorial issued this warning:

> The mayor's early response to the work of his task force is hugely disappointing. It nibbles around the edges instead of embracing

the enormous interrelated challenges at the heart of the report. It fails to commit to the transformative change this moment demands—and that Emanuel has promised.

Later would come a report from the U.S. Department of Justice that detailed excessive use of force, corruption, and other misconduct within the Chicago Police Department, which largely targeted the city's African American and Latino/a American residents.[21]

Tamir Rice (November 2014): Two Seconds and a Child is Killed

The sense that the police and vigilante killings of African Americans could not get any more outrageous was shattered only a few months after the fatal shooting of the teenager Michael Brown, and just one month after the—at that time—largely video-blacked-out killing of teenager Laquan McDonald. For this time, it was not a teenager but a twelve-year-old child. As Tamir Rice was playing in a Cleveland park with a friend's toy gun, someone called 911 and reported "a guy in here with a pistol," "probably fake," and "probably a juvenile." Unfortunately, none of those details got further than the dispatcher, who instead sent out a "Code 1" which instructed officers to respond with their highest level of urgency. And that is exactly what Officer Timothy Loehmann and his partner did. The *New York Times* reported that "within two seconds of the car's arrival, Officer Loehmann shot Tamir in the abdomen from point-blank range, raising doubts that he could have warned the boy three times to raise his hands, as the police later claimed." If that was not enough, when the boy's fourteen-year-old sister ran to the scene she was tackled and placed in handcuffs, and when his mother arrived the officers threatened to arrest her if she did not calm down. There is more: neither officer checked Rice's vital signs or provided first aid, and it took eight minutes for medical personnel to arrive from a fire station a block away. And still more: a check of police department records showed that Officer Loehmann was hired despite having lost his previous job with another police department as a result of his "dangerous loss of composure" while being trained in the use of firearms.[22]

Again, socio-historical context is important for understanding how such killings are perceived, both nationally and, especially, within local African American communities. Because it occurred just two days prior to the announcement of a grand jury decision not to indict the police officer who killed Michael Brown in Ferguson, Missouri, the Rice killing was at the center of a huge wave of protest, not only in Cleveland but nationwide. Moreover, the litany of errors that led to Rice's death was just the latest piece of evidence that the Cleveland Police Department (CPD) was broken. Just twenty-one and a half months earlier Ohio's attorney general had used the words "systemic failure" to describe the condition of the department, and less than two weeks after Rice was killed the U.S. Justice Department made public the results of an investigation begun prior to his killing which found that police officers were rarely disciplined despite a clear pattern of use of excessive force which included punching, kicking, and shooting at people for no good reason. Based on those findings, the following year the CPD was pressured into accepting new policy guidelines and the appointment of an independent monitor.[23]

While that settlement may have seemed encouraging to some, it came just days after a judge found another Cleveland police officer, Michael Brelo, innocent of the 2012 killing of an unarmed African American couple, Timothy Russell and Malissa Williams, prompting investigations of the CPD by both the Ohio state attorney general and the U.S. Justice Department. In that incident, following a car chase, police officers fired 137 shots into the car after mistaking its exhaust backfiring for gun shots. Brelo, who jumped on the hood of the car and fired repeatedly, and five other officers were dismissed.[24]

As is often the case in such killings, although a grand jury declined to bring charges against Officer Loehmann for killing Tamir Rice, the city settled with the victim's family for six million dollars, without any admission of wrongdoing and with the understanding that there would be no civil suit. Finally, as was true in Chicago, the power of what was at that time commonly known as the Black Lives Matter movement was felt when the county prosecutor, Tim McGinty, was voted out of office in the next election.[25]

Walter Scott (April 4, 2015): Videotaped Being Shot Eight
Times as He Ran Away

This brief overview of cases of police and vigilante violence against African Americans has uncovered one of the reasons why such killings, especially when they are done with impunity, carry such weight as acts that terrorize, as they are absorbed into the collective consciousness and memory of African Americans: each new killing seems to be more outrageous than the last. Just four and a half months after the killing of Tamir Rice sent shockwaves through African American communities there was yet another example of what, like the shooting of Michael Brown, appeared to be an execution-style killing of an African American; this time, however, there was a very different early response from the criminal justice system and the politicians to which it answers. In North Charleston, South Carolina, officer Michael T. Slager was caught on video firing eight shots at Walter Scott, a fifty-year-old father of four who had warrants out for missing child support payments, as he fled by foot after being stopped and questioned for a broken taillight. That killing was so blatant, and so close in its temporal proximity to so many other outrageous police killings of African Americans, that within days the officer was charged with murder, two months later he was indicted by a grand jury, and *Time* magazine placed pictures of Scott running and Slager shooting him, on a mostly black cover, under the large words, in white, "BLACK LIVES MATTER," followed in smaller, gray-colored print with the words "THIS TIME THE CHARGE IS MURDER."[26]

Once again, in a nation where attempted police cover-ups of such actions are becoming increasingly exposed, it is likely that the only reason Officer Slager was charged with a crime was because his actions were caught on a smartphone video by someone who happened to be walking by. Without that video, Slager's claim that he shot Scott because he feared for his life—usually an effective way for police in the United States to avoid prosecution when they kill someone—backed by collaborative statements from other officers who arrived on the scene later, would have likely been enough for him to avoid prosecution. Unfortunately for Slager, the video did not support his claim that a struggle over his Taser prompted the shooting. Instead it showed Taser wires coming from Scott, Slager standing between fifteen and twenty feet from Scott as he shot the latter while he tried to flee, and then Slager picking up an object from the area where he had scuffled with Scott and dropping it near Scott's body. The video also discredited police reports that claimed officers gave Scott CPR. Instead, it revealed that after the shooting Officer Slager handcuffed Scott behind his back, left him face-down for several minutes, and did not provide CPR. A second officer and then a third arrived; neither provided CPR.[27]

The Scott killing was so blatant, so well publicized, and so ill timed in terms of the growing African American outrage over such slayings that it was condemned at all levels of administration and governance, including by the police chief, mayor, governor, and the state's two U.S. senators. North Charleston city officials avoided a civil suit by authorizing the city to pay a 6.5 million dollar settlement to Scott's family. The *Time* magazine reporter was so convinced that the Scott killing must signal a turning point in recognizing the need for criminal justice reform that he concluded: "The shooting ought to put police departments on the same side with the protestors who are demanding change." Unfortunately, it didn't. Twenty months after Scott was killed, the Slager state murder trial, which was to be decided by a jury with only one African American member, ended in a hung jury—just one vote shy of the unanimous verdict needed for a conviction. Two years after Officer Slager killed Scott, he accepted a plea bargain in a federal case in which he admitted to violating Scott's civil rights in exchange for the State of South Carolina agreeing to drop its murder charge and the federal government dropping its remaining charges against him. As a part of that agreement Slager reversed his previous position that he shot Scott in self-defense and admitted that he used excessive force against him.

Two weeks after Walter Scott was fatally shot, yet another police-related death shocked the nation.[28]

Freddie Gray (April 19, 2015): "A Rough Ride," a Severed Spine, and a Violent Rebellion

Like most large American cities, Baltimore has a well-earned reputation within its African American community for having a racist, corrupt, and out-of-control police department. What distinguishes the poverty-plagued city of Baltimore from most of the other cities so far discussed is the fact that it was ruled by an African American mayor and an African American police chief, and much of its police misconduct involves African American police officers.

The city's long-simmering resentment at such blatant abuse within what was ostensibly a black power-governing structure—which appeared useless to stop it—came to a head on April 19, 2015 with the death of twenty-five-year-old Freddie Gray from a severed spine, after having been taken into police custody a week earlier. Like the killing of Walter Scott and many others, Gray's death left people wondering why he was stopped and arrested in the first place. His "crimes" were running from a police officer with whom he had established eye contact, and later the possession of a pocket knife, which was in fact legal. A video showed that Gray did not resist being arrested by three European American officers, Garrett E. Miller, Edward M. Nero, and Lieutenant Brian W. Rice, and he seemed to be in pain from an injured leg as he was dragged to a police van. The video also caught someone off-camera protesting about how Gray was being treated, given what appeared to them to be his broken leg. Gray was also ignored when he asked for his asthma inhaler. The police van—which was driven by an African American officer, Caesar R. Goodson, Jr.—made several stops before Gray was taken to a police station. At some point, Goodson asked African American officer William G. Porter to check on Gray's condition. Porter asked Gray if he needed help, to which Gray replied yes. The officer helped him onto the metal bench of the van, but did not call for medical assistance. During one of those stops an African American female sergeant, Alicia D. White, checked Gray's condition and found him to be unresponsive, but did nothing to help him.[29]

Shortly after those six officers were indicted on various charges related to Gray's death, including the driver giving Gray what the state prosecutors called "a rough ride" (one intentionally meant to cause the passengers discomfort), the *Baltimore Sun* reported that his autopsy found that he "suffered a single 'high-energy injury' to his neck and spine—most likely caused when the police van in which he was riding suddenly decelerated." It also determined that Gray, who had both his wrists and angles shackled and who was placed face down in the van, was not secured by a seat belt. An excerpt from the autopsy indicated that Gray, who "could be heard yelling and banging," "died of a **Neck Injury.**" That autopsy also indicated that the van made a total of five stops before Gray was taken to the police station and then to a hospital. It concluded that because Gray's neck injury occurred while he was in the van, appropriate safety procedures were not followed, and available safety equipment was not used, his "manner of death" could not be characterized as an unforeseen event or accident, but "is best certified as **Homicide.**"[30]

Baltimore was already a city ready to explode—and that is exactly what happened after Freddie Gray's death. Although the news of his demise was followed by mostly peaceful protests, that relative tranquility did not last. The afternoon following Gray's funeral, which began earlier that morning, flyers appeared, purportedly from a local high school, announcing that a "purge" was about to begin. Some demonstrators threw bottles at the police, others severely damaged a police car; looters broke into a local CVS, a massive fire was started at an intersection, the pharmacy was burned to the ground, by 7 p.m. the governor declared a state of emergency, and by 8 p.m. the mayor had announced a citywide curfew. From April 25 through May 3 more than thirty businesses were seriously damaged, and fifteen buildings and 144 vehicles were destroyed by fire. Damage in the city during that period totaled an estimated nine million dollars.[31]

Soon after that city returned to some semblance of normalcy, Mayor Stephanie Rawlings-Blake requested and was granted an investigation by the U.S. Justice Department to determine if the Baltimore City Police Department "engaged in a pattern of unconstitutional policing." That fall the Baltimore Board of Estimates approved a 6.4 million dollar settlement for Freddie Gray's family, and within the same week the mayor announced that she would not seek re-election in order to devote more time to the city's problems. After failing to win convictions on any of the charges against the first four of the six officers tried, with one of those trials ending in a hung jury, the state's attorney concluded that the local police and court system were stacked against that happening and dropped all charges against the remaining officers. In August of 2016 the Civil Rights Division of the U.S. Department of Justice released a report on its investigation of the Baltimore City Police Department, which documented a pattern of intentional and systemic discrimination against the city's African American residents at every stage of their contact with the police, "from the initial decision to stop individuals on Baltimore streets to searches, arrests, and uses of force."[32]

There have, of course, been many egregious killings of African Americans since Freddie Gray's death. However, publishing a moderate-size, single-volume book manuscript in a timely fashion requires that the reasonably brief overview of selected killings I provide in this chapter indeed remains brief. That means my choosing not only when the case examples should begin, but also, somewhat arbitrarily, when they should end. Applying that same logic, although I will cover additional killings in the chapters that come, I will not attempt to analyze every major killing up to the manuscript going to press. Instead, I draw most of the case examples for this book from the Amadou Diallo to the Freddie Gray killings, over the sixteen-year period of 1999-2015 which I have discussed in this chapter. Given both the importance and the persistence of this issue, there will of course be other books, reports, articles, and essays that will analyze other fatal incidents.

The State's Complicity in Keeping the Killings Statistically Invisible and the Role of Technology in Amplifying their Terror

What African Americans are now experiencing almost routinely in the way of police and vigilante violence is so outrageous that many of the more recent incidents I reviewed make the Amadou Diallo shooting discussed at the beginning of this chapter look mild by comparison. Ironically, however, while often highly dramatic and well publicized, such killings are for the most part statistically invisible. This is true because state complicity in such violence is not limited to the fact that it disproportionately targets African American communities through its "War on Drugs" and other policing actions and allows it to happen with virtual impunity. It is also evident in the fact that despite the often flagrant, execution-style disregard for African American lives and decades of social protests by African Americans and others, ranging from peaceful demonstrations to violent urban rebellions, "black lives" still don't "matter" enough politically for there to be a federally mandated national reporting mechanism for police killings. At best, we have only unofficial counts complied by news organizations and activist groups. For example, in their analysis of police killings in 2015, a team of *Washington Post* reporters found that although African American men constituted only 6 percent of the U.S. population that year, they comprised 40 percent of unarmed men shot by the police. Based on that data set and U.S. Census data, it has been estimated that 3.2 times as many African American men aged eighteen to forty-four have been killed by the police as their European American counterparts in the same age range. Moreover, a widely cited report compiled by an organization of African American activists indicates that in 2012, 313 African Americans were killed by the police, security guards, or vigilantes; that is, one African American was killed every twenty-eight hours. And as you will see, the end of the cumulative effects of such traumatic "collective memories" is nowhere in sight. Consequently, the impression such killings give to African Americans seems to be little short of state-sponsored or -sanctioned domestic terrorism. Indeed, today the terror threat level provoked by the increasingly routine nature of such spectacular and systemically supported killings has risen to a point where, for many African Americans, their apparent racial control functions and consequences are hard to ignore, as they have become America's twenty-first-century lynchings.[33]

Again, it is important to remember that the problem of police and vigilante killings of African Americans is certainly not just a late twentieth and early twenty-first-century phenomenon. It existed back in the days of the slave patrols to catch runaway slaves and to terrorize those who might otherwise have the temerity to contemplate escaping or organizing an insurrection. And because no credible statistics on such killings are kept, we cannot say for certain that their numbers have increased, or indeed decreased. However, using data based on police reports, which reflect biases such as non-reporting and underreporting, the Centers for Disease Control and Prevention found that the rate of police killings of African Americans has actually declined by 70 percent over the past forty to fifty years. Consistent with that data, Keeanga-Yamahtta Taylor cites an article in a Detroit newspaper as evidence that the types of highly racialized police abuse that exist today were commonplace in northern cities at least as early as the 1920s. That article reported that fifty-five African Americans had been shot, with "a few of them" appearing to have been "executed," by the police in just that one city during the first half of 1925 alone, and many more had been subjected to random stops and searches.[34]

Two things have changed. First, there is now an expectation on the part of African Americans, especially among the young, that, decades after the civil rights movement and with evident progress such as that symbolized in the election of Barack Obama as the nation's first African American president in 2008 and his re-election in 2012, they should be treated as first-class citizens who no longer must be mindful of their "place." That is, they are not inclined to remain within the prescribed boundaries of white racial control. Second, there is the spread of technology such as the video camera, which, in 1991, enabled the brutal beating of Rodney King by members of the Los Angeles Police Department to be captured; and more recently the widespread use of camera-ready smartphones, surveillance cameras, the internet, twenty-four-hour cable-news television stations, and social media that make such killings national news, where they would have previously been known of by only a relatively few people residing within the local communities in which they occurred. So ironically, just as African Americans' refusal to now "know" and remain in what is deemed to be their rightful racial place during a time of generally improved race relations has made them more vulnerable, the more widespread visibility of such killings that has brought the issue to public attention also radically increases their power as acts of racial terrorism.[35]

What These Case Examples Don't and Do Tell Us

Some readers may be concerned that I have chosen the most outrageous and highly publicized examples to illustrate the contemporary police and vigilante killings of African Americans. To that criticism, I must confess: I stand guilty as charged. Indeed, one important way in which the cases I have selected are different from most other such killings is, of course, in the societal reaction they provoked. Most of the police and vigilante killings of African Americans never see the light of day beyond the local communities in which they occur, and where the killers' accounts typically go unquestioned by those in power. But because they were so outrageous, were more likely to have been caught on video, were so well publicized, and often provoked mass protests as part of a growing and increasingly well-organized movement against such killings, the cases I have discussed were more likely to result in charges being brought against the police and vigilantes, and in some cases even convictions.

So why did I choose them? There are three reasons I have selected some of the most extreme examples of the police and vigilante killings of African Americans for examination in this chapter and the rest of this book. First, they are the cases that are the most powerful in the terroristic message they send to African Americans, as a racial control mechanism, that remind us to "stay in our lane"—the pothole-ridden slow lane that doesn't go very far, or to many nice places. Second, it is these most outrageous killings that periodically offer the nation the best chance to reform its criminal justice system, and scholars such as myself the best opportunity to examine why it doesn't. And finally, it is such extreme cases that most profoundly reflect and affect race relations at any particular point in time. I neither claim this study is, nor intend it to be, an empirically based analysis of a representative sample of police and vigilante killings of African Americans. That is a different study for another scholar.

However, despite the limitations of the cases I have examined, from reading these numerous case examples of the police and vigilante killings of African Americans since 1999—the closing year of the twentieth century—through the first few months of 2015, one can discern some clear patterns of similarities which all, or at least most, share. Hopefully some of these will have changed by the time this book is published. These conclusions are, of course, not meant to be representative of most police and vigilante killings of African Americans. Instead, they represent the cases that have been most highly publicized, because they were deemed to be so egregious as to significantly reflect and impact American race relations.

1. *The victims of such killings tend to be young, unarmed, low-income, African American males,* whereas those who kill them are most likely to be European American men who are older and more affluent. This does not mean that older African American men and African American women are not victims and that African Americans are never perpetrators; only that they are less likely to be so in these high-profile cases.[36]

2. *Police and vigilantes racially profile their victims.* That is, they often use their highly racialized discretion to stop and otherwise engage individuals who have not committed any serious wrongdoing and who, if they were not African American, would probably not have been confronted.

3. *The police and vigilantes and African Americans tend to offer radically different accounts of such killings.* While the police and vigilantes argue that such killings are necessary to protect themselves in situations where they fear for their lives, and have nothing to do with "race," African Americans view them as part of an old and persistent pattern of racial profiling, discrimination, and violence.

4. *The police are rarely prosecuted for killing unarmed African Americans.* Of course, this is also true, to a lesser extent, for other people they kill. They tend to be charged only when there is irrefutable video evidence combined with massive and extensive social protest.

5. Even when the charges are severe and the evidence is strong, *when the police do face criminal prosecution they are rarely convicted.*

6. *To avoid civil suits* that require a lesser burden of proof, can expose systemic problems within departments and local governments, and can therefore be embarrassing to elected officials, *cities and towns often provide large cash settlements to the victims' families.*

7. *There is a "blue code" of silence, lies, and other cover-up norms and tactics that protect police officers from prosecution in such cases.* The police tend to protect their own, no matter what they do.

8. *Vigilantes who kill African Americans are more likely to be prosecuted and convicted than is the case for police officers.* This is less likely to be the case in states where there are highly racialized self-defense statutes such as the "Castle" and "Stand Your Ground" laws.

9. Both non-violent and violent *social protest of such killings by African Americans is a response not to a single incident but to a long history of perceived police racism and misconduct.*

10. *No matter how outrageous the killings and how intense the racial crises they provoke, they tend not to result in national reform of the criminal justice system.* And even when reform is mandated by national entities such as the U.S. Department of Justice, it tends to be limited to specific local governments and their police departments.

As you have seen, few social issues have received as much conventional and social media attention in the United States over the past few years as the police and vigilante killings of African Americans. Conflict over this issue has often strained race relations to near breaking point. The recent election of Donald Trump as president was fueled by his highly racialized, pro-police campaign that called for "law and order" and attacked activists who pushed for police reform. However, a determined and increasingly well-organized African American community has shown no inclination to back down from their insistence that, indeed, Black Lives Matter. Consequently, there seems to be no end in sight for this intense racial conflict. The outcome of this struggle, now international in scope, may profoundly impact every aspect of American life, including its criminal justice system, politics, race relations, and culture.

An Invitation to Take a Closer Look

As you have probably already discerned from what I have said thus far, and how I have said it, this book is not written from the perspective of a somehow "objective" social scientist who claims to be "value-neutral" about this highly controversial subject matter. As a concerned African American father, grandfather, and scholar with relative job security and a decent pension, I have committed myself to doing what I can to stop the madness of these highly racialized killings that terrorize our communities, cause unimaginable suffering to the loved ones of their victims, and deny all African Americans our basic rights as full citizens. Toward that end, an important goal of this book is to provide an informed and progressive African American perspective on what is happening, why, and how it can be stopped.

The overview of more than a dozen police and vigilante killings of African Americans, from Amadou Diallo to Freddie Gray, presented in this chapter provides a few hints as to what such a perspective looks like: hopefully enough to entice you to take a closer look at what is all too obvious for millions of us African Americans. First, the police and vigilante killings of African Americans are not only a serious social malady but a reflection of deeply engrained systemic racism. Second, such killings must ultimately be understood as not just a social issue but ultimately a political issue, because they can persist at such a large magnitude only because they are normally not just protected by this nation's political system and its criminal justice apparatus, but encouraged by them. In brief, they can best be understood as part of a nation's "necropolitics" of who lives and who dies. And, finally, regardless of the intent of the individual actors involved, such killings function as a racial control mechanism which, when left unchallenged, terrorizes many African Americans into curtailing their aspirations for full and safe freedom of movement beyond what has historically been deemed their proper racial "place."[37]

A Preview of the Chapters to Come

In this book's remaining chapters I develop and apply a racial control argument and conceptual framework for better understanding the pervasive, disproportionate, and persistent police and vigilante killings of African Americans. That racial control perspective takes into account the interrelationship of such macro-level factors as systemic racism, economic and political neoliberalism, and highly racialized politics;

interpersonal-level factors such as racial animus, hypermasculinity, police and vigilante attitudes and culture, and negative emotions; and social movements and other challenges to such violence.

In Chapter 2, "Making Sense of the Killings: Theoretical Insights, Conceptual Framework, and My Racial Control Argument," I forge the theoretical and conceptual tools that guide my analysis. I begin with a review of a dozen relevant bodies of theoretical and substantive literature, which I organize into three broad categories of scholarship that explain the workings of: social oppression; race relations, systemic racism, and the racial state; and violent interpersonal interactions. Building upon that review, I lay out the study's key theoretical assumptions, identify existing concepts, and develop new ones that comprise the study's conceptual framework. I conclude by presenting my argument that the excessive police and vigilante killings of African Americans function as a racial control mechanism. I also present a set of propositions around which I organize the remaining chapters.

In Chapter 3, "Violence-Centered Racial Control Systems and Mechanisms in U.S. History," I explain my historical sociological method and examine the similarities and differences of the violence-centered racial control *systems* of slavery, peonage, Jim Crow, and systemic racism and their *mechanisms* of lynchings, the death penalty, and mass incarceration. By doing so I bring to the surface what they reveal about the persistence and dynamics of racial control-focused violence that aids our understanding of how today's police and vigilante killings of African Americans function as racial control mechanisms for systemic racism.

In Chapter 4, "Police and Vigilante Killings of African Americans as a Racial Control Mechanism," I return to my main argument that the police and vigilante killings of African Americans, like police and vigilante violence generally, function as a racial control mechanism for systemic racism. It is here that I take the ideas, concepts, and lessons of history presented in Chapters 1 and 2 and apply them to better understand the various economic, social status, and political functions that contemporary police and vigilante killings of African Americans serve for members of the dominant racialized group.

In Chapter 5, "Viewing the Killings Through an Economic Lens: Hypercapitalism and the Growth of the American Police State," I bring class-based oppression to the center of my analysis and make it clear that, while the main focus of this study is the racial control functions of the police and vigilante killings of African Americans, rising economic inequality in the United States and other nations means that the class control functions of such violence cannot be overlooked. Indeed, when combined with their racial control functions, which have intensified under the Trump administration, the magnitude and consequences of such actions could increase exponentially if left unchecked.

In Chapter 6, "Ground Zero: The Vicious Cycle of Fatal Dominative Encounters," I examine the interpersonal-level factors that set the stage for such killings and that are present in both the actual encounter between a particular police officer or vigilante and the person he or she kills, and in its aftermath. It is here that I analyze the impact of racial bias, violence-centered notions of what it means to be a man, police and vigilante attitudes and culture, and negative emotions on those deadly encounters, as well as how their outcomes reinforce or loosen the strength of police and vigilante killings as a violence-centered racial control mechanism.

I begin the final chapter of *Killing African Americans*, "Making Black Lives Matter: Lessons Learned and Unfinished Business," by placing the current efforts to make "black lives matter" within the larger sociohistorical context of the struggles of African Americans against racial violence throughout their history in the United States. In the remainder of the chapter I discuss not only what needs to be done to address the issue of the disproportionate, pervasive, and persistent police and vigilante killings of African Americans, but also what those who want progressive and fundamental change must do politically to *force* the nation's dominant racialized group to act.

Notes

1. Noel A. Cazenave, *The Urban Racial State: Managing Race Relations in American Cities* (Lanham, MD: Rowman and Littlefield, 2011), 142; W.E.B. DuBois, *The Souls of Black Folk* (Greenwich, CT: Fawcett, 1961), v.
2. Cazenave, *The Urban Racial State*, 139–42, 145; Alan Feuer, "$3 Million Deal in Police Killing of Diallo in '99," *New York Times*, January 7, 2004, www.nytimes.com/2004/01/07/

nyregion/3-million-deal-in-police-killing-of-diallo-in-99.html?_r=0, Accessed April 27, 2016; Manning Marable, *Race, Reform, and Rebellion: The Second Reconstruction and Beyond in Black America, 1945-2006* (Jackson, MS: University Press of Mississippi, 2007), 221. Because race/color terms such as "black," "white," and "race" used to racialize groups of people are erroneous and injurious, and because their uncritical use reifies them, I will not use them as if they are not problematic. Instead, when referring to groups of people I will typically use pan-ethnic designations such as African American, European American, Latino/a American, or Asian American, or more specific ethnic terminology like Irish American, Puerto Rican, or Jamaican. When I do use words such as black, white, and race I will usually place them within quotation marks to remind the reader that their uncritical use is problematic. I will not use quotation marks, however, if I am referring to highly racialized social and historical phenomena and events such as white power, white backlash, white power structure, black power, black nationalism, the Black Lives Matter movement and slogan, and white nationalism, or if I make it clear that such designations refer to perceptions one racialized group has of another. For more on my reasons for not uncritically using race/color terminology to refer to groups of people see my *Conceptualizing Racism* book: Noel A. Cazenave, *Conceptualizing Racism: Breaking the Chains of Racially Accommodative Language* (Lanham, MD: Rowman and Littlefield, 2016), 136, 146–48, 213–14, note # 2.

3. Noel A. Cazenave, "Understanding Our Many Fergusons: Kill Lines—The Will, the Right and the Need to Kill," *Truthout*, September 29, 2014, www.truth-out.org/opinion/item/26484-understanding-our-many-fergusons-kill-lines-the-will-the-right-and-the-need-to-kill, Accessed April 29, 2016; Earl E. Pollock, *Race and the Supreme Court* (Sarasota, FL: Peppertree Press, 2012), 36.

4. Cazenave, The Urban Racial State, 161.

5. Associated Press, "Cincinnati Officer is Acquitted in Killing that Ignited Unrest," *New York Times*, September 27, 2001, www.nytimes.com/2001/09/27/us/cincinnati-officer-is-acquitted-in-killing-that-ignited-unrest.html, Accessed April 25, 2016; Cazenave, *The Urban Racial State*, 161; Associated Press, "Cincinnati Settles Suits against Police," *New York Times*, May 23, 2003, www.nytimes.com/2003/05/23/us/cincinnati-settles-suits-against-police.html?ref=topics&pagewanted=print, Accessed May 12, 2016.

6. *Report of the National Advisory Commission on Civil Disorders* (New York: Bantam Books, 1968), 1, 11, 143; Chris Hayes, *A Colony in a Nation* (New York: W.W. Norton, 2017), 30–32.

7. Cazenave, *Conceptualizing Racism*, 119; Harvard Sitkoff, *The Struggle for Black Equality* (New York: Hill and Wang, 2008), 44.

8. Cazenave, Conceptualizing Racism, 119.

9. Cazenave, *Conceptualizing Racism*, 119; Glenn Kessler, "Was the 'Stand Your Ground' Law the 'Cause' of Trayvon Martin's Death?" *Washington Post*, October 29, 2014, www.washingtonpost.com/news/fact-checker/wp/2014/10/29/was-the-stand-your-ground-law-the-cause-of-trayvon-martins-death/?utm_term=.c1e15ce7001f, Accessed March 10, 2017; Lizette Alvarez and Cara Buckley, "Zimmerman is Acquitted in Trayvon Martin Killing," *New York Times*, July 13, 2013, www.nytimes.com/2013/07/14/us/george-zimmerman-verdict-trayvon-martin.html, Accessed June 15, 2017; Keeanga-Yamahtta Taylor, *From #BlackLivesMatter to Black Liberation* (Chicago, IL: Haymarket Books, 2016), 151; Christopher J. Lebron, *The Making of Black Lives Matter: A Brief History of an Idea* (New York: Oxford University Press, 2017), xi.

10. Cazenave, *Conceptualizing Racism*, 120; Lizette Alvarez, "Florida Self-Defense Law Complicated Jury's Job in Michael Dunn Trial," *New York Times*, February 16, 2014, www.nytimes.com/2014/02/17/us/florida-self-defense-law-hung-over-jury-in-michael-dunn-trial.html, Accessed March 10, 2017; Rick Neale, "Loud-Music Shooter's

Murder Conviction Upheld," *USA Today*, November 17, 2016, www.usatoday.com/story/news/nation-now/2016/11/17/loud-music-shooter-michael-dunn-murder-conviction-upheld/94030386/, Accessed June 16, 2017; Lizette Alvarez, "Florida Man is Convicted of Murdering Teenager in Dispute over Loud Music," *New York Times*, October 1, 2014, www.nytimes.com/2014/10/02/us/verdict-reached-in-death-of-florida-youth-in-loud-music-dispute.html?_r=0, Accessed April 26, 2016.

11. Mary M. Chapman, "Theodore Wafer Sentenced to 17 Years in Michigan Shooting of Renisha McBride," *New York Times*, September 3, 2014, www.nytimes.com/2014/09/04/us/theodore-wafer-sentenced-in-killing-of-renisha-mcbride.html?_r=0, Accessed April 26, 2016.

12. Cazenave, *Conceptualizing Racism*, 120; Al Baker, J. David Goodman, and Benjamin Mueller, "Beyond the Chokehold: The Path to Eric Garner's Death," *New York Times*, June 13, 2015, www.nytimes.com/2015/06/14/nyregion/eric-garner-police-chokehold-staten-island.html, Accessed April 26, 2016; Ford Fessenden, "New Perspective on Eric Garner's Death," *New York Times*, December 3, 2014, www.nytimes.com/interactive/2014/12/03/us/2014-12-03-garner-video.html, Accessed June 16, 2017; J. David Goodman and Al Baker, "Wave of Protests after Grand Jury Doesn't Indict Officer in Eric Garner Chokehold Case," *New York Times*, December 3, 2014, www.nytimes.com/2014/12/04/nyregion/grand-jury-said-to-bring-no-charges-in-staten-island-chokehold-death-of-eric-garner.html, Accessed April 26, 2016.

13. Cazenave, *Conceptualizing Racism*, 120; J. David Goodman, "Eric Garner Case Is Settled by New York City for $5.9 Million," *New York Times*, July 13, 2015, www.nytimes.com/2015/07/14/nyregion/eric-garner-case-is-settled-by-new-york-city-for-5-9-million.html?login=email&mtrref=www.google.com&assetType=nyt_now, Accessed April 26, 2016.

14. Julie Bosman and Emma G. Fitzsimmons, "Grief and Protests Follow Shooting of a Teenager," *New York Times*, August 10, 2014, www.nytimes.com/2014/08/11/us/police-say-mike-brown-was-killed-after-struggle-for-gun.html?_r=0, Accessed April 30, 2016; Frances Robles and Julie Bosman, "Autopsy Shows Michael Brown Was Struck at Least 6 Times," *New York Times*, August 17, 2014, www.nytimes.com/2014/08/18/us/michael-brown-autopsy-shows-he-was-shot-at-least-6-times.html, Accessed April 30, 2016; Cazenave, *Conceptualizing Racism*, 121; Wesley Lowery, *"They Can't Kill Us All": Ferguson, Baltimore, and a New Era in America's Racial Justice Movement* (New York: Little, Brown and Company, 2016), 24.

15. Cazenave, *Conceptualizing Racism*, 121; Emily Brown, "Timeline: Michael Brown Shooting in Ferguson, Mo," *USA Today*, August 10, 2015, www.usatoday.com/story/news/nation/2014/08/14/michael-brown-ferguson-missouri-timeline/14051827/, Accessed April 27, 2016.

16. Wilson Andrews, Alicia Desantis, and Josh Keller, "Justice Department's Report on the Ferguson Police Department," *New York Times*, March 4, 2015, www.nytimes.com/interactive/2015/03/04/us/ferguson-police-racial-discrimination.html?_r=0, Accessed May 4, 2016; Max Ehrenfreund, "The Risks of Walking While Black in Ferguson," *Washington Post*, March 4, 2015, www.washingtonpost.com/news/wonk/wp/2015/03/04/95-percent-of-people-arrested-for-jaywalking-in-ferguson-were-black/?utm_term=.47005ee5e2b6, Accessed March 10, 2017; John Eligon, "Ferguson Police Chief Thomas Jackson Joins Exodus of City Officials," *New York Times*, March 11, 2015, www.nytimes.com/2015/03/12/us/police-chief-joins-exodus-in-ferguson.html, Accessed May 4, 2016; Matt Apuzzo and Monica Davey, "Ferguson Nears Deal with Justice Dept. to Overhaul Police Force," *New York Times*, December 16, 2015, www.nytimes.com/2015/12/17/us/ferguson-nears-deal-with-justice-dept-to-overhaul-police-force.html, Accessed May 4, 2016; Hayes, *A Colony in a Nation*, 38.

17. Chicago Tribune Staff, "Laquan McDonald Police Reports Differ Dramatically from Video," *Chicago Tribune*, December 5, 2015, www.chicagotribune.com/news/ct-laquan-mcdonald-chicago police reports met 20151204-story.html, Accessed May 9, 2016; Monica Davey and Mitch Smith, "Video of Chicago Police Shooting a Teenager Is Ordered Released," *New York Times*, November 19, 2015, www.nytimes.com/2015/11/20/us/laquan-mcdonald-chicago-police-shooting.html, Accessed May 5, 2016; Steve Schmadeke, Jason Meisner, and Bill Ruthhart, "Shooting Video Latest Stain on Chicago's Policing Record," *Chicago Tribune*, November 25, 2015, www.chicagotribune.com/news/local/breaking/ct-chicago-cop-shooting-laquan-mcdonald-murder-charge-1125-20151124-story.html, Accessed May 5, 2016.

18. Schmadeke, Meisner, and Ruthhart, "Shooting Video Latest Stain on Chicago's Policing Record."

19. John Kass, "If Police Shooting Video Had Been Released Sooner, Would Emanuel Be Mayor?," *Chicago Tribune*, November 26, 2015, www.chicagotribune.com/news/ct-laquan-mcdonald-emanuel-kass-met-1126-20151125-column.html, Accessed May 5, 2016; Jeff Coen and John Chase, "Top Emanuel Aides Aware of Key Laquan McDonald Details Months Before Mayor Says He Knew," *Chicago Tribune*, January 14, 2016, www.chicagotribune.com/news/local/politics/ct-rahm-emanuel-laquan-mcdonald-shooting-met-20160113-story.html, Accessed May 5, 2016; Bill Ruthhart, Bob Secter, and David Kidwell, "Four New Laquan McDonald Shooting Videos Raise More Questions," *Chicago Tribune*, November 26, 2015, www.chicagotribune.com/news/ct-laquan-mcdonald-new-videos-met-20151125-story.html, Accessed May 9, 2016; Jeremy Gorner, "Chicago Officials Release Burger King Video from Laquan McDonald Shooting," *Chicago Tribune*, December 4, 2015, www.chicagotribune.com/news/ct-shooting-laquan-mcdonald-burger-king-video-met-20151203-story.html, Accessed May 9, 2016; Chicago Tribune Staff, "Laquan McDonald Police Reports Differ Dramatically from Video"; Monica Davey, "Officers' Statements Differ from Video in Death of Laquan McDonald," *New York Times*, December 5, 2015, www.nytimes.com/2015/12/06/us/officers-statements-differ-from-video-in-death-of-laquan-mcdonald.html?_r=0, Accessed May 9, 2015.

20. Davey and Smith, "Video of Chicago Police Shooting a Teenager Is Ordered Released; Chicago Tribune Staff, "Laquan McDonald Police Reports Differ Dramatically from Video"; Nausheen Husain, "Laquan McDonald Timeline: The Shooting, the Video and the Fallout," *Chicago Tribune*, January 13, 2017 and apparently updated since then, www.chicagotribune.com/news/laquanmcdonald/ct-graphics-laquan-mcdonald-officers-fired-timeline-htmlstory.html, Accessed April 8, 2017.

21. Monica Davey, "Prosecutor Criticized over Laquan McDonald Case is Defeated in Primary," *New York Times*," March 16, 2016, www.nytimes.com/2016/03/16/us/prosecutor-criticized-over-laquan-mcdonald-case-is-defeated-in-primary.html, Accessed May 9, 2016; Jeanne Kuang, "Group Slams Police Union Hire of Officer Charged in Laquan McDonald Shooting," *Chicago Tribune*, March 31, 2016, www.chicagotribune.com/news/laquanmcdonald/ct-laquan-mcdonald-jason-van-dyke-court-met-20160323-20160331-story.html, Accessed May 9, 2016; Chicago Police Accountability Task Force, "Police Accountability Task Force Recommendations for Reform: Restoring Trust between the Chicago Police and the Communities They Serve," Executive Summary, April 7, 2016, chicagopatf.org/, Accessed May 9, 2015; Editorial Board, "Editorial: Chicago Police Reforms: Mayor Emanuel's Meager 'Down Payment,'" *Chicago Tribune*, April 22, 2016, www.chicagotribune.com/news/opinion/editorials/ct-chicago-police-task-force-laquan-emanuel-edit-0425-jm-20160422-story.html, Accessed May 9, 2016; Julie Bosman and Mitch Smith, "Chicago Police Routinely Trampled on Civil Rights, Justice Dept, Says," *New York Times*, January 13, 2017, www.nytimes.com/2017/01/13/us/chicago-police-justice-department-report.html, Accessed April 9, 2017.

22. Shaila Dewan and Richard A. Oppel, Jr., "In Tamir Rice Case, Many Errors by Cleveland Police, Then a Fatal One," *New York Times*, January 22, 2015, www.nytimes.com/2015/01/23/us/in-tamir-rice-shooting-in-cleveland-many-errors-by-police-then-a-fatal-one.html?_r=0, Accessed May 1, 2016.

23. Dewan and Oppel, Jr., "In Tamir Rice Case, Many Errors by Cleveland Police, Then a Fatal One"; Plain Dealer Staff, "Cleveland Police Chase, Shooting a 'Systemic Failure' by the Department, Attorney General Mike DeWine Says (Video)," *Plain Dealer*, February 5, 2013, www.cleveland.com/metro/index.ssf/2013/02/cleveland_police_chase_shootin_1.html, Accessed June 20, 2017; Mitch Smith and Matt Apuzzo, "Cleveland Police to Accept Tough Standards on Force," *New York Times*, May 27, 2015, A1, A13.

24. Smith and Apuzzo, "Cleveland Police to Accept Tough Standards on Force"; Mitch Smith, "Six Cleveland Officers Fired for Role in Killing of Couple," *New York Times*, January 26, 2016, www.nytimes.com/2016/01/27/us/six-cleveland-officers-fired-for-role-in-2012-fatal-shooting-of-couple.html, Accessed May 4, 2016.

25. Timothy Williams and Mitch Smith, "Cleveland Officer Will Not Face Charges in Tamir Rice Shooting Death," *New York Times*, December 28, 2015, www.nytimes.com/2015/12/29/us/tamir-rice-police-shootiing-cleveland.html, Accessed May 3, 2016; Mitch Smith, "Tamir Rice's Family to Receive $6 Million from Cleveland," *New York Times*, April 25, 2016, www.nytimes.com/2016/04/26/us/tamir-rice-family-cleveland-settlement.html?_r=0, Accessed May 3, 2016; The Editorial Board, "Voters Tell Prosecutors, Black Lives Matter," *New York Times*, March 18, 2016, www.nytimes.com/2016/03/18/opinion/voters-tell-prosecutors-black-lives-matter.html, Accessed May 17, 2016.

26. Alan Blinder and Timothy Williams, "Ex-South Carolina Officer is Indicted in Shooting Death of Black Man," *New York Times*, June 8, 2015, www.nytimes.com/2015/06/09/us/former-south-carolina-officer-is-indicted-in-death-of-walter-scott.html, Accessed May 10, 2016; David Von Drehle, "Line of Fire: An Unarmed Black Man is Shot by a Police Officer—And This Time a Video Records the Killing. Where the Debate on Racism and Law Enforcement Goes from Here," *Time*, April 20, 2015, 24–28.

27. Michael S. Schmidt and Matt Apuzzo, "South Carolina Officer is Charged with Murder of Walter Scott," *New York Times*, April 7, 2015, www.nytimes.com/2015/04/08/us/south-carolina-officer-is-charged-with-murder-in-black-mans-death.html?_r=0, Accessed May 10, 2016.

28. Von Drehle, "Line of Fire: An Unarmed Black Man is Shot by a Police Officer—And This Time a Video Records the Killing," 27; Alan Blinder, "Mistrial for South Carolina Officer Who Shot Walter Scott," *New York Times*, December 5, 2016, www.nytimes.com/2016/12/05/us/walter-scott-michael-slager-north-charleston.html, Accessed April 6, 2017; Pete Williams, Craig Melvin, and Daniel Arkin, "Michael Slager, Ex-Cop Who Shot Walter Scott, to Plead Guilty in Civil Rights Case," NBC News, May 2, 2017, www.nbcnews.com/storyline/walter-scott-shooting/michael-slager-ex-cop-who-shot-walter-scott-plead-guilty-n753786, Accessed May 2, 2017; Holly Yan, Khushbu Shah, and Emanuella Grinberg, "Ex-Officer Michael Slager Pleads Guilty in Shooting Death of Walter Scott," CNN, May 2, 2017, www.cnn.com/2017/05/02/us/michael-slager-federal-plea/, Accessed May 2, 2017.

29. David A. Graham, "The Mysterious Death of Freddie Gray," *The Atlantic*, April 22, 2015, www.theatlantic.com/politics/archive/2015/04/the-mysterious-death-of-freddie-gray/391119/, Accessed May 11, 2016; Sheryl Gay Stolberg, "Police Officers Charged in Freddie Gray's Death to be Tried in Baltimore," *New York Times*, September 10, 2015, www.nytimes.com/2015/09/11/us/freddie-gray-trial-baltimore.html, Accessed May 11, 2016; Eliott C. McLaughlin and Amanda Watts, "Charges against Baltimore Officers in

Freddie Gray Case," CNN, December 16, 2015, www.cnn.com/2015/12/15/us/charges-against-baltimore-officers-freddie-gray-trials/, Accessed May 11, 2016.

30. Lynh Bui and Derek Hawkins, "Baltimore Prosecutors Say Freddie Gray Was Given 'Rough Ride' in Police Van," *Washington Post*, June 9, 2016, www.washingtonpost.com/local/public-safety/trial-of-officer-charged-with-murder-in-death-of-freddie-gray-set-to-begin/2016/06/08/25090374-2cc8-11e6-9b37-42985f6a265c_story.html?utm_term=.c41dd11e996b, Accessed April 10, 2017; Justin Fenton, "Autopsy of Freddie Gray Shows 'High-Energy' Impact," *Baltimore Sun*, June 24, 2015, www.baltimoresun.com/news/maryland/freddie-gray/bs-md-ci-freddie-gray-autopsy-20150623-story.html, Accessed May 11, 2016; *Baltimore Sun*, "Freddie Gray Autopsy: Excerpt from the Report," *Baltimore Sun*, June 24, 2015, www.baltimoresun.com/news/maryland/freddie-gray/bal-read-the-freddie-gray-autopsy-report-text-story.html, Accessed April 10, 2017. Bold letters in original.

31. Joshua Berlinger, "Baltimore Riots: A Timeline," CNN, April 28, 2015, www.cnn.com/2015/04/27/us/baltimore-riots-timeline/, Accessed May 11, 2016; Sabrina Toppa, "The Baltimore Riots Cost an Estimated $9 Million in Damages," *Time.com*, May 14, 2015, time.com/3858181/baltimore-riots-damages-businesses-homes-freddie-gray/, Accessed May 11, 2016.

32. Matt Apuzzo and Sheryl Gay Stolberg, "Justice Department Will Investigate Baltimore Police Practices," *New York Times*, May 7, 2015, www.nytimes.com/2015/05/08/us/politics/justice-department-will-investigate-baltimore-police-practices-after-freddie-gray-case.html?_r=0, Accessed June 22, 2017; Sheryl Gay Stolberg, "Freddie Gray Settlement Approved by Baltimore Officials," *New York Times*, September 9, 2015, www.nytimes.com/2015/09/10/us/freddie-gray-baltimore-police-death.html, Accessed June 22, 2017; Sheryl Gay Stolberg, "Baltimore's Mayor, Stephanie Rawlings-Blake, Won't Seek Re-Election," *New York Times*, September 11, 2015, www.nytimes.com/2015/09/12/us/baltimores-mayor-stephanie-rawlings-blake-wont-seek-re-election.html, Accessed August 8, 2017; Derek Hawkins, Lynh Bui, and Peter Hermann, "Baltimore Prosecutors Drop All Remaining Charges in Freddie Gray Case," *Washington Post*, July 27, 2016, www.washingtonpost.com/local/public-safety/baltimore-prosecutors-drop-all-remaining-charges-in-freddie-gray-case/2016/07/27/b5c10f34-b655-4d40-87e6-80827e2f0e2d_story.html, Accessed July 27, 2016; U.S. Department of Justice, *Investigation of the Baltimore City Police Department* (Washington, DC: Civil Rights Division, U.S. Department of Justice, August 10, 2016), 7, http://s3.documentcloud.org/documents/3009471/Bpd-Findings-8-10-16.pdf, Accessed August 10, 2016.

33. Kimberly Kindy, Marc Fisher, Julie Tate, and Jennifer Jenkins, "A Year of Reckoning: Police Fatally Shoot Nearly 1,000," *Washington Post*, December 26, 2015, http://www.washingtonpost.com/sf/investigative/2015/12/26/a-year-of-reckoning-police-fatally-shoot-nearly-1000/, Accessed April 24, 2016; Will Greenberg, "Here's How Badly Police Violence Has Divided America," *Mother Jones*, March 19, 2017, http://www.motherjones.com/media/2017/03/police-shootings-black-lives-matter-history-timeline, Accessed March 20, 2017; Malcolm X Grassroots Movement, "Operation Ghetto Storm: 2012 Annual Report on the Extrajudicial Killings of 313 Black People by Police, Security Guards and Vigilantes," April 4, 2013, mxgm.org/operation-ghetto-storm-2012-annual-report-on-the-extrajudicial-killing-of-313-black-people/, Accessed April 23, 2016; Maurice Halbwachs, *Maurice Halbwachs On Collective Memory* (Chicago, IL: University of Chicago Press, 1992), 22.

34. Mike Males, "Who Are Police Killing?," Center on Juvenile and Criminal Justice, August 26, 2014, www.cjcj.org/news/8113, Accessed March 8, 2017; Taylor, *From #BlackLives-Matter to Black Liberation*, 114.

35. Cazenave, Conceptualizing Racism, 110.
36. Percentage-wise, African American police officers are more likely to kill African Americans than European American police officers are. This is probably due to the fact that they are more likely to patrol inner-city neighborhoods with large concentrations of African Americans. Paul Butler, *Chokehold: Policing Black Men* (New York: The New Press, 2017), 33–34.
37. Achille Mbembe, "Necropolitics," *Public Culture*, 2003, 15 (1), 11.

2

MAKING SENSE OF THE KILLINGS: THEORETICAL INSIGHTS, CONCEPTUAL FRAMEWORK, AND MY RACIAL CONTROL ARGUMENT

Let us begin with a tale of two mothers. Imagine that you are an African American woman who has just been informed that your worst nightmare has come true. An hour earlier, your sixteen-year-old son—a good kid who has struggled with bipolar disorder—was shot to death by a police officer in a neighborhood playground after someone called 911 to complain that he was acting strangely. While the killing of your child was, indeed, the realization of your worst nightmare and of the anxiety that caused you to hug and kiss him each morning before he left home as if you might never see him again, it is not a concern shared by mothers in a more affluent and "whiter" part of town, who not only do not fear the police but are in fact grateful that they are there "to protect and to serve" them and their families. How does she—how do we—account for the radically different worlds inhabited by those two mothers, who live only a mile and a half from each other?

And there are still other questions that beg for answers. How do we make sense of the large numbers of often highly dramatic, and always real, police and vigilante killings of usually unarmed African Americans and the fact that such violence is rarely punished? How do we comprehend the post-Ferguson protests attitude expressed about the killing of Michael Brown in that Missouri town by St. Louis County Police Department police officer Dan Page, who after helping to police the protests there boasted to a right-wing group that "I'm . . . a killer . . . If you don't want to get killed, don't show up in front of me." How do we mentally process the warning by another officer, one with a Ph.D., who, also in response to the national uproar by African Americans about what happened in Ferguson, wrote an op-ed essay for the *Washington Post* titled: "I'm a Cop. If You Don't Want to Get Hurt, Don't Challenge Me?" And how do we comprehend how such an attitude could be asserted so assuredly in a nation where the police are so often "challenged" by European Americans, some of whom are clearly armed, who boldly proclaim their constitutional rights without facing such fatal consequences? In this chapter, I provide a conceptual framework, argument, and methodology that moves us closer to such understanding.[1]

Theoretical Insights from What We Already Know

I begin assembling and crafting the analytical tools for this study by reviewing a dozen bodies of scholarship that fit three broad and overlapping theoretical frameworks: social oppression theories; race relations, systemic racism, and racial state theories; and interaction theories that explain interpersonal violence.

But before I begin, a word of caution. Literature reviews are quite simplistic in their necessary slicing and dicing of social phenomena into conceptually and analytically convenient categories. As the movement toward intersectional research has stressed, however, in the real world it can be quite difficult to separate overlapping forms of oppression. In this study, you will find this to be especially true when it comes to the impact of police and vigilante killings as instruments of racial and class-based social control—factors which, when combined, can have their power increased exponentially. The class dimensions of racial oppression have been obvious from the beginning of the development of racist ideology to justify systems of economic exploitation such as colonialism and slavery. Then and now, economic elites have been able to mobilize racial animus against the racially oppressed to further their own economic interests and to stifle any possibilities of interracial alliances of the economically oppressed based on a shared class consciousness. So, as I review these various bodies of relevant literature, please remember that they should be viewed as convenient and oversimplified categories of overlapping social phenomena that cannot in fact be so easily separated.

Social Oppression Theories

Social oppression theories explain why and how groups of human beings oppress other groups of humans, how they keep them oppressed, and what those who are oppressed do to challenge such oppression. Oppression has been defined as "those attitudes, behaviors, and pervasive and systematic social arrangements by which members of one group are exploited and subordinated while members of another group are granted privileges." An important analytical feature of the concept that is evident in that definition is its ability to explain phenomena at the individual, interpersonal, group, institutional, and systems levels and to account for often interrelated forms of oppression such as those based on "race," class, gender, and sexual orientation. Theories of social oppression help us to understand why and how police and vigilante killings are used to maintain the power and privileges one social group enjoys at the expense of another. In this section of my literature review I examine two major categories of oppression-focused theories: class-centered theories and a more general and multidisciplinary social dominance theory.[2]

Class-Centered Theories of Oppression

Marxist theory. One of the oldest and most influential theories of oppression is contained within the work of the nineteenth-century radical intellectual Karl Marx. Marx, whose writings were not intended to provide a general theory of social oppression, has been called an economic determinist. According to Marx, all of a society's other major and interrelated institutions (e.g., family, religion, government, and education), its culture (e.g., art, music, literature, etc.), and other components comprise a superstructure that rests on its economic institutional base, which consists of the economic mode (e.g., capitalism, socialism, or communism) and means (e.g., money, factories, equipment, and labor) of production and the class relations (e.g., the bourgeoisie and the proletariat) they produce.[3]

Not surprisingly, Marx's main interest is oppressive class relations. An oversimplified, but useful, illustration of Marx's theory of oppression is that the factory-owner capitalists (the bourgeoisie) profit economically by gaining and keeping control of a society in such ways that allow them to pay their workers (the proletariat) as little as possible and have them work under whatever conditions they set for them. The bourgeoisie and other privileged classes rely on the police, and if necessary the military, as the ultimate instruments of social, political, and economic control to keep workers from getting out of hand either by engaging in individual acts of crime, such as theft or robbery, or rebellion, such as sabotage, or by trying to collectively organize a strike or a revolution. But more routinely they rely on system-sustaining ideologies generated and disseminated by the various components of the superstructure that the upper classes control, such as government, religion, education, the media, and the related ideas pervasive within popular culture.[4]

In his classic statement of how the material conditions under which one lives even shape one's consciousness of those conditions, Marx concludes that "it is not the consciousness of men that determines their existence, but their social existence that determines their consciousness." That is, it is not what they think that fashions their social location and circumstances, but their social location and circumstances that shape what they think. With this insight, we can better appreciate why groups of mothers born into very different racial and class circumstances view the police so differently—why some see them with fear and dread while others welcome them with open arms.[5]

Although Marxist theory offers a useful analytical perspective and set of concepts for understanding various forms of social oppression, it should be remembered that Marx was a nineteenth-century figure whose ideas were developed to explain how capitalism worked at that time. A major flaw in his theory is its assumption that capitalism had within itself the seeds of its own destruction. It assumed, for example, that as capitalism extracted more and more profit from exploited workers, they would eventually develop the kind of class consciousness that would lead to a worker's revolution through which they would seize control of the economy and the rest of society. In *Capital in the Twenty-First Century*,

Thomas Piketty documents how, because of its flexibility and adaptability, capitalism has not only survived but thrived into the twentieth and twenty-first centuries. As African American intellectual W.E.B. DuBois made clear more than eight decades ago, another important reason most European American workers have not developed class consciousness is their willingness to accept the "psychological wage" of whiteness, consisting of racial consciousness and privileges, rather than uniting as an oppressed class with working- and lower-class African Americans and other racially and economically oppressed people to obtain real *economic* wages.[6]

Neo-Marxist explanations of economic neoliberalism. Various neo-Marxist scholars have attempted to salvage the essentials of Marxist social thought while making the modifications needed for it to more accurately explain what is happening today, such as the central role that racism has played in the United States in preventing its working classes from uniting in the pursuit of their own class interests and the rise of a new form of extreme free-market capitalism known as economic neoliberalism.

In his essay on the history of neoliberalism, George Monbiot traces the origin of the term, which its advocates rarely use today, to a 1938 meeting in Paris of right-wing delegates who equated the social democracy of the British welfare state and Roosevelt's New Deal in the United States with what they considered to be the collectivist tyranny of Nazism and communism. During the following decade of the 1940s, intellectuals who shared the view that "government planning, by crushing individualism, would lead inexorably to totalitarian control" wrote books that disseminated those ideas to wealthy individuals who, because they found them useful in their fight against what they saw as oppressive government taxes and regulations, funded think tanks, academic positions within university departments, and other entities to promote their cause. As the movement grew in the 1950s and became "more strident," it shed its name. After remaining largely dormant during the tumultuous 1960s it anonymously reasserted itself in the 1970s and 1980s and has ever since been a major player in the economic elite's use of governments to institute monetary and social policies that radically redistribute income and wealth upward throughout much of the world.[7]

The term neo*liberalism* is deceptive. While liberalism has always had
as one of its chief goals the making of the minimum changes necessary
to maintain a socio-economic system essentially as it is, as you have
seen, advocates of neoliberalism found the status quo unacceptable. They
particularly resented a progressive tax system that financed the government's social contract with the middle and working classes—and the
poor—in terms of providing a welfare state set of social programs that
gave them both a safety net and educational and other opportunities
for social advancement. Consequently, the shifting of American politics farther and farther to the right required that the term "liberal" be
discredited as a left-wing call for wasteful government spending on the
poor and other "bleeding-heart" policies. The rise of neoliberalism as
both an ideology and a set of economic and political policies and practices has helped propel the rightward movement of governments today
by promoting an extreme form of hypercapitalism. At the core of neoliberalism is the assumption that what is good for the market is good for
society, and there should therefore be no regulation, taxes, or other limits
placed on assumed "free" markets. Of particular importance to this study
is the neoliberal mandate that *while the safety nets that provide for those
who are struggling economically are eliminated, the social control apparatus
of repressive laws, police, courts, and prisons that protect the property and
other interests of the rich and wealthy are greatly expanded.* So, the apparent
irony of neoliberalism, as a form of extreme capitalism, is that while it
insists on no regulation of the markets that benefit the well-to-do, it
requires very tight management of nearly every facet of the lives of those
who are not affluent.

Some observers noted the racial implications of the radical shift in
the nation's political economy just as African Americans seemed to have
gained some real power with the successes of the civil rights movement.
In 1970 sociologist Sidney Wilhelm published *Who Needs the Negro?*,
with its ominous conclusion that, like Native Americans before them,
African Americans faced the threat of genocide. For African Americans, their perilous status was not driven by the desire of members of
the racially dominant group for their land, but arose because while white
racial animus continued, due to automation and other changes in the

economy, African American labor was no longer needed. The "African Americans as economically obsolete" argument was also captured a year later in a book published by Samuel Yette, an African American journalist, titled *The Choice: The Issue of Black Survival in America*, in which Yette warned: "Black Americans have outlived their usefulness. Their *raison d-etre* to this society has ceased to be a compelling one. Once an economic asset, they are now an economic drag." Given America's violent and racist history, for Wilhelm, Yette, and many concerned African Americans, the notion of African Americans now being both "black" and useless evoked the specter of genocide. Following that argument and sentiment, Wilhelm concluded that the real function of Richard Nixon's "law and order" campaign slogan and policies—which nearly a half century later Donald Trump skillfully placed at the center of his own campaign and presidency—was providing "ideological justification for their otherwise indefensible deeds," and Yette denounced it as nothing more than "a euphemism for the total repression and possible extermination of those in the society who cry out for justice where little justice can be found." Both men seemed to have anticipated the post-civil rights movement era of mass incarceration and highly publicized police and vigilante killings of African Americans. This is Yette raising the issue of African Americans choosing to live only with dignity, which seems to be so central to the drama of so many of today's encounters between African Americans and the police and vigilantes who confront them. "They want to survive, but only as men and women—no longer as pawns or chattel."[8]

Decades later, as the ominous consequences of what Wilhelm and Yette warned about—the increasing economic obsolescence of many African Americans—had become all too obvious, French sociologist and Marxist scholar Loic Wacquant provided important insights into the racial and other social consequences of neoliberal policies and practices. Wacquant focused specifically on the dramatic increase in the mass incarceration of African Americans, a phenomenon which I will go on to show is inextricably linked to the current police and vigilante killings of African Americans. As Michele Alexander would do later in her groundbreaking *The New Jim Crow*, and I do in this study, in an article he published in 2000 Wacquant placed what he saw happening to

African Americans within the larger political-economic context of the exploitation they have faced throughout American history. In making his case that for African Americans, prison is the nation's new "peculiar institution," Wacquant argues:

> Not one but several 'peculiar institutions' have operated to define, confine, and control, African Americans in the history of the United States: chattel slavery from the colonial era to the Civil War, the Jim Crow system in the agrarian South from Reconstruction to the Civil Rights revolution; the ghetto in the northern industrial metropolis; and, in the post-Keynesian age of desocialized wage labor and welfare retrenchment, the novel institutional complex formed by the remnants of the dark ghetto and the carceral apparatus with which it has become joined by a relationship of structural symbiosis and functional surrogacy. In the 1970s, as the urban 'Black Belt' lost its economic role of labor extraction and proved unable to ensure ethnoracial closure, the prison was called upon to shore up caste division and help contain a dishonored and supernumerary population viewed both as deviant and dangerous.[9]

Nearly a decade later, in *Punishing the Poor: The Neoliberal Government of Social Insecurity*, Wacquant characterizes repressive state control actions as "penal pornography" to make an important point about how they are used to terrorize African Americans.

> The rampant gesticulation over law and order is conceived and carried out not so much for its own sake as *for the express purpose of being exhibited and seen*, scrutinized, ogled: the absolute priority is to put on a spectacle, in the literal sense of the term. For this, words and deeds proclaiming to fight crime and assorted disorders must be methodologically orchestrated, exaggerated, dramatized, even *ritualized*. This explains why, much like the staged carnal entanglements that fill pornographic movies, they are extraordinarily repetitive, mechanical, uniform, and therefore eminently *predictable*.[10]

As highlighted by the outrageous and almost theatrical case examples of police and vigilante killings of African Americans which I examined in Chapter 1, for African Americans the terror value of such killings seems to be enhanced by their performance as an all too predictable "spectacle" of drama, with its carefully scripted plot and cast of characters.

More recently, radical African American scholars such as Sundiata K. Cha-Jua and Keeanga-Yamahtta Taylor have included the neoliberal explanation of contemporary African American exploitation in analyses which also place systemic racism at their core. Their analyses stress how racism works under today's colorblind ideology and how the growing class cleavages among African Americans make its lower classes more vulnerable to exploitation and abuse.[11]

Social Dominance Theory

A recent trend in the behavioral sciences is the effort to develop a more general, multidisciplinary theory of oppression. In their book *Social Dominance: An Intergroup Theory of Social Hierarchy and Oppression*, psychologists Jim Sidanius and Felicia Pratto detail what they refer to as an integrative intergroup theory of social hierarchy and oppression that incudes theoretical and empirical insights from social psychology, political sociology, political science, and evolutionary psychology. As you will see, Sidanius and Pratto's work provides an impressive body of empirically grounded theory that is chock full of ideas that can be applied to an analysis of police and vigilante killings of African Americans.[12]

Building on its assumption that "all human societies tend to be structured as systems of *group-based social hierarchies*," social dominance theory (SDT) "attempts to identify the various mechanisms that produce and maintain" it "and how these mechanisms interact." One of the key mechanisms for the maintenance of such inequality is *systematic terror*, "the use of violence or threats of violence disproportionately directed against subordinates." Such terror can take three forms: *official terror* (e.g., government-executed police violence), *semiofficial terror* (e.g., police violence that, while not officially sanctioned by government, is tolerated), or *unofficial terror* (e.g., unsanctioned private vigilante violence), and "is likely to be most ferocious when subordinates directly challenge and confront the hegemonic control of dominants."[13]

From their review of cross-national evidence, Sidanius and Pratto identify the key role that criminal justice systems play in social oppression.

They note, for example, that "as we look around the world and across human history, we consistently see that subordinates are prosecuted and imprisoned at substantially higher rates than dominants." And, in stressing the crucial link between the law and terror, they conclude that "the criminal justice system's differential treatment of dominants and subordinates is clearly *systematic* and essentially inseparable from the expression of group-based power. Not only does the law function to maintain the group-based social order, but it also helps to reproduce this group-based social order." From their review of the empirical evidence, they conclude that group discrimination within the criminal justice follows basic principles or laws so common across social systems that they can be characterized as "laws of law." The fourth of those five laws, "The Tolerance of Abuse Principle," is especially relevant to this study because it explains why prosecution, much less conviction, of the police for wrongdoing against members of socially oppressed groups is so rare. As Sidanius and Pratto put it, "the degree of negative sanctions against security forces for abuses of power will tend to be exceedingly small, especially in cases of abuse against subordinates."[14]

Another key assumption of SDT is that the oppressed play a key role in both reinforcing their oppression (e.g., though their internalization of negative stereotypes, by resigning themselves to the self-fulfilling prophecy of engaging in behavior such as crime that is used to justify their oppression, or by more affluent African Americans supporting harsh actions against the African American poor from whom they try to distance themselves) and challenging it (e.g., through social protest).[15]

Race Relations, Systemic Racism, and Racial State Theories

The next category of theories I review explains the workings of American race relations and the highly organized system of race-based oppression known as systemic racism, as well as the role of the state, and its numerous appendages, in the construction and maintenance of racial oppression. These theories can help us understand why African Americans are targeted for the type of surveillance, harassment, and other actions that lead to their being so disproportionately killed by the police and vigilantes.

Race Relations Theory

Racial oppression theory. As I have just reviewed social oppression theories, I begin my discussion of race relations theory by examining a theory of racial oppression that fits both categories. In their book *A Socio-History of Black–White Relations in America*, sociologists Jonathan H. Turner, Royce Singleton, Jr., and David Musick define oppression as

> a situation in which one, or more, identifiable segments of the population in a social system systematically and successfully act over a prolonged period of time to prevent another identifiable segment, or segments, of the population from attaining access to the scarce and valued resources of that system.

Turner et al identify four variables—all of which apply to the police and vigilante killings of African Americans—that account for the success and persistence of social oppression. They are:

> (1) the degree to which an oppressed population can be readily identified, (2) the degree of emotional arousal of oppressors, (3) the respective degrees of power of the oppressed and oppressors, and (4) the degree to which oppression can be institutionalized in key social structures and prevailing cultural beliefs.

As you may recall, all four of these were evident in George Zimmerman's killing of Trayvon Martin and other case examples of police and vigilante killings detailed in Chapter 1.[16]

Group position theory. As you have seen, this book is organized around the premise that police and vigilante violence targeted at African Americans functions as a violence-centered *racial control mechanism*. Although it may seem radical, the concept of racial control is in no way a significant departure from mainstream American sociological theory. Indeed, because social control has been a central concern of the discipline since its inception, it is not surprising that one of the most empirically tested propositions about race relations is that its social controls are tightened when there is a perceived threat to the racial status quo. In his attempt to provide a more sociological explanation of prejudice than was commonly accepted at that time, in the late 1950s, symbolic interactionist

Herbert Blumer argued in his group position theory of racial relations that, rather than being viewed as animus held by bigoted individuals, prejudice could best be explained as having its origin in a "sense of group position." That is, "race prejudice is fundamentally a matter of relationship between racial groups," in that it is a "defensive reaction" and "protective device" that serves "to preserve the integrity and the position of the dominant group." In brief, Blumer concluded, as I would put it, that prejudice—such as the racist stereotype of African Americans as criminals—exists and persists because it functions as a psycho-emotional mechanism of racial control.[17]

The racial threat hypothesis. Sociological research has found that one of the most powerful predictors of continuity and change in social phenomena is demographics, i.e., population size, composition, and change. Consistent with that fact, in the late 1960s, nearly a decade after Blumer's article, which emphasized subjective meanings, sociologist Hubert M. Blalock, Jr. brought those more macro-level and objective factors into his "threat" theory (also known as group threat theory and racial threat theory) of what he referred to as "minority-group relations." In that way, Blalock was able to account for the simultaneous workings of both objective and subjective factors by hypothesizing that there are two "psychological mechanisms" that link the percentage of minority group members in a given geographic area with the "discriminatory behavior" they face: "a fear of economic competition" and "a power threat based on the fear that the minority might gain political dominance."[18]

Decades later, in a book he edited titled *Social Threat and Social Control*, Allen E. Liska made his case for the centrality of both concepts to sociology and our understanding of social phenomenon. First, in specific reference to the criminal justice system, he observes that social threat impacts "the pattern and shape of deviance and crime control institutions, organizations, programs, and policies" and, in turn, those things "substantially affect the structure and organization of society and people's daily lives." He then states that because "originally, the concept was defined as any structure, process, relationship, or act that contributes to the social order . . . the study of social order and social control were indistinguishable."[19]

While the social control emphasis of sociology has deep roots in the concern with breakdown of social order and stability expressed by its more conservative founders, such as Auguste Comte and Emile Durkheim, Liska points out that since the turbulent mid-1960s the dominant explanation of the phenomenon within American sociology has come from adherents of the more left-leaning conflict-theoretical perspective. Within such an approach, "lawmaking is assumed to reflect the interests of the powerful" and "the greater the number of acts and people threatening to the interests of the powerful, the greater the level of deviance and crime control." For Liska the most extreme form of such control is fatal control, which entails killing the "threatening population." From there he moves to his review of Blalock's racial threat hypothesis and makes the case for the need for the chapters that follow by noting that not only are the existing studies that set out to test it inconclusive, but their methodology has not changed significantly since Blalock formulated his ideas in the late 1960s. Of particular relevance to this study is Liska's functional-equivalence hypothesis, which states that "some forms of deviance and crime control are functionally equivalent; that is, they perform similar control functions, and, therefore, as one form increases the others decrease." For example, with the abolition of slavery there has been a succession of violence-centered and criminalization-justified control mechanisms targeted at African Americans that meet Liska's criterion, including group vigilantism and lynching, the death penalty, mass incarceration, and, of course, today's police and vigilante killings.[20]

In another article in that collection, Liska and his co-author, Jiang Yu, outline how the racial threat hypothesis can be applied specifically to the contemporary police killings of African Americans. That is, as African Americans, who are routinely subjected to racist stereotypes such as their being dangerous black criminals, reach a larger proportion of the population, that "affects the threat perceived by police and thereby the police homicide rate." Six years after Liska released that edited collection of racial threat hypothesis-focused papers, David Jacobs and Robert M. O'Brien published an article in a leading sociology journal which examined political and threat explanations of "the state's use of internal violence" which

suggest that killings by the police would be "greatest in stratified jurisdictions with more minorities." Their analysis of police killings in 170
cities found that "racial inequality" provides the best explanation for such
killings. When Jacobs and O'Brien specifically analyzed the police killings of African Americans, they found that "cities with more blacks and
a recent growth in the black population have higher police killing rates of
blacks, but the presence of a black mayor reduces these killings." They also
found that, contrary to class-centered theories, their results held up when
they controlled for "economic disparity," and that such racial differences
remained when the overall amount of interpersonal violence the police
encountered was taken into account.[21]

In a more recent analysis of 721 police shootings in the United States
from 2011 to 2014, Cody Ross found that, after controlling for other
relevant factors, not only were unarmed African Americans three and a
half times more likely to be shot by the police than unarmed European
Americans, but *un*armed African Americans were as likely to be shot as
armed European Americans. Consistent with the racial threat hypothesis, as well as the literature I have reviewed on neoliberalism, Ross also
found that "racial bias in police shootings is most likely to emerge in
police departments in large metropolitan counties with low median
incomes and a sizable portion of black residents, especially when there
is high financial inequality in that county."[22]

Although, as has been seen, the racial threat hypothesis has important
heuristic value for this study, given its insufficient attention to racist
attitudes and emotions it provides only a partial explanation of police
and vigilante killings of African Americans. And, in the absence of a
fully fleshed-out systemic racism theory, even studies that include more
racism-centered variables would be at a loss to provide an adequate
explanation of what is actually happening—one that goes beyond simply assuming that racial animus is purely reactive and solely in response
to economic competition and political threat.

More recent "macropsychological" research has found that the disproportionate killings of African Americans vary with regional differences
in racial bias. Eric Hehman, Jessica K. Flake, and Jimmy Calanchini
found from their analysis of both implicit and explicit bias, based on a

sample of more than two million residents from across the United States, that when relevant demographic variables were controlled for, "only the implicit racial prejudices and stereotypes of White residents" explained such regional differences in the disproportionate police use of lethal force against African Americans. This finding suggests that in understanding such killings the focus should not be on the implicit or explicit bias of individual officers, as if they are somehow isolated or, indeed, deviant from society-wide racial attitudes and stereotypes. Instead, consistent with my racial control argument, in the use of lethal force, individual police officers are actually implementing the expectations of the larger European American community. As former federal prosecutor and Georgetown University law professor Paul Butler put it in his book *Chokehold: Policing Black Men*, "The work of police is to preserve law and order, including the racial order." In brief, they serve as agents of racial control.[23]

Such macropsychological research is moving the implicit bias research of psychologists into the larger social context of systemic racism more commonly articulated by sociologists. As this book's readers will see, it was the modern civil rights movement that challenged existing race relations thinking by forcing into the national discourse and social science theory its view, long held by African Americans, that racism is systemic.

Systemic Racism Theory

Kwame Ture and Charles Hamilton's institutional racism theory. One of the most important precursors to systemic racism theory was published in 1967 by two African Americans. One of them, Stokely Carmichael, was a young civil rights activist who later changed his name to Kwame Ture, and the other, Charles Hamilton, was a political science professor. In *Black Power*, they introduced the concept of institutional racism. Because a social system is composed of all of a society's interrelated institutions, the concept of institutional racism was an important step towards a systemic racism perspective.[24]

Ture and Hamilton conceptualized racism as being something much larger than the then dominant view; the prejudiced attitudes and actions of bigoted individuals. Moreover, their definition of racism as "the predication of decisions and policies on considerations of race for the purpose of *subordinating* a racial group and maintaining control over that group" fits the racial control focus of this study. Finally, by viewing racism as a phenomenon that goes well beyond intentional actions, they stress that it can manifest itself in ways that are largely invisible and very impersonal.

> Racism is both overt and covert. It takes two, closely related forms ... individual racism and institutional racism. The first consists of overt acts by individuals ... The second type is less overt, far more subtle, less identifiable in terms of *specific* individuals committing the acts. But it is no less destructive of human life. The second type originates in the operation of established and respected forces in the society, and thus receives far less public condemnation than the first type.[25]

For example, Ture and Hamilton would characterize the overtly racist actions of a rogue police officer as *individual* racism, whereas they would view the systemic racial profiling of African Americans by the police in the enforcement of highly racialized policies and practices such as the War on Drugs and Stop-and-Frisk as examples of *institutional* racism.

The contours of the emerging systemic racism perspective were also evident in the findings of President Johnson's National Advisory Commission on Civil Disorders, released the year after Ture and Hamilton published *Black Power*. In explaining the pervasiveness and intensity of violent unrest in American cities during the "long hot summer" of 1967, the document—which came to be known as the Kerner report, after Otto Kerner, the Illinois governor who chaired the commission—found that due to the nation's "white racism," racial tensions had reached the point where the country was splitting into "two societies, one black, one white—separate and unequal." In explaining how white racism worked, the Kerner commission report focused specifically on the containment of many African Americans in racially segregated ghettoes: "white society is deeply implicated in the ghetto. White institutions created it, white institutions maintain it, and white society condones it." What became known as systemic racism theory was more fully developed in the 1970s by European American scholars such as Joel Kovel, Robert

Blauner, David Wellman, and Joe Feagin, who had by the end of that decade become its leading exponent.[26]

Joel Kovel's White Racism: A Psychohistory. Joel Kovel treats the United States as "a 'racist society,'" in which its "racism evolves historically, and may be expected to appear in different phases in different epochs and locales." He fleshes out this idea in three psycho-historical stages of white racism: dominative racism, aversive racism, and metaracism. Dominative racism, which was characteristic of the South during slavery, entailed overt physical and sexual oppression. Aversive racism explains, for example, the racial animus of highly segregated Northern cities and their suburbs, which combined racial ghettoization with an attitude of emotional repulsion and coldness toward African Americans. Finally, the metaracism of the late twentieth century to the present is covert and highly institutionalized, operating largely through the invisible and impersonal, but highly racialized, mechanizations of the economy and technology.[27]

Kovel's psychohistorical stages offer a useful analytical tool for better understanding what criminalization-justified racial control mechanisms operate during which period of American economic history and race relations, and how. The slave patrol precursors of modern policing in the United States emerged to protect slavery and its dominative form of racism. Corrupt sheriffs and other elements of the criminal justice system enforced the labor needs of the debt peonage/Jim Crow economy of the South under a hybrid dominative/aversive racism. Group vigilante violence by European American residents of "white" neighborhoods ensured the ghettoization of African Americans driven by aversive racism, and it was such ghettoization that made a racially targeted War on Drugs and its mass incarceration offshoot possible. Finally, under today's meta-racism, it is the ostensibly colorblind, hyperaggressive policing of African American communities, due to a host of circumstances rooted in their often precarious economic position, that justifies their being treated as occupied territories in which any African American who makes a fuss about being treated inhumanely can be killed by anxiety-, anger-, and fear- driven and trigger-happy police officers and vigilantes.[28]

Robert Blauner's Racial Oppression in America. In his book, which was published two years after Kovel's study, sociologist Robert Blauner also stressed that because contemporary racism was institutionalized, it could not be reduced to the prejudiced attitudes of racially bigoted individuals. To explain racism as "a system of racial oppression," Blauner combined elements of the "racism as domestic colonialism" metaphor with Marxist theory and concluded that "racism is a system of domination as well as a complex of beliefs and attitudes."[29]

David Wellman's Portraits of White Racism. Drawing upon data collected for a research project he directed for Blauner, David Wellman also stressed the need to move beyond the discipline's dominant prejudice-centered explanation of racism. This is how Wellman described racial stratification in the United States:

> I view racial stratification as part of the structure of American society, much like class division. Instead of being a remnant from the past, the social hierarchy based on race is a critical component in the organization of modern American society. The subordination of people of color is functional to the operation of American society as we know it and the color of one's skin is a primary determinant of a person's position in the social structure. Racism is a structural relationship based on the subordination of one racial group by another. Given this perspective, the determining feature of race relations is not prejudice toward blacks, but rather the superior position of whites and the institutions—ideological as well as structural—which maintain it.[30]

Consistent with this perspective, one need not find individual racial bigots acting in overtly racist ways to demonstrate the existence of racism. Indeed, in his study of police treatment of African American men, Paul Butler cites studies that have found that African American police officers, perhaps due to the fact that they are more likely to work in largely African American inner-city neighborhoods, are proportionately more likely to kill African Americans than European American police officers. Therefore, *this study does not focus on the racial attitudes and behavior of individual police officers and vigilantes.* As you will see, racism, as a highly organized *system* of race-justified oppression embedded in each of the overlapping institutions which collectively comprise society, can work fine without them. Police and vigilantes of any racialized ethnicity, and with a wide range of racial attitudes, can and do carry out highly racialized killings. This also means that demonstrating the existence of racism entails an examination of the working of racist social structures, not the impossible task of somehow "proving" what is in the hearts and minds of the individual police officers or vigilantes.[31]

Joe Feagin's systemic racism theory. The most prolific and influential exponent of systemic racism theory today is sociologist Joe Feagin. In his 1977 article "Indirect Institutionalized Discrimination," Feagin fleshed out a typology and other details of Ture and Hamilton's institutional racism concept in a way that made explicit the conceptual links required for its transition to what would become a more fully developed systemic racism theory. Because a social system is simply the organization all of a society's interrelated social institutions and other social entities, the distance between an institutional and a systemic racism perspective is not very far. At the core of that analytical expansion is the fact that racism is both systemic in its organization and workings and cumulative in its effect. In explaining the systemic nature of racism and other forms of discrimination, Feagin states that such oppression entails "the interaction between direct and indirect discrimination, and between discrimination in various institutional sectors," which "takes on a complex form which can be termed 'systemic discrimination' or the 'web of discrimination.'" Feagin then shines his analytical spotlight on the cumulative nature of social oppression by stressing that in addition to its being "interlocking," it is also "cumulative, involving many institutional sectors at the same point in time." In this way, he highlights both the highly structured and dynamic nature of systemic racism.[32]

In *Discrimination American Style: Institutional Racism and Sexism*, which Feagin published that following year with his wife Clairece as his co-author, the Feagins went into greater detail in explaining the four-fold typology of discrimination based on the two dimensions of scale (i.e., social embeddedness) and intent. The first discrimination type, *isolate discrimination*, is the form that is smallest in its sociological scope, and is intentional. An example is a racially bigoted and rogue police officer or lone vigilante whose actions are out of line with departmental and/or community standards. While *small-group discrimination* is identical to isolate discrimination in the fact that it is also intentional and violates social norms against such behavior, instead of being limited to the actions of a lone individual, it is behavior engaged in by a small group of people. Here we might have a small group of racially bigoted police officers or vigilante members. *Direct institutionalized discrimination* exists when a group of people intentionally discriminates against members of another group with widespread social support for their actions. This would include the actions of police officers and vigilantes who used deadly force to enforce Jim Crow and Apartheid laws and other norms in the United States and in South Africa, respectively, as well as the mayors and top police administrators in New York City who, until recently, pressured the city's police officers to target African Americans in their stop-and-frisk actions and other hyperaggressive policing methods. Finally, in *indirect institutionalized discrimination*—the form of discrimination in which the Feagins are most interested—there is a high level of social organization but a lower level of intent. An example is a criminal justice system which, while ostensibly colorblind, treats people of African American descent more harshly at every point of contact (e.g., the initial encounter, arrest, prosecution, conviction, sentencing, and parole) and level (the police, the courts, legislation), including making them more likely targets of police and vigilante killings.[33]

Indirect institutionalized discrimination has two subcategories. The first, *side-effect discrimination*, refers to discrimination occurring in one institutional arena that manifests itself in another where no discrimination is evident. For example, racial discrimination in employment may negatively impact the overall socio-economic status of many African Americans, making them more vulnerable to the operations of the criminal justice system by placing them in the ranks of the poor, whose neighborhoods are more likely to be heavily patrolled by the police. The second subcategory of indirect institutionalized discrimination is *past-in-present discrimination*, in which past acts of racial discrimination negatively impact members of historically racially oppressed groups today.

For example, because in many cities African Americans tended not to be hired as police officers in significant numbers until fairly recently, many African American job applicants do not have the same knowledge of how to enter into and advance through the system as European American applicants who come from generations of family members who have worked in the local police department—for example, when and where to apply, how to prepare for civil service tests, how to keep or get clean police records. Moreover, due to seniority provisions in their union contracts, African Americans are more likely to face the "last hired–first fired" conundrum: because they are relatively new hires, when the city, town, or state faces tough times financially they may be among the first to be laid off. In these and other ways, past overt and direct institutional discrimination often manifests itself today as past-in-present discrimination in police departments that, because they do not reflect the racial makeup of the communities they serve, are more likely to treat their African American residents and other residents of color in ways that are racially bigoted, inhumane, and sometimes fatally violent.[34]

My Conceptualizing Racism book. In *Conceptualizing Racism*, I discuss my own approach to systemic racism. For example, I note that in an early lecture of the White Racism course I have taught at the University of Connecticut since the mid-1990s, I state that "unlike what is generally assumed, racism is a group and societal-level phenomenon . . . one that cannot be reduced to the prejudice and behavior of individuals." In that book, I also include a figure that graphically summarizes my conceptualization of racism as a "highly organized system of 'race' justified oppression." That figure maps out the relationship between systemic racism's racist historical foundation; its interrelated major institutions of economics, politics, education, family, and religion; and "race" and other racist ideologies, including racist stereotypes and images, which bind it all together at its core. It suggests that to understand the police and vigilante killings of African Americans, we must place those killings within the context of a long history of violence-centered racial control systems and mechanisms targeted at African Americans and recognize that they persist because they are supported directly or indirectly by every interrelated institution of American society, and are fueled and justified by racist notions of who African Americans are (e.g., dangerous black criminals) and, therefore, how they should be treated.[35]

The lesson of systemic racism theory is clear: racism can occur at various points and levels of the police and vigilante killings of African Americans. While some of that racism may be overt, much of it is hidden within highly organized social structures and processes. However, the reason why such disproportionate killings exist and persist is not nearly so complex or hard to explain. The fact that they are encouraged by a highly racialized criminal justice system, with strong links to politics and every other institution of society, enables them to occur with relative impunity, compared to how the nation treats its other citizens and residents who are not citizens. Such actions persist, therefore, because they are both racially normative and prescribed. With that in mind, in this study my focus is on systemic racism as highly organized, society-wide, and historically rooted racist attitudes, policies, and practices that can in no way be reduced to the question of whether an individual police officer or vigilante is intentionally or unintentionally racially bigoted. In brief, systemic racism theory rejects the explanation that what is happening entails no more than "a few bad apples," and instead directs us to examine the entire "bag" of social structures and processes to see where the rot comes from.

Figure 2.1 illustrates the key factors involved in the disproportionate police and vigilante killings of African Americans, and their various reciprocal relationships, from a systemic racism perspective.

That figure shows that *racist stereotypes*, including but not limited to the view of African Americans as dangerous criminals, justify the *racial discrimination* African Americans experience and the resulting *racial disparities* they endure. Such disparities include resources (e.g., income, wealth, education, job, and housing opportunities) that would normally shelter them from negative experiences within the criminal justice system (e.g., in racial profiling, arrests, prosecutions, convictions, and sentencings) and fatal encounters with its police. The reciprocal relationship between these three factors makes African American prime targets for the *disproportionate police and vigilante killings* which, for all

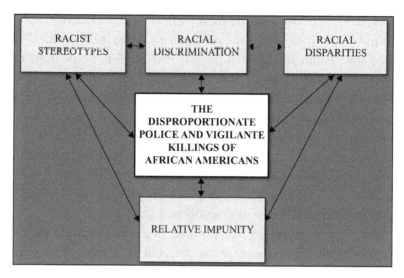

Figure 2.1 Racist Stereotypes, Racial Discrimination, Racial Disparities, Relative Impunity, and the Disproportionate Police and Vigilante Killings of African Americans

of the reasons mentioned above, are most likely to happen with *relative impunity* compared to the treatment of other American citizens or non-citizen residents. Finally, when such killings happen with impunity, that reinforces the entire system of reciprocal relationships, as the cycle of killing African Americans with impunity strengthens as it repeats itself. To better understand how that happens, we must examine a critical administrative component of systemic racism: the political institution and its various non-governmental appendages.

Racial State Theories

Michael Omi and Howard Winant's racial state theory. Although the term "racial state" may have been first used in the 1940s to help explain the genocide and other highly racialized atrocities committed by Nazi Germany, the concept went largely underdeveloped until the mid-1980s, when Michael Omi and Howard Winant included a chapter called "The Racial State" in their book *Racial Formation in the United States*. The authors note that throughout U.S. history it has been the state, i.e., the various levels and branches of governments and their non-governmental appendages, that has been the focal point of "the politics of race," and that today it is "increasingly the pre-eminent site of racial conflict." That is, the state is inherently racial because it is racial not only in its consequences, but in its goals. This is consistent with my argument that ultimately politics is the reason why the disproportionate police and vigilante killings of African Americans is so pervasive and persistent. Moreover, the authors' observation that "every transformation of the racial order—is constructed through a process of clash and compromise between racial movements and the state" supports the assumption of the Movement for Black Lives that both the ultimate cause of and the solution to such killings is inextricably political.[36]

Glenn Bracey's critical race theory of state. In a recent article in which he proposes a critical race theory of the state, Glenn Bracey rejects what he sees as Omi and Winant's pluralistic and optimistic view of the state as an agent for positive racial change and insists that it is more accurate to view the state as being not only inherently *"racial,"* but inherently *"racist."* Indeed, Bracey views the state "as a tool whose foundations, basic assumptions, and perpetual *raison d'etre* are the promotion of white supremacy." In explaining how the state works as "a vital instrument of racism," Bracey contends that "through it, whites: define, unify, and organize themselves; arbitrate intra-racial disputes; mobilize and legitimize force; coerce people of color; and relieve their emotional costs by laundering racial oppression through a formal, 'impersonal' apparatus." Bracey seems to answer the question of how long African Americans can expect to be targets of police and vigilante violence when he concludes that "so long as whites retain the power to determine people of color's rights, there can be no assurance that whites will not use their instrumental control of the state to retract those rights."[37]

Although Bracey rejects the power-pluralist view of the state as a neutral arbitrator of race relations in favor of his assumption that the state is indeed racist, he does allow for the fact that the racist state is adaptable enough to change when it is in its own interest to do so. This is an idea that Carter A. Wilson explored years earlier, in greater depth, in his implicit theory of the racial state. Wilson explains that state responses to challenges to the racial status quo are both "indeterminate" and "paradoxical." They are indeterminate in that their outcome may be shaped by a number of factors, including social movement activity. They are paradoxical in that although the state is normally committed to the maintenance of the racial status quo, when forced to do so it will adapt in response to the demands of the racially oppressed. This perspective acknowledges that while movements such as the Movement for Black Lives may not fundamentally change the state's commitment to white supremacy, they can force it to make significant reforms.[38]

Devonya Havis' application of Michael Foucault's concept of state racisms. Philosopher Devonya N. Havis has applied French theoretician Michael Foucault's concept of "state racisms" to explain the role that "stand your ground" laws in the United States play in state-sanctioned vigilantism against African Americans. According to Havis, the underlying premise of Foucault's conceptualization of state racisms is that "the modern state requires racism as a means of exercising power." In explaining why that is the case, Havis states that "according to Foucault, modern states have a system of population management based on a hierarchy of 'human species.'" To elucidate the workings of such state *disciplinary power* in population management, Havis turns to Foucault's concept of *biopower*.

> Under the framework of biopower, some human "subspecies" are identified as more valuable than others, based on positive traits that regularly occur within the population. Meanwhile, other human subspecies regularly exhibit undesirable traits. In Foucault's words, populations thus become a 'political problem': there is a direct relationship between the flourishing of populations with the desirable traits and the withering of populations with undesirable traits. To address that problem, modern states take control over life by "making live and letting die": they make desirable populations live and let undesirable populations die. It is only through the death of undesirables that desired elements—and the state itself—can flourish.[39]

Havis makes it clear that this type of social Darwinism-infused racial eugenics is not just a passive process based on the neglect of those deemed to be unworthy of living. Instead, that "form of public hygiene" may "in some cases . . . involve actively bringing about the death of members of an undesirable subspecies," such as African Americans who, through pervasive racist images, have been racially profiled as dangerous black criminals. As an illustration of how the state does this work, Havis examines the ostensibly "race-neutral" but in fact highly racialized "Stand Your Ground" laws in Florida and elsewhere that helped set the stage for George Zimmerman's killing of Trayvon Martin by providing significant leeway for the slayings of those who are perceived to be a threat, even when an individual could easily escape such "threat" by simply leaving the situation. Her analysis is consistent with Ken Neubeck's and my finding in *Welfare Racism* that welfare reform legislation in the United States has been used as a form of procreation- and immigration-focused "race population control." It also fits Achille Mbembe's extension of Foucault's notion of biopower through his conceptualization of "necropolitics" as the state's ability to determine who lives and who dies.[40]

My urban racial state theory. In *The Urban Racial State*, I provide a perspective and set of concepts for analyzing what states do in their racial management capacity through different branches and at various levels of government. However, as the title of my book suggests, my main focus is the *urban* racial state, which I define as "the political structure and processes of a city and its suburbs that manage race relations in ways that foster and sustain both its own immediate political interests, and ultimately, white racial supremacy." To show how the racial state, more generally conceived, works at that and other levels of government, I build on Louis Althusser's elaboration of Marx's idea of state apparatus and on Antonio Gramsci's concept of hegemony. I argue that aside from its routine use of its various "ideological state apparatuses (ISAs) like public schools and various social programs that can buttress its legitimacy without resorting to violence," "a state's power" ultimately rests in its "repressive state apparatuses (RSAs) like the police, the courts, and prisons."[41]

Such a racial management framework can be useful in explaining how states, in their racial state capacity, ensure their own survival by balancing the rights of police and vigilantes to kill African Americans with near impunity against the rights of African Americans not to be slain as if their lives don't matter. My urban racial state theory also provides the conceptual tools needed to track how, when, and why the racial state shifts modalities in keeping with the current state of race relations. For example, under the administration of President George W. Bush, the federal racial state assumed its default position as a largely invisible, *racially oblivious* protector of the status quo, when there was no large-scale, national movement that insisted that "black lives matter." Then later, due to pressure from that movement, under the presidency of Barack Obama it shifted to a *racially ameliorative* federal racial state that allowed for some reform of the criminal justice system. Then, in sync with the major white backlash Donald Trump generated as fuel for his successful presidential campaign, the federal racial state reverted to its *racially repressive* mode, characteristic of the more overtly racist eras of American history, which deploys its coercive power under highly racialized slogans like "law and order" and "blue lives matter."[42]

As part of my conceptualization of the urban racial state I delineated nine analytical points where the various, complex, sometimes conflicting activities of the racial state occur, based on the branch (executive, legislative, or judicial) and level (federal, state, or local) of its governmental core. To understand the racial state actions that ignore, ameliorate, or actively encourage police and vigilante violence against African Americans, we can examine the actions of the President, Congress, and courts and prosecutors at the federal level. For example, an analysis of the Trump administration entails focusing on the *executive branch of the federal racial state*. We can also zero in on the actions of governors, legislators, and various courts and prosecutors at the state level. For example, if we focus on the actions of the state legislature that would be the *legislative branch of the state-level racial state*. Finally, we can examine the racial state actions of mayors, city and town councils, courts, and prosecutors at the local level. For example, an examination of the role of municipal courts would entail bringing into focus the actions of the *judicial branch of the local (or urban) racial state*. Because the various branches and levels of the racial state usually work in sync, it can be especially revealing when one branch and level of it challenges the actions of another. A case in point is when the U.S. Justice Department investigates, brings charges against, and/or monitors the actions of a local police department, as it did under the Obama administration in cities and towns such as Chicago, Cleveland, Ferguson, Missouri, and Baltimore.[43]

Interaction Theories

When there is a police or vigilante killing of an African American person, what is often most visible to public scrutiny is what is thought to be known about the immediate situation leading up to that killing and the various attitudes, fears, and expectations that came to be embedded within it. While I stress in this study that such a situational analysis does not, and cannot, explain the pervasiveness, disproportionality, and persistence of such killings, when properly framed to encompass the larger macro- (e.g., economic, political, and demographic) level factor influences I have discussed, meso- (i.e., group) and micro- (i.e., interpersonal) level interaction theories can provide insights that go way beyond the intentions of the groups or individual actors involved in particular incidents.

Athens' Radical Interactionist Theory

Lonnie Athens' radical interactionist theory offers an alternative to the more mainstream power and conflict-evasive symbolic interactionist conceptual framework within American sociology. By accounting for not only cooperation but also the conflict component of collective action, it is better able to explain phenomena such as power, conflict, and dominance, and especially our shared interest in interpersonal violence.[44]

Athens defines a "collective act" as one that requires the participation of at least two people, and "domination" as occurring "when an individual or group participating in a collective act steers the direction of its development according to their particular preferences." That is, "if a certain individual or group sways the path of a collective act's construction to their liking, then it could be said that they dominated it." He also stresses that such *dominative encounters* have profound social consequences for the relative hierarchical ranking of the individuals and groups involved that are far removed from the actual encounter itself.[45]

While not all police and vigilante killings involve dominative encounters, when they do occur they always include an act of rebellion on the part of a member or members of the subordinated group, and often the failure of dominant group members to realize the extent of the resentment held by those who are oppressed. For, as Athens notes, "superordinates are notorious for failing to detect the seething resentment and disdain that subordinates often feel toward them." This helps explain explosive encounters between the police and African Americans who resist what they consider to be harassment, and yet another show of disrespect, by shouting in frustration something like "Why are you always fucking with me!" As readers will see later when I discuss hypermasculinity, when males are involved such dominative encounters can be understood as high-stakes masculinity contests, where the penalty for African American men or boys asserting their masculinity, or even humanity, can be death.[46]

Athens' radical interactionist approach is also useful in analyzing violent dominative encounters as sequentially unfolding processes. Here I describe only the first five of the eight stages he identifies—those most relevant to the interpersonal-level interactions between a police officer or vigilante and the person he or she kills. During that *role-claiming* stage a person or group asserts a superordinate status that requires another person or group to accept the position of the subordinate. For example, when police officers drive by a group of African American teenage boys hanging out near a corner store in their neighborhood, stare at them, and drive pass them, this routine is commonly understood as meaning that when they have circled the block and returned, the boys will have let them "have the corner" by dispersing and leaving the area. During the *role-rejection* stage one of those youngsters rebels, as he refuses to accept the role of a compliant subordinate, by disobeying that unspoken directive and remaining on the corner. When the police officers exit their vehicle and one of them orders him to "assume the position"—which means to spread his hands and feet out on the patrol car, a wall, or the ground to be searched—and when he is slow to respond and questions the way he is being treated, the *role-sparring* stage begins. This is followed by the *role-enforcement* stage, when the officers attempt to force him to comply. Finally, the dominative encounter reaches its climax with the *role-determination* stage, when an officer, who feels he is losing control of what has escalated into a scuffle, fatally shoots the young man who has challenged his authority. The same sequence of events may occur in a dominative encounter between a vigilante and an African American he confronts.[47]

The Sociology of Emotions

As you have seen, the deadly dominative encounters between the police or vigilantes and African Americans are often emotions-driven, and, as I have indicated, the various categories of literature I review in this chapter overlap. This is certainly true for the literatures on systemic racism and the sociology of emotions, as is evident in Joe Feagin's conceptualization of systemic racism as having at its cognitive-affective core—which fuels racist institutions and practices—not only attitudes, ideologies, and images, but also negative emotions.[48]

Emotions are important, not only as an essential component of attitudes, but also because of their own impact on human behavior. Unfortunately, all too often, sociologists and others write as if racism and other systems of oppression are inanimate objects, and as such are devoid of emotions. This study categorically rejects that assumption and maintains that because oppressive systems are composed of people, and because people are emotional beings, such systems are driven, at least in part, by emotions. As the "*All* Lives Matter!" rejection of the African American insistence that "Black Lives Matter!" illustrates, system-sustaining emotions become obvious when oppressive systems, and the privileges they bring, are challenged. One of the aims of this book is to place such emotions at the center of systemic racism theory.[49]

As you will see, even when emotions are placed front and center of scholarly interest, the analysis tends to be limited to individuals and their interpersonal relations. With that limitation clearly in mind, let's take a look at what the growing body of literature on the sociology of emotions can contribute to our understanding of the fatal interactions of police and vigilantes and the African Americans they kill. The sociology of emotions differs from psychological, biological, and other explanations of the phenomenon in that it "places the person in a context and examines how social structures and culture influence the arousal and flow of emotions in individuals." For example, sociologist Jonathan Turner stresses that, like other social resources, emotions are not distributed equally; positive emotions are more readily available to those who are affluent and otherwise more privileged, and negative emotions are more likely to be accessible to a society's middle and lower stratas, such as the police, most vigilantes, and the people they kill. Earlier in this chapter I mentioned that in their theory of oppression, Turner et al identified emotional arousal as a key factor necessary to explain discriminatory behavior. Consistent with the racial threat hypothesis I discussed earlier, they conclude that "the greater the level of threat experienced, the more likely are people to be aroused emotionally and attuned to the distinctive feature of a target population." Equally as important is the lack of emotional empathy caused by that racial stereotyping and animus, resulting in large segments of the European American population not caring if African Americans are killed, while remaining comfortable in their belief that they somehow deserved it.[50]

Some of the scholarship on the sociology of emotions provides important macro-level insights as to how American culture is ripe with negative emotions that can encourage what is often racially targeted police and vigilante violence. For example, in his book *Angry White Men*, Michael Kimmel says the following about what he refers to as "the new American anger" as *aggrieved entitlement*: the type of white male anger that is widely articulated in American culture through media outlets like Fox News television and Rush Limbaugh's talk radio.

> The new American anger is more than defensive; it is reactionary. It seeks to restore, to retrieve, to reclaim something that is perceived to have been lost. Angry White Men look to the past for their imagined and desired future. They believe that the system is stacked against them. Theirs is the anger of the entitled: we are entitled to those jobs, those positions of unchallenged dominance. And when we are told we are not going to get them, we get angry.[51]

In *Harvest of Rage*, Joel Dyer analyzes the similarly reactionary anger behind the Oklahoma City bombing of the mid-1990s, by white supremacists who were consumed with a rage which, he argues, goes way beyond that single act of those domestic terrorists on that day. Instead it reflects, he stresses, a much large social malaise that affects many rural Americans who are unable to adjust to the radical changes in the global economy that have sent their lives into turmoil. The point Kimmel, Dyer, and others make in such studies of the negative emotions so prevalent in American culture today is that the emotional state of many violent individuals cannot be understood outside of the larger socio-historical context that impacts them—including what is happening in terms of changing racial, economic, and gender relations.[52]

Other scholarship on the sociology of emotions can help us better understand how emotions impact police and vigilante killings of African Americans at the group and interpersonal levels. With Jan Stet, Jonathan Turner reviews a number of theories of the sociology of emotions that connect human emotions to social structures. One of them, Theodore Kemper's power-status model, conceptualizes power as "the ability to compel others to follow one's wishes and directives" and status as "the giving and receiving of unforced deference, honor, and respect." I would add here that, as in the case of police and vigilante killings, power in the form of deadly force may be used to enforce status demands. Examining such killings as power-status battles helps reveal why the emotional stakes are so high that people are willing to risk killing or dying to achieve the positive emotions from winning, which include "*satisfaction, security,* and *confidence,*" and to avoid those negative emotions that come from losing, such as "*anxiety, fear,* and *loss of confidence.*" And because these power-status encounters most commonly involve men or men and boys, it does not require much of a leap to view them as masculinity contests, as I stress in my discussion of the relevant hypermasculinity literature.[53]

Hypermasculinity

From the previous bodies of literature reviewed in this chapter, it can be seen that no explanation of emotionally charged battles over who will be dominant and who will submit in encounters between the police, vigilantes, and the African Americans they kill is complete without an examination of hypermasculinity. Although masculinity is best viewed as a social construction, such an inquiry must begin with the important biological roots of maleness. In their review of the evolutionary psychology research, Sidanius and Pratto found that humans share with primates "male domination" of "intergroup relations," "hostile and agonistic relations between groups," and "stalking, attacking, and killing of outgroup males." All of this is "intimately connected to and bound up with the male predisposition for group boundary maintenance, territorial defense/acquisition, and the exercise of dominion." Not surprisingly, therefore, they found that males tend to have a higher social dominance orientation and concluded that "intergroup aggression is primarily a male enterprise." This helps explain why, indeed, many of the high-profile police and vigilante killings of African Americans seem to be the deadly endgames of testosterone-driven clashes.[54]

As useful as such insights are, biology has its limits in explaining the behavior of men and boys. For example, it does not explain different levels of aggression in different cultures and for groups of men of different socio-economic status within the same society and culture or subculture. For such an explanation, we must examine the gender roles assigned to men as well as the resources available to them to achieve their manhood in socially prescribed ways. In brief, we must bring into our analysis the *social construction of masculinity*. For example, in an article I published some time ago on the all too often precarious "quest for manhood" for African American men, I noted that masculinity in America is an extremely competitive and "volatile" undertaking. Because it must "be earned and proved" daily, "masculine attainment" cannot be taken for granted; instead, it can best be viewed as a lifelong quest. I also stressed that many low-income African American men find themselves caught in the "double bind" of having accepted society's notions of what it means to *be a man*, to "be somebody," then finding that, due to racial discrimination and its multiple effects, they do not have the legitimate means to achieve their manhood in socially acceptable ways. Some consequently resort to violence as a more readily available means of proving their manhood; and even those who don't are not inclined to passively accept being treated with disrespect by the police or vigilantes.[55]

I believe that pressure for masculine attainment also applies to many police and vigilantes, who do not have the sufficient class position or other resources to be secure in their manhood and who have immersed themselves in very macho occupations and gun-centered worldviews. As Kimmel notes, the intensity of their quest for masculine attainment has grown in recent decades, as angry "white" men cling to their guns and extreme right-wing politics while reacting, sometimes violently, to their loss of status economically, politically, racially, and in gender terms. That move to a volatile form of perpetually insecure hypermasculinity has been exacerbated by the United States' involvement in numerous wars, including a domestic war against terrorism, that have resulted in the militarization of police.[56]

Finally, as I will discuss in greater detail in Chapter 6, hypermasculinity, or what might otherwise be described as masculine insecurity, is not only acted out in police and vigilante treatment of other men and boys. It is also a factor in violence against women and against LGBTQ people, who are often punished for deviating from what are deemed to be their appropriate gender roles. These and other hypermasculinity issues are at the center of police and vigilante attitudes and culture.

Police and Vigilante Attitudes and Culture

As I noted earlier, when there is rare acknowledgment by police or local governmental officials that a police officer or vigilante has engaged in racially targeted misconduct, the focus—consistent with the popular misconceptualization of racism as individual prejudice—is on that "one rotten apple" of a lone bigot, with no real effort to understand where such attitudes come from, how pervasive they are among his or her fellow officers or citizens, and why they persist. There is also little embrace of the fact that, as I show in the next chapter, throughout American history—going back to the slave patrols of the nation's Southern colonies which were an important precursor in the development of modern U.S. policing—the police, like vigilantes, have played a major role in keeping African Americans in their proper racial place. In this section, and more extensively in Chapters 4 and 6, I review some of the evidence of racial bias embedded in the attitudes and culture of American police officers that I believe convincingly makes the case that the racist legacy of policing in the United States continues. Such scholarship points to the importance of examining police culture as an incubator of the racist attitudes associated with the disproportionate killings of African Americans.[57]

In one of his studies of racist attitudes and culture within police departments in the mid-1970s, John Teahan found that racist attitudes among police offers actually *increased after* they had undergone a program of racial sensitivity training. In another longitudinal study of police officers which considered the time they entered the police academy, thirteen weeks later when that training was complete, and a year and a half after they graduated, he found that the racial attitudes of African Americans and European Americans had hardened and become more divisive; with a dramatic increase in the racial prejudice of European American police officers toward their African American colleagues. And in their study of campus police officers, Dennis Leltner and William Sedlacek found evidence that their department reinforced negative racial attitudes. Such attitudes were found to be associated with officers receiving the most commendations, being rated by their top supervisor as being closest to an ideal officer, getting the highest ratings by supervisors, and receiving the most promotions. They also found higher peer ratings for officers who were authoritarian.[58]

Despite intense racial divisions within police departments, the police do manage to function as a powerful force in defending the actions of their own. That is routinely done legally through the political clout, legal resources, and other support of their unions. Many police officers also rely on illegal cover-ups of their actions through a "blue wall" or "blue code"-of-silence norm that requires them to protect their own even when that entails lying, filing false reports, and giving false testimony. This norm is similar to the "no snitching" mores criminals violently enforce against residents of low-income neighborhoods who have witnessed a crime, to keep them from cooperating with the police.[59]

A premise of this study is that such police attitudes and culture, and their deadly consequences, could not exist without significant support from not only other elements of the criminal justice system, such as legislators, prosecutors, and judges—as well as the leaders of the various branches and levels of the racial state, such as mayors, governors, and presidents—but also tens of millions of Americans. For example, internet fundraisers for police officers and vigilantes charged with killing African Americans are generously supported, as was the case for George Zimmerman, the vigilante who killed Trayvon Martin, and Darren Wilson, the police officer who fatally shot Michael Brown. In addition, such causes sometimes attract money from wealthy right-wing donors to cover the killer's legal defense costs.[60]

Conceptual Framework, Propositions, and My Racial Control Argument

With the theoretical and substantive insights culled from the literatures I have reviewed, I am now ready to propose a conceptual framework, set of propositions, and argument that I think can help us make sense of the numerous, disproportionate, and outrageous police and vigilante killings of African Americans both historically and today in twenty-first century America.

Conceptual Framework

The analytical concepts I borrow (e.g., ideology, ideological state apparatus, repressive state apparatus, neoliberalism, racial threat, systemic racism, systemic terror, racial state, dominative encounters, hypermasculinity, masculine attainment) or have created (e.g., the urban racial state; the racially oblivious, ameliorative, and repressive racial state; three levels and branches of the racial state, racial control system, racial control mechanism) that are relevant to this study do not exist in intellectual isolation. Indeed, the reason they can be crafted into a coherent conceptual framework is because they share underlying assumptions about how the social world operates. To that end, I begin by summarizing what we have learned about that conceptual perspective from the theoretical and substantive insights provided us by the various literatures I have reviewed in this chapter.

Conceptual frameworks, also known as theoretical perspectives, provide a broad outline of how social phenomena work based on their different assumptions about what it is important to focus on. Because the basic assumption of this study is that the pervasive, disproportionate, persistent, and usually unpunished police and vigilante killings of

African Americans are best viewed as a racial control mechanism, I use the conflict theoretical approach to explain the key role played by power in the way that oppressive social structures such as systemic racism are "set up, sustained, and changed."[61]

As I noted earlier, the dominant narrative—the one that is most often pushed by the police and elected officials—when a police or vigilante killing occurs, which seems hard to justify, is that it was the act of "one bad apple" among the many in a criminal justice system and society that are basically good. This approach keeps the focus on the assumed aberrant and deviant actions of individuals and off the workings of highly organized social systems and processes. As can be seen from the preceding literature review, the very different assumption of this study, consistent with its conflict-theoretical perspective, is that the disproportionate and pervasive police and vigilante killings of African Americans are not deviant or otherwise aberrant behavior. Instead they are *normative*, with strong and highly racialized ideological and institutional support from millions of Americans at every level of society. And as I noted earlier, the normative support for killings by the police is most evident in the fact that officers are rarely punished. I also concluded that because neither the pervasiveness nor the disproportionality of police or vigilante killings can be explained by focusing on the prejudices of bigoted individuals, this study will not engage in the pointless, and near impossible, task of trying to figure out what is in the hearts and minds of individual police and vigilantes who kill African Americans. Bigotry or membership in the dominant racialized group are not requirements to engage in such actions. So, consistent with this perspective, since neither is a necessary or sufficient condition to explain the phenomenon, we could almost—despite the growing research evidence to the contrary—treat the racial attitudes and behaviors of the individual killers as being irrelevant. While such a conclusion would be extreme, my point is simply that what is more analytically important is the highly racialized criminal justice system, politics, and overall social system that both encourage and condone those killings. The literature I reviewed suggests that an adequate explanation of police and vigilante killings of African Americans must account for relevant actions at multiple levels, including the individual, group, organizational, institutional, and systemic levels, as well as interrelated forms of oppression based not only on "race," but also on class, gender, and sexual orientation.

Because my method is historical sociology, it should not be surprising that in this book I stress that equally as important as understanding the social context of such killings is placing them within their proper historical milieu. What seems, when viewed ahistorically, to be a recent spate of highly racialized police and vigilante killings of African Americans that has been made very visible by technological advances such as smartphone cameras and videos, social media, and twenty-four-hour cable news can instead best be understood within the context of a long history of racial control systems and their violence-centered mechanisms, dating back to slavery. By examining them through the lens of history we can better appreciate the role played by perceived threat, not only in the sociology of individual police officers and vigilantes who kill African Americans, but in the dominant racialized group's tightening up of whatever means of racial control is available to it. That is, the various criminalization-justified mechanisms of state-sponsored or -sanctioned terror are most likely to be deployed when there is a perceived challenge to the control of the dominant racialized group, both at the interpersonal and the societal levels. In brief, such killings often happen when the racially oppressed, either individually or collectively, are perceived as not knowing and/or remaining in what is deemed to be their proper racial "place."

It has also been seen that such threat is heightened by economic neoliberalism as a form of ruthless hypercapitalism which, because it includes political ideologies, policies, and practices that radically redistribute the economic and other resources of a nation upward to a tiny percentage of the population, requires increasingly repressive police and vigilante violence to keep those already at the bottom of society, for racial and other reasons, contained, controlled, and divided, and therefore far away from potential class-based political alliances that could threaten such actions. With the election of Donald Trump as president, we can expect that, if left unchecked, the combined power of economic and racial oppression will increase exponentially in ways that encourage still more police and vigilante violence.

The literature I have reviewed in this chapter also suggests that such violence and social divisions are fueled by racist notions such as the idea that African Americans are and should be treated as "dangerous black criminals." It suggests that the killings persist because they are supported directly or indirectly by each of the interrelated institutions of American society that collectively comprise its social system, beginning of course with the criminal justice system, which includes racist police and vigilante attitudes and culture. That interpersonal/interaction-centered literature also stresses the importance of bringing highly racialized emotions to the center of those killings that involve struggles for dominance and respect, which often take the form of high-stakes battles to assert masculinity.

The literature I have reviewed here suggests not only that power, and its politics, policies, and practices offshoots, are the main causes of the pervasive and disproportionate killings of African Americans, but also that resolution can only come with a change in American race relations and politics. In brief, the disproportionate police and vigilante killings of African Americans can best be understood as acts of political violence.

Key Propositions

From these theoretical and substantive insights, I propose the following five propositions, each of which I will explore in its own chapter.

Proposition # 1 (Chapter 3). *The pervasive and disproportionate police and vigilante killings of African Americans can best be understood as one of a number of violence-centered racial control systems and mechanisms used to oppress African Americans throughout the history of the United States.*

Proposition # 2 (Chapter 4). *The pervasive and disproportionate police and vigilante killings of African Americans can best be understood as a violence-centered racial control mechanism.*

Proposition # 3 (Chapter 5). *The extreme economic and political policies and practices of political neoliberalism that have exacerbated economic inequality and racial tensions require police and vigilante violence to control what is seen as a surplus and dangerous population.*

Proposition # 4 (Chapter 6). *The immediate interpersonal-level factors that are often associated with such violence include racial bias, displays of hypermasculinity, police and vigilante attitudes and culture, and the expression of negative emotions.*

Proposition # 5 (Chapter 7). *Because, as actions of oppression, power and politics best explain why such killings are so pervasive and target African Americans so disproportionately, it is only by African Americans and other people of goodwill organizing in movements to change race relations and politics that they can be significantly reduced.*

Racial Control Argument

Once again, this book's main argument is that the pervasive and disproportionate police and vigilante killings of African Americans can be best understood as a racial control mechanism. That is, they must be understood as being part of the highly racialized "necropolitics" of who lives and who dies in American society that have made it necessary for activists to proclaim what otherwise would be obvious: "Black Lives Matter!"[62]

The best way to flesh out this argument is to explain what I mean and what I don't mean by "racial control mechanism."

The Racial Control Mechanism Concept

I begin with what racial control does *not* mean. My use of the terms "racial control systems" and "mechanisms" does not assume that members of the racially dominant group intentionally create them for the purpose of racial control—although that may well be the case, as the historical evidence suggests was true for racial control systems such as slavery, debt peonage, and Jim Crow and their mechanisms such as lynchings, the death penalty, mass incarceration, and police and vigilante violence (including, but not limited to, killings). Here my assumption is that proving *intent* or the existence of a racial conspiracy is not necessary because, regardless of any individual's intentions, that is the way they *function* for systemic racism and the members of the dominant racialized group who benefit from it. Such functions include the economic function of containing a population which includes many people who have been kept out of the labor market to the benefit of members of the dominant racialized group, and who, in that and other ways, have been denied the opportunity to accumulate wealth. They also include the social status function by, for example, the labeling of African Americans as dangerous criminals, which creates a grouping of people that all European Americans can look down upon. Finally, there is the political function for both politicians and their constituents, who benefit, both careerwise and in asserting their political will in the election process, from keeping African Americans marginalized politically and otherwise.

In placing police and vigilante killings in historical context, I make the distinction between *racial control systems* and their *mechanisms*. Social *systems* are large, highly institutionalized, and enduring social structures and processes such as slavery, debt peonage, Jim Crow, and contemporary systemic racism which encompass smaller, less institutionalized, and less durable criminalization-justified structures and processes that function as their enforcement mechanisms. *Merriam-Webster's Collegiate Dictionary* defines a mechanism as "a piece of machinery"—for our purposes, a piece of social machinery that is but one component of much larger structures—and as "a process or technique for achieving a result."[63]

Such mechanisms—lynchings, the highly racialized death penalty, mass incarceration, and the pervasive and disproportionate police and vigilante killings of African Americans—are larger in scope than any single individual or organization, but not as large, well-structured, or enduring as the social institutions which collectively comprise a social system. So, in this study I suggest that just as police and vigilante violence in the past served as an enforcement mechanism that has supported such overtly racist systems of oppression as slavery, peonage, and Jim Crow, today it is a criminalization-justified mechanism that serves similar economic, social status, and power functions for a much more covert, and at times seemingly colorblind, program of systemic racism.

I discuss racial control systems and their mechanisms in greater detail in Chapter 3, in which I contextualize today's police and vigilante violence, and more specifically the killings of African Americans, as but one of many violence-centered racial control mechanisms used in the United States from the era of slavery to the present.

Notes

1. Greg Botelho, "Missouri Police Officer on Leave over Video in Which He Says: "I'm . . . a Killer," CNN.com, August 23, 2014, www.cnn.com/2014/08/22/us/missouri-police-officer-suspended/, Accessed May 14, 2016; Sunil Dutta, "I'm a Cop. If You Don't Want to Get Hurt, Don't Challenge Me," *Washington Post*, August 19, 2014, www.washingtonpost.com/posteverything/wp/2014/08/19/im-a-cop-if-you-dont-want-to-get-hurt-dont-challenge-me/, Accessed May 20, 2016.
2. Susanne Bohmer and Joyce L. Briggs, "Teaching Privileged Students about Gender, Race, and Class Oppression," *Teaching Sociology*, 1991, 19 (April), 155.
3. Karl Marx, *A Contribution to the Critique of Political Economy* (New York: International Publishers, 1970), 20–21; Davita Silfen Glasberg and Deric Shannon, *Political Sociology: Oppression, Resistance, and the State* (Thousand Oaks, CA: Pine Forge Press, 2011), 31.
4. Marx, *A Contribution to the Critique of Political Economy*, 20–21.
5. Marx, *A Contribution to the Critique of Political Economy*, 20–21.
6. Jonathan Sperber, *Karl Marx: A Nineteenth-Century Life* (New York: Liveright, 2013), xiii–xv; Glasberg and Shannon, *Political Sociology*, 31–32; Thomas Piketty, *Capital in the Twenty-First Century* (Cambridge, MA: Belknap, 2014), 9–10; W.E.B. DuBois, *Black Reconstruction in America, 1860–1880* (New York: Touchstone, 1995, first published in 1935), 700. For more on the limitations of class theory see Glasberg and Shannon, *Political Sociology*, 32–33.
7. George Monbiot, "Neoliberalism: The Ideology at the Root of All Our Problems," *Truthout*, April 19, 2016, www.truth-out.org/opinion/item/35692-neoliberalism-the-ideology-at-the-root-of-all-our-problems, Accessed May 21, 2016.
8. Sidney M. Wilhelm, *Who Needs the Negro?* (Hampton, VA: U.B. and U.S. Books, 1993), xv, 3; Samuel F. Yette, *The Choice: The Issue of Black Survival in America* (New York: Putnam's Sons, 1971), 18–19.
9. Loic Wacquant, "The New 'Peculiar Institution:' On the Prison as Surrogate Ghetto," *Theoretical Criminology*, 2004, 4 (3), 377.
10. Loic Wacquant, *Punishing the Poor: The Neoliberal Government of Social Insecurity* (Durham, NC: Duke University Press, 2009), xi–xii.
11. Sundiata K. Cha-Jua, "The New Nadir: The Contemporary Black Racial Formation," *The Black Scholar*, 2010, 40, 1 (Winter), 38–39; Keeanga-Yamahtta Taylor, *From #BlackLivesMatter to Black Liberation* (Chicago, IL: Haymarket Books, 2016), 6, 7.
12. Jim Sidanius and Felicia Pratto, *Social Dominance: An Intergroup Theory of Social Hierarchy and Oppression* (Cambridge: Cambridge University Press, 1999), 4.
13. Sidanius and Pratto, *Social Dominance*, 31–32, 41. Italics in original.
14. Sidanius and Pratto, *Social Dominance*, 202, 205, 207, 218. Italics in original.
15. Sidanius and Pratto, *Social Dominance*, 43–44.
16. Jonathan H. Turner, Royce Singleton, Jr., and David Musick, *Oppression: A Socio-History of Black-White Relations in America* (Chicago, IL: Nelson-Hall, 1984), 1–2, 4.
17. Herbert Blumer, "Race Prejudice as a Sense of Group Position," *The Pacific Sociological Review*, 1958, 1, 1 (Spring), 3, 5.
18. Hubert M. Blalock, Jr., *Toward a Theory of Minority-Group Relations* (New York: John Wiley and Sons, 1967), 29.
19. Allen E. Liska, "Introduction to the Study of Social Control," in Allen E. Liska, ed., *Social Threat and Social Control* (Albany, NY: SUNY Press, 1992), 1, 3. For an informative set of theory-focused essays specifically on crime and social control see George S. Bridges and Martha A. Myers, eds., *Inequality, Crime, and Social Control* (Boulder, CO: Westview Press, 1994).
20. Liska, "Introduction to the Study of Social Control," 17–19, 29.

21. Allen E. Liska and Jiang Yu, "Specifying and Testing the Threat Hypothesis: Police Use of Deadly Force," in Liska, ed., *Social Threat and Social Control*, 53–55; David Jacobs and Robert M. O'Brien, "The Determinants of Deadly Force. A Structural Analysis of Police Violence," *American Journal of Sociology*, 1998, 103 (4), 837, 858–59.
22. Cody T. Ross, "A Multi-Level Bayesian Analysis of Racial Bias in Police Shootings at the County-Level in the Unites States, 2011–2014," *PLOS One*, 2015, 10 (11), 1, 6, 20.
23. Eric Hehman, Jessica K. Flake, and Jimmy Calanchini, "Disproportionate Use of Lethal Force in Policing is Associated with Regional Racial Biases of Residents," *Social Psychological and Personality Science*, released online 2017 (July 27), 1; Paul Butler, *Chokehold: Policing Black Men* (New York: New Press, 2017), 3.
24. Stokely Carmichael and Charles V. Hamilton, *Black Power: The Politics of Liberation in America* (New York: Vintage Books, 1967); Noel A. Cazenave, *Conceptualizing Racism: Breaking the Chains of Racially Accommodative Language* (Lanham, MD: Rowman and Littlefield, 2016), 71–73.
25. Carmichael and Hamilton, *Black Power*, 3–4. Italics in original.
26. National Advisory Commission on Civil Disorders, *Report of the National Advisory Commission on Civil Disorders* (New York: Bantam Books, 1968), 1–2, 10; Joel Kovel, *White Racism: A Psychohistory* (New York: Columbia University Press, 1984, 1st edition published 1970); Robert Blauner, *Racial Oppression in America* (New York: Harper and Row, 1972); David T. Wellman, *Portraits of White Racism* (Cambridge: Cambridge University Press, 1993, 1st edition published, 1977); Joe R. Feagin and Clairece Booher Feagin, *Discrimination American Style: Institutional Racism and Sexism* (Englewood Cliffs, NJ: Prentice-Hall, 1978); Cazenave, *Conceptualizing Racism*, 76–79, 85–90.
27. Kovel, *White Racism*, ix–xi.
28. More than two and a half decades later, Carter A. Wilson expanded upon Kovel's work by adding an additional psycho-historical stage and some other useful concepts. Carter A. Wilson, *Racism: From Slavery to Advanced Capitalism* (Thousand Oaks, CA: Sage, 1996), 58, 78, 118, 172.
29. Blauner, *Racial Oppression in America*, 277, 280.
30. Wellman, *Portraits of White Racism*, xii, 54–55.
31. Butler, *Chokehold*, 33–34.
32. Joe R. Feagin, "Indirect Institutionalized Discrimination: A Typological and Policy Analysis," *American Politics Quarterly*, 1977, 5, 2 (April), 192; Cazenave, *Conceptualizing Racism*, 73; Noel A. Cazenave, "Joe R. Feagin: The Social Science Voice of Systemic Racism Theory," in Ruth Thompson-Miller and Kimberley Ducey, eds., *Systemic Racism: Making Liberty, Justice, and Democracy Real* (New York: Palgrave Macmillan, 2017), 17, 27–33.
33. Cazenave, *Conceptualizing Racism*, 87–90; Feagin and Feagin, *Discrimination American Style*, 28–31; Cazenave, "Joe R. Feagin: The Social Science Voice of Systemic Racism Theory," 28–29.
34. Feagin and Feagin, *Discrimination American Style*, 31–33; Cazenave, *Conceptualizing Racism*, 90.
35. Cazenave, *Conceptualizing Racism*, 160, 169, 176–77.
36. Noel A. Cazenave, *The Urban Racial State: Managing Race Relations in American Cities* (Lanham, MD: Rowman and Littlefield, 2011), 22 and note # 28; Michael Omi and Howard Winant, *Racial Formation in the United States: From the 1960s to the 1980s* (New York: Routledge and Kegan Paul, 1986), 70, 72, 75, 76.
37. Glenn E. Bracey II, "Toward a Critical Race Theory of State," *Critical Sociology*, 2015, 41 (3), 561, 564–65. Italics in original.
38. Bracey II, "Toward a Critical Race Theory of State," 563–64, 566; Wilson, *Racism*, 16, 20, 165; Cazenave, *The Urban Racial State*, 23.

39. Devonya N. Havis, "'Seeing Black'" through Michel Foucault's Eyes," in George Yancy and Janine Jones, eds., *Pursuing Trayvon Martin: Historical Contexts and Contemporary Manifestations of Racial Dynamics* (Lanham, MD: Lexington Books, 2014), 118, 122–23. Italics in original.
40. Havis, "'Seeing Black' through Michel Foucault's Eyes," 123; Kenneth J. Neubeck and Noel A. Cazenave, *Welfare Racism: Playing the Race Card against America's Poor* (New York: Routledge, 2001), 148–52; Achille Mbembe, "Necropolitics," *Public Culture*, 2003, 15 (1), 11–12.
41. Cazenave, *The Urban Racial State*, 24–25. Italics in original.
42. Cazenave, *The Urban Racial State*, 28–31. Italics in original.
43. Cazenave, *The Urban Racial State*, 27–28.
44. Lonnie Athens, *Domination and Subjugation in Everyday Life* (New Brunswick, NJ: Transaction Publishers, 2015), 1, 4.
45. Athens, *Domination and Subjugation in Everyday Life*, 132, 153, 157. Italics in original.
46. Athens, *Domination and Subjugation in Everyday Life*, 140, 158.
47. Athens, *Domination and Subjugation in Everyday Life*, 175–85. Italics in original.
48. Joe R. Feagin, *Racist America: Roots, Current Realities, and Future Reparations* (New York: Routledge, 2014), xiv.
49. Lisa B. Spanierman and Nolan L. Cabrera, "The Emotions of White Racism and Anti-Racism," in Veronica Watson, Deirdre Howard-Wagner, and Lisa Spanierman, eds., *Unveiling Whiteness in the Twenty-First Century: Global Manifestations, Transdisciplinary Interventions* (Lanham, MD: Lexington Books, 2015), 9.
50. Jonathan H. Turner and Jan E. Stets, *The Sociology of Emotions* (Cambridge: Cambridge University Press, 2005), 2; Jonathan H. Turner, *The Problem of Emotions in Societies* (New York: Routledge, 2009), xi; Turner, Singleton, and Musick, *Oppression*, 4–5; Feagin, *Racist America*, 288.
51. Michael Kimmel, *Angry White Men: American Masculinity at the End of an Era* (New York: Nation Books, 2013), 21, 32. Italics in original.
52. Joel Dyer, *Harvest of Rage: Why Oklahoma City is Only the Beginning* (Boulder, CO: Westview Press, 1997), 5.
53. Turner and Stets, *The Sociology of Emotions*, 216. Italics in original.
54. Sidanius and Pratto, *Social Dominance*, 49, 51, 55.
55. Noel A. Cazenave, "Black Men in America: The Quest for 'Manhood,'" in Harriette McAdoo, ed., *Black Families* (Beverly Hills, CA: Sage, 1981, 1st ed.), 177–78, 181. Italics in original.
56. Kimmel, *Angry White Men*, xii, xiv, 16; James William Gibson, *Warrior Dreams: Violence and Manhood in Post-Vietnam America* (New York: Hill and Wang, 1994), 9, 11, 17, 33; Radley Balko, *Rise of the Warrior Cop: The Militarization of America's Police Forces* (New York: Public Affairs, 2013), xii, xvi.
57. Kristian Williams, *Our Enemies in Blue: Police and Power in America* (Oakland, CA: AK Press, 2015), 63–75; Robin Shepard Engel, "Police: History," *Encyclopedia of Crime and Justice*, 2002, 5, www.encyclopedia.com/doc/1G2-3403000181.html, Accessed August 13, 2017; William A. Westley, *Violence and the Police: A Sociological Study of Law, Custom, and Morality* (Cambridge, MA: The MIT Press, 1970), 96, 100–1, 104; David Weisburd, Rosann Greenspan, et al., "Police Attitudes toward Abuse of Authority: Findings from a National Study," National Institute of Justice, Research in Brief, May 2000, 4, 9, www.ncjrs.gov/pdffiles1/nij/181312.pdf, Accessed February 20, 2017; E. Ashby Plant and B. Michelle Peruche, "The Consequences of Race for Police Officers' Response to Criminal Suspects," *Psychological Science*, 2005, 16 (3), 180; B. Michelle Peruche and E. Ashby

Plant, "The Correlates of Law Enforcement Officers' Automatic and Controlled Race-Based Responses to Criminal Suspects," *Basic and Applied Social Psychology*, 2006, 28 (2), 193.

58. John E. Teahan, "Role Playing and Group Experience to Facilitate Attitude and Value Changes among Black and White Police Officers," *Journal of Social Issues*, 1975, 31 (1), 35; John E. Teahan, "A Longitudinal Study of Attitude Shifts among Black and White Police Officers," *Journal of Social Issues*, 1975, 31 (1), 47, 49–50; Dennis W. Leltner and William E. Sedlacek, "Characteristics of Successful Campus Police Officers," *Journal of College Student Personnel*, 1976, 17 (July), 304–5, 307.

59. Balko, *Rise of the Warrior Cop*, 334.

60. Amanda Robb, "George Zimmerman, Darren Wilson, and the Kickstarted Defense: You Call This Justice?," *The Guardian*, October 1, 2014, www.theguardian.com/commentisfree/2014/oct/01/george-zimmerman-darren-wilson-crowd-sourced-legal-fees. Accessed May 6, 2016.

61. Cazenave, *Conceptualizing Racism*, 181.

62. Mbembe, "Necropolitics," 11.

63. Merriam-Webster, *Merriam-Webster's Collegiate Dictionary, Deluxe Edition* (Springfield, MA: Merriam-Webster, 1998), 1135.

3

VIOLENCE-CENTERED RACIAL CONTROL SYSTEMS AND MECHANISMS IN U.S. HISTORY

African American abolitionist Frederick Douglass had this to say to the American Anti-Slavery Society in 1865 about the adaptability of racial oppression: "It has been called by a great many names, and it will call itself by yet another name; and you and I and all of us had better wait and see what new form this old monster will assume, in what new skin this old snake will come forth next."[1]

Racial oppression is, indeed, a strange animal. It is a shape-shifter that not only survives but thrives through its ability to take different forms as the need arrives. It can be highly visible as it lets out a frightening lion-like roar, as it did during American slavery. It can trample its victims beneath its hooves like a rumbling herd of wildebeest, as it did during this nation's deadly white race riots. Or it can be as quiet and stealthy as a mouse, as systemic racism usually works in the United States today. But no matter how it manifests itself, there is one enduring mechanism that remains at its core: violence.

At the analytical center of this study, right next to its substantive focus on lethal violence, I have placed the concept of racial control. As I noted earlier, by "racial control" I mean the actions of members of a racially dominant group, and their allies, that keep members of racially oppressed groups in a socially subordinated position. In this chapter, I examine the many forms taken by the savage beast of racial oppression and its violence, from slavery to the present, as a way for us to better understand today's police and vigilante killings of African Americans as systemic racism's mechanism of racial control. In this way, the concept of racial control is given socio-historical context and depth by my exploration of the study's Proposition # 1, that *the pervasive and disproportionate police and vigilante killings of African Americans can best be understood as one of a number of violence-centered racial control systems and mechanisms used to oppress African Americans throughout the history of the United States.* To that end, this chapter continues with some additional conceptual work.

More about Violence-Centered Racial Control Systems and Mechanisms

As you have seen, an important assumption upon which my analysis of racial control systems and mechanisms is built is that racial oppression persists in the United States and other highly racialized societies because of its ability to take different forms during different historical periods. As Frederick Douglass made clear many years ago, this is not a new revelation for African American intellectuals and leaders. Moreover, it is also a perspective that persists. Here is what Michelle Alexander has to say about that shape-shifting process in *The New Jim Crow.*

> Since the nation's founding, African Americans repeatedly have been controlled through institutions such as slavery and Jim Crow, which appear to die, but then are reborn in new form, tailored to the needs and constraints of the time . . . there is a certain pattern to this cycle. Following the collapse of each system of control, there has been a period of confusion—transition—in which those who are most committed to racial hierarchy search for new means to achieve their goals within the rules of the game as currently defined. It is during this period of uncertainty that the backlash intensifies and a new form of racialized social control begins to take hold. The adoption of the new system of control is never inevitable, but to date it has never been avoided.[2]

Another scholar suggests, as does Alexander elsewhere in her book, that what happens as racial control systems and mechanisms take on new forms entails much more than white racial backlashes. In explaining how political groups can snatch victory out of what initially appears to be the jaws of defeat by issue-switching, Vesla M. Weaver introduces the concept of a *frontlash*: "the process by which formerly defeated groups may become dominant issue entrepreneurs in light of the development of a new issue campaign." For example, as will be seen later in this chapter when I discuss the origins of highly racialized mass incarceration, facing defeat in the area of civil rights, segregationists skillfully managed resentment against social protests, civil disobedience, and urban unrest to shift the focus to crime—an issue they could win on while being able to deny that their actions were in any way racial. By doing so, they were able to move public policy away from social reforms that benefited African Americans to punishment that targeted them. As distinguished from a backlash, which is reactive and conservative and expresses emotional sentiments that originate with the masses, a frontlash is "preemptive, innovative, proactive, and, above all strategic." Moreover, it is designed and executed by elites. Weaver illustrates those differences through the following metaphors: "Instead of a bungee cord recoiling when stretched too far, we can think of frontlash as water moving swiftly through a path that comes to an end, forcing the water to seek alternative routes or as a weed that after being killed by weed killer mutates into a new variety, becoming resistant."[3]

Another guiding assumption of this study, which I discussed in the previous chapter, is that because lethal violence is the ultimate means through which systems of oppression are established and maintained, *the pervasiveness, disproportionality, and persistence of violence against African Americans can best be understood when viewed through the analytical lens of political violence.* It is important to note here, however, that while all oppressive systems and mechanisms are ultimately violence-dependent, they differ in the degree to which their enforcement relies on police, vigilante, and other very overt forms of physical, and often fatal, violence.

Another premise of this study is that the state, in its racial state capacity, authorizes, sponsors, or otherwise sanctions both the formal (e.g., the police) and informal (vigilante) racial control agents who are employed, or at least protected, by its various branches and levels. An especially strong thread tying together various racial control systems and mechanisms is the U.S. Supreme Court's various rulings, which have tended to support racially repressive federal, state-level, and local laws, policies, and practices.

Speaking of the state, by focusing on what these violence-centered racial control systems and mechanisms share in common in terms of their cumulative political, psychological, and emotional impact on African Americans, we can better appreciate the centrality of the implicit threat of genocide to the African American experience. Consistent with that fact is this study's supposition that *for African Americans the threat of genocide, the ultimate racial control enforcement mechanism, is at the ideological and psycho-emotional core of all forms of violence-centered oppression.* That threat has been very real and was reinforced by the fact that the United States did not sign the United Nations pact against genocide until 1988, nearly forty years after it was approved by that organization's Genocide Convention. Indeed, African American concern about genocide was the subject of an appeal to the United Nations nearly four decades before the United States accepted its anti-genocide pact. In making clear the basis of its charge of genocide against the government of the United States, the *We Charge Genocide* petition clarified that

> it is sometimes incorrectly thought that genocide means the complete and definitive destruction of a race or people. The Genocide Convention, however, adopted by the General Assembly of the United Nations on December 9, 1948, defines genocide as any killings on the basis of race, or, in its specific words, as "killing members of the group." Any intent to destroy, *in whole or in part,* a national, racial, ethnic or religious group is genocide, according to the Convention. Thus, the Convention states, "causing serious bodily or mental harm to members of the group" is genocide as well as "killing members of the group."[4]

And in the preface to the 1970 edition of that petition, actor and activist Ossie Davis cautioned, as did Samuel Yette a year later in his book *The Choice* (discussed in Chapter 2), that at the time of its writing African Americans may have been facing more than such a "limited genocide" because "for the first time, black labor is expendable, the American economy does not need it anymore."[5]

A fifth assumption about racial control systems and mechanisms as state-sponsored or -sanctioned political violence is that the form they take at any point in time is shaped largely by the prevailing race relations and both the rational and emotional responses of the racially dominant group to perceived threats to the racial status quo. Indeed, Michelle Alexander argues that different racial control systems and mechanisms are characterized by diverse meanings and significances of "race," e.g., African Americans as slaves under slavery, as second-class citizens under Jim Crow, and as criminals under peonage; vigilantism and lynching; the death penalty; mass incarceration; and today's police and vigilante killings of African Americans. In his study of the history of "lawlessness and violence" in the United States, after identifying seven periods of race relations in the United States from slavery through the post-World War II period, Allen D. Grimshaw states his thesis that "in each of these periods the patterns of race relations and social racial violence were determined more by reaction of the dominant white community to attacks on the accommodative pattern by Negroes than by any conscious determination of policy by the white group." Grimshaw's emphasis on the emotional was likely a reflection of the fact that his focus was on lawless violence rather than the more highly institutionalized state-sponsored or -sanctioned violence. While I see no need to take either side of a debate as to whether rational interests or negative emotions are more important in the violence-centered racial control systems and mechanisms I study, I take from Grimshaw's thesis the perspective that, contrary to the simplistic view of these systems and mechanisms as conspiratorial in their origin and entirely rational in their planning and goals, negative emotions play a crucial role in their origins and evolution.[6]

Another premise upon which this study is based has to do with the difference between a sociological and an historical perspective in the conceptualization of racial control systems and mechanisms. Whereas the sociological perspective, while treating them as overlapping social structures and processes, is more likely to focus on what is unique and distinct about each, the historical approach stresses that they are all part of one continuous and nearly seamless historical process of oppression.

Although it may be useful to treat the racial control systems and mechanisms as somewhat distinct social structures, with their own processes, and in that way to focus on their similarities and differences, it is also *important to view them as one interconnected, and ever changing, historical process of racial oppression,* running like a common thread throughout U.S. history. Such a more fluid view is consistent with what Alan Liska refers to as the functional-equivalence hypothesis: that because different social control systems and mechanisms serve similar functions, "as one form increases the other decreases," e.g., from lynchings to legal executions. In brief, analyses of historical *processes* can be just as revealing as those of social *structures*. Although my approach is primarily sociological, because it is based on the historical sociology method, it incorporates both.[7]

Because the violence-centered racial control systems and their enforcement mechanisms that I examine in this chapter justify their actions through the assumption that African Americans are largely a dangerous and criminal race of people, *they all require, to one degree or another, the criminalization of African Americans.* With this focus, I assume that what on the surface appear to be simply crime control mechanisms are, upon closer examination, actually racial control mechanisms. The three violence-centered racial control systems that I examine in this chapter are slavery, peonage, and Jim Crow and the three heavily criminalized racial control mechanisms I analyze are highly racialized vigilantism and lynching, the death penalty, and mass incarceration. I will also examine the enforcement role that police and vigilante killings of African Americans play in each.[8]

Violence-Centered Racial Control Systems and Mechanisms in Historical Perspective

In this section I examine the characteristics of the three violence-centered racial control systems of slavery, peonage, and Jim Crow. Then I discuss the three highly racialized, criminalization-justified, and violence-centered crime-control mechanisms of vigilantism and lynching, the death penalty, and mass incarceration which African Americans have encountered both prior to and, for some, concurrently with the crisis they face today: that of systemic racism and police and vigilante killings. Let's start at the beginning, with slavery.

Slavery (1654–1865)

Slavery is an ancient and highly organized system of social and economic exploitation in which members of a dominant group use violence, laws, ideologies, customs, and other instruments of power to place and hold those of a physically subordinated group in bondage as their property. It is the oldest, most highly institutionalized, most encompassing, and most oppressive system of racial control the people now known as African Americans have faced. It evolved from the indentured servitude status of about twenty African slaves who were brought to Jamestown, Virginia in 1619 to work the tobacco fields more than a century and a half before the former British colonies became the United States of America. It was not, however, until 1654 that John Casor became the first legally recognized slave, when a Virginia court declared him property for life. American slavery lasted for a total of 211 years and ended in 1865 with the ratification of the Thirteenth Amendment to the U.S. Constitution. Indeed, it was the arrangement under which tens of millions of people of African descent lived during most of the time in which members of that group have resided in the United States. In 1860, five years before slavery was abolished following the North's victory over the South in the Civil War, 94 percent of people of African descent living in the United States were slaves. That is 3,839,000 people, compared to only 258,000 who were free. For African Americans, freedom from shackles is still relatively new. As I noted in the previous chapter, politically, slavery was a system of "*dominative* racism" that was maintained through the pyschocultural mechanism of direct physical domination and oppression based on violence.[9]

Although the main function of slavery in the United States was the accumulation of wealth for members of the racially dominant group through labor exploitation, for them and others not wealthy enough to own slaves it also served the important social status and prestige function of providing a group to which they could all feel superior. Slavery also attained the political function of providing their government leaders a system of privilege and a way of life around which they and their followers could unite in a way that built group solidarity by, in part, masking the very real class, ethnic, and other differences that might have otherwise divided them.

To keep slaves in line, their "owners" and overseers deployed every type of violence imaginable, including whipping, torture, mutilation, rape, breaking up families, and killings. Because slaves had no legal rights, such actions—whether they could best be characterized as official, semi-official, or unofficial—were at, a minimum, state-sanctioned and often state-sponsored terrorism.

Oppressive systems are held together by ideologies that explain and justify their existence and actions. Although slavery has a long history in world affairs, and still persists under various names, what made the bondage system in the Americas unique, and what made it so insidious and its impact so enduring, is the fact that it was so successfully organized around the concept of race: the idea that there are physically distinct groups of people who, based on their biology, could be deemed superior or inferior, destined to rule or to be ruled. For much of world history, slavery was so common, had such historically deep and geographically expansive roots, and happened to people so routinely that there was no need for an explanation, other than perhaps, "Remember that war we had? We won. You lost. And you are now our slaves." However, in a land built on the egalitarian belief that all men, at least, were created equally, how does one justify placing men, women, and children in such inhumane bondage? That conundrum was resolved by the crafting of the race concept, with its logic that because they are not human, or at least not fully so, there is no need to treat these members of an inferior biological race humanely, much less as equals.[10]

To say that police and vigilante actions were essential to the enforcement of the norms, customs, and laws necessary for the maintenance of slavery would be more than a slight understatement. Indeed, scholars of the history of American policing include among its main roots the slave patrols that ensured that slaves neither escaped nor revolted nor did anything else that might threaten what became known as America's "peculiar institution." Moreover, as W.E.B. DuBois explained, slave patrols not only provided the "special police force" needed to ensure the survival of slavery but, by providing employment and status for poor European Americans, fostered both a sense of racial belonging and solidarity with slave owners and a hatred for slaves of African descent that kept them from realizing and organizing against their own class-based exploitation. When even more ruthless means of protecting slavery were needed, e.g., in cases of a suspected or real slave insurrection, there was the "vigilance committee," which has been described as "a corrupted form of the patrol system" that, in the form of "lynching parties," engaged in search-and-destroy missions against suspected African American insurgents. This legacy continues, with police and their unions and vigilantes most inclined to align themselves with reactionary American politics, especially when it comes to racial issues.[11]

Like contemporary police and vigilante killings of African Americans, such terrorism was in no way merely an issue of private actions of slave owners and other local European Americans aligned with them. Instead, in its racial state capacity, every branch and level of the state was deeply involved in both state-sponsored or -sanctioned terrorism and in the everyday regulation of slavery. For example, nearly every aspect of slave life was carefully controlled by numerous slave codes enacted by state legislatures which authorized their enforcement by slave owners and slave patrols. And if their power proved insufficient to keep slaves in line, as in the case of insurrections, it was backed up by state militia and, ultimately, the U.S. army. Indeed, the historical relationship between American slavery and the state is so fundamental that some scholars have suggested that the protection of the right of British colonies in North America to continue to engage in slavery after a court ruling in England outlawed the practice there in 1772 was a major reason for the American revolution and the establishment of the United States of America—not as a bastion of democracy for all, but as a slave state. Later, its Southern states would fight a bloody civil war to maintain their peculiar institution.[12]

As bad as slavery was, for some people of African descent the worst was yet to come. While it is generally thought that African Americans have never experienced racial violence as cruel and brutal as that which happened under slavery, other, more careful observers of African

American life and history have questioned that simplistic assumption. For example, this is what the anti-lynching crusader Ida B. Wells-Barnett concluded about racial violence during slavery and afterward, only a few decades after slavery was abolished:

> During the slave regime, the Southern white man owned the Negro body and soul ... While slaves were scourged mercilessly ... the white owner rarely permitted his anger to go so far as to take a life, which would entail upon him a loss of several hundred dollars ... But Emancipation came and the vested interests of the white man in the Negro's body were lost.

As you will see, this was certainly true for African Americans in the system of oppression that was crafted to replace slavery: peonage.[13]

Peonage (1865–1940s)

Like slavery, peonage is a system of involuntary labor exploitation; in this case it is one justified by what is deemed to be a debt which an individual is mandated by law, the threat or use of physical force, or both, to pay through servitude to his or her debtor. Peonage, also known as "debt peonage," "debt servitude," or "debt slavery," occurs mainly in rural areas with an agrarian or other land-based economy like that of much of the American South of the mid-nineteenth to mid-twentieth centuries. Although peonage was officially outlawed by the U.S. Congress in 1867, it persisted into the 1940s, with some cases documented into the 1960s. During its reign it took different forms in the United States, including share-cropping and other types of exploitative tenant farming, convict leasing, and depth peonage, and was set in place largely through a series of black codes pushed by planters and others with an interest in retaining their ability to generate as much as possible of the economic wealth that they enjoyed from African American labor prior to the abolition of slavery. During this period of American race relations, racial oppression was expressed politically and psychoculturally as a "dominative aversive racism" that required both direct domination, as was true for slavery, as well as physical, psychological, and emotional distance between the racially dominant and racially subordinated groups.[14]

To understand the history behind the emergence of the peonage system we should begin with what happened in the South in the wake of the enactment of the Thirteenth Amendment to the U.S. Constitution, which abolished slavery, following the South's defeat by the North in the Civil War. After slavery, the South was economically devastated. Members of the wealthy planter class witnessed the crumbling of a system of labor exploitation that served as the foundation of their often opulent lifestyles; working-class European Americans faced an uncertain future of high unemployment and the threat of looming competition from former slaves who were now free; and former slaves found themselves both landless and penniless, with no means of supporting themselves and their families or even of leaving the South. With the end of Reconstruction and the willingness of Northern business interests and the various branches of the federal racial state to support their efforts to regain dominance over their former slaves, the South's planter class encouraged terrorism on the part of white supremacist organizations in order to take back control of state and local governments, which then enacted the "black codes" they used to return the economically and politically vulnerable African Americans, and their labor, to a condition as close to slavery as possible.[15]

Here is a description of just some of the black codes passed by Southern legislatures that "severely restricted black freedom, forcing blacks to work the white man's land on the white man's terms."

> If a black man was found to be unemployed, he could be arrested as a vagrant and fined; if he failed to pay his fine, he was turned over to a planter who paid it and then forced him to work off his debt. Anyone who refused to sign a labor contract was imprisoned and forced to work without pay. Blacks who broke contracts could be shipped, fined, and sold into labor for a year. Orphaned children and even children of families could be taken away from their homes, forced to work as apprentices, and even whipped by their employers . . . To ensure that blacks would remain farmers and servants, some codes prohibited them from seeking any employment other than agricultural labor or domestic work without a special license. They could not lease or rent land, nor were they allowed to buy it.[16]

Although many of the black codes focused, as in the quote above, on regulation of the labor of African Americans after slavery, there were other codes that restricted almost every aspect of their lives, including, in some states, denying them "the right to vote, hold office, and work and travel when they wanted to," and even "to live in cities without a special permit."[17]

Like slavery, peonage is a highly organized system of oppression; one which includes a number of types of inter-related, debt-based exploitation that were justified through law and enforced by legal, extralegal, and illegal violence. Tenant farming included: the least exploited "cash tenants," who rented land and owned their own animals and tools; the more oppressed "share tenants," who also owned their own animals and tools but, because they had no money, were required to give a percentage of their crops to rent land; and the most subjugated "sharecroppers." Because they had nothing but their labor to offer, needed to make use of animals and tools, had to provide a much higher percentage of crops to the land owner, and depended on their honesty in bookkeeping, sharecroppers were likely to be in a state of perpetual debt. Although there were impoverished European American tenant farmers, a higher proportion of African Americans were landless and therefore dependent on tenant farming, and these were the most likely to be caught in the most exploitative forms of tenant farming, especially share cropping. Convict leasing was an extreme form of labor exploitation under which "planters, mine owners, railroad construction companies, and other employers would bid on state contracts to employ large numbers of convicts on chain gangs for a few pennies a day per prisoner." Those convicts were disproportionately African Americans and for many their only crime was a charge of vagrancy, usually without the benefit of a trial, by a corrupt local sheriff who benefited financially, along with other local officials, from rounding up laborers for those eager to purchase their contracts when those caught in the net of that cruel labor-extraction system were unable to pay their fines. Finally, debt-peonage laws were passed by states which forbade any slaves from leaving a plantation without paying back advances and other debts their former owners claimed were due them.[18]

The racial ideology used to justify such actions was that African Americans were lazy, shiftless, irresponsible, and immoral criminals who did not repay their debts. Here we see the roots of the racial criminalization that is at the core of the subsequent racial control enforcement mechanisms of highly racialized vigilantism and lynchings, the death penalty, mass incarceration, and the police and vigilante killings of African Americans.

Although throughout its history African Americans challenged peonage in the courts and elsewhere, it lingered into the 1940s and even beyond, eventually collapsing as the modern civil rights movement began to take shape and such atrocities in the American South were more likely to be exposed, both nationally and internationally. Unfortunately, however, its legacy remains. Investigations prompted by recent police killings of African Americans have uncovered what is apparently widespread debt exploitation of low-income African Americans to fund town and city services, including the salaries of police, who are pressured to target such motorists on petty and sometimes trumped-up charges that result in their being burdened with fines which, if not paid, lead to even further, economically draining trouble with the police and courts. For example, in its investigation of the Ferguson, Missouri city government and police department after the killing of Michael Brown, the U.S. Department of Justice found that such fines were a major source both of town revenue and of community–police conflict.[19]

More recently there was the July 2016 police killing of thirty-two-year-old cafeteria worker Philando Castile during a routine traffic stop in a St. Paul, Minnesota suburb, which his girlfriend live streamed on Facebook. That video and a police dashcam video showed that Castile was shot after informing officer Jeronimo Yanez that he had a gun he was licensed to carry. Castile is heard to say on the police-car dashcam video, "Sir, I have to tell you, I do have a firearm on me." Officer Yanez responded "'OK, don't reach for it then,' and 'Don't pull it out.'" As Officer Yanez shot him, Castile was heard to say "I'm not pulling it out." His last words were: "I wasn't reaching for it." Aside from raising the issue of racial profiling and the question of whether the Second Amendment right to carry a firearm applies to African Americans, the

Castile killing, like the fatal shooting of Michael Brown in Ferguson, Missouri, exposed the existence of a modern form of criminal justice peonage. An examination of police records by National Public Radio (NPR) found that over a fourteen-year period Castile had been stopped at least forty-six times and given more than $6,000 in fines in "a seemingly endless cycle of traffic stops, fines, court appearances, late fees, revocations and reinstatements in various jurisdictions." Only a half-dozen of those stops were due to violations a police officer would have been able to notice without first stopping him, and most (e.g., suspended licenses and the lack of insurance) had to do with the debt spiral that arose from these frequent stops for no apparent reason.[20]

Jim Crow (1877–1964)

Like slavery and peonage, "Jim Crow" was a highly organized system of "race"-justified oppression. Because Jim Crow existed concurrently with peonage for many years and the two systems fed off one another, it is best to view them as somewhat distinct but overlapping systems of oppression. As "a system of segregation and discrimination that barred black Americans from a status equal to that of white Americans," Jim Crow laws, customs, and norms not only kept the "races" separated but also removed African Americans from the opportunities and privileges from which members of the racially dominant group benefited from in every arena of life.[21]

My knowledge of Jim Crow is much more than academic. I lived the formative years of my life in New Orleans, where my family and I were required to sit in the back of buses and streetcars, drink out of "Negro"-designated water faucets, use segregated restrooms, be seated in the back-balcony areas of "white" movie theaters (or anywhere in those for colored only), and take a very long bus ride past a lovely "white" amusement park to a not-so-nice rat-infested one ironically called Lincoln Beach. My sister and I went to all-"Negro" schools with inferior facilities and attended mass with other African Americans at a church that was presided over by European American priests and nuns. All public facilities, such as the hospitals we were born in, restaurants, and libraries, were segregated, and almost all of the city government jobs, such as police officer and bus driver, were reserved for European Americans. Even the cemeteries in which our relatives were buried were segregated.

Although Jim Crow covered much of the same historical ground as peonage, placing brackets around its beginning and end is difficult. The racist image of the shuffling and smiling Jim Crow minstrel character for which the system was named was created in 1828. However, that actual system of legal segregation took much longer to fully crystallize: first with the passage of segregation laws in the North that denied "Negroes" or "colored" people the vote, restricted where they could live and go to school, required them to use segregated public accommodations, kept them out of all but the most menial of jobs, and in some cases even banned them from entering the state; then in the South, as an extension of the slave codes—and building on the black codes enacted after the abolition of slavery—with the Supreme Court's 1896 *Plessy v. Ferguson* decision, the even more rigid and encompassing system of Jim Crow segregation was made official as the law of the land. While the *Brown* decision of 1954 overturned *Plessy v. Ferguson* as the chief remaining legal pillar upholding Jim Crow, it took the modern civil rights movement to put the final nail in its coffin, at least as far as its being legally mandated. Because Jim Crow was especially intense in the South, I (somewhat arbitrarily) begin that era with the end of Reconstruction in 1877—when the North's removal of federal troops from the South set the stage for the return of its control to white supremacists—and end my discussion a little after the passage of the Civil Rights Bill of 1964. In addition to being most pronounced in the South, as with peonage, Jim Crow can best be characterized politically as dominative aversive racism that was enforced psychoculturally by emotional distance that encouraged physical and social segregation. Unlike peonage, however, it was not a phenomenon that was confined largely to rural areas.[22]

Why was physical and emotional distance at the core of this new system of oppression, when this was not nearly so much the case with peonage and slavery? First of all, the supervision under relative close proximity required by slavery and peonage was no longer needed. And also, as one historian put it, "So long as blacks were slaves, so long as they posed no threat to the political and economic supremacy of whites, people were content to live with them on terms of relative intimacy." All that changed, however, with the passage of the Thirteenth, Fourteenth, and Fifteenth Amendments, which, in theory at least, freed African Americans and gave them full citizen rights—including, for men, the right to vote.[23]

Like slavery and peonage, Jim Crow was a totalitarian form of social organization that regulated most aspects of the lives of the African Americans it controlled. It was not, however, as rigid and encompassing as slavery or peonage, with African Americans having more freedom in and control over their daily lives within their segregated communities than they did previously under slavery or the black codes. Moreover, for some, there was a more readily available escape route from the most restrictive form of Jim Crow that existed in the American South: a bus or train ticket North.[24]

Another similarity Jim Crow shared with slavery, which distinguished it from peonage, was the fact that it targeted *most* African Americans, and for their *entire* lives. While, as was true for peonage, the terror that enforced Jim Crow was highly institutionalized into law and the criminal justice system, it was also enforced by the extralegal and illegal violence of police, white supremacist organizations, vigilante groups who engaged in lynching, and the actions of individual "white" men and women who took it upon themselves to violently punish any African Americans who violated laws, customs, or norms such as drinking from a "whites only" water fountain. The chief ideology that fueled and confirmed racial segregation was the notion that there were distinct biological races of people that were so unequal in their intellectual, moral, and other essential abilities that they must be kept separate and socially and politically unequal.[25]

Of course, Jim Crow could not have been so highly organized and tightly regulated without the active involvement of every branch and level of the state in its racial state capacity. State legislatures passed the Jim Crow laws enforced by local counties, towns, and cities. Those laws were supported by local and state courts and ultimately the U.S. Supreme Court, with the 1896 *Plessy v. Ferguson* decision being but one example. And eventually it was the 1954 Brown decision, and federal

laws spurred by the civil rights movement such as the Civil Rights Act
of 1964, the Voting Rights Act of 1965, and the Fair Housing Act of
1968 that were passed by Congress under the leadership of President
Johnson, that dismantled it.[26]

Each of the three major violence-centered racial control systems just
discussed were buttressed by one or more of the three violence-centered
and criminalization-justified racial control mechanisms which I will discuss next: vigilantism and lynching, the death penalty, and mass incarceration. And of course, for each, as I will continue to show, police and
vigilante violence generally, and killings more specifically, had a major
presence.

Vigilantism and Lynching (1877–1955)

Vigilantism has been defined as the violent actions of an individual or
a group that entail "taking the law into one's own hands and attempting to effect justice according to one's own understanding of right and
wrong." And because vigilantism—as opposed to revolutionary violence,
for example—is usually "designed to maintain the established socio-
political order," it has also been described as a form of "establishment
violence." Whereas "'legitimate' coercion" by a political regime (e.g.,
through its police or other security forces) is regulated by laws and other
"formal boundaries" for appropriate behavior, the "'illegitimate' coercion"
of private vigilante individuals and groups is not, although it may be
unofficially sanctioned, or even sponsored, by the state. My focus in this
section is the history of vigilantism engaged in by groups, which tends
to be most strongly associated with lynchings, rather than the acts of
well-armed vigilante individuals who simply shoot their victims, which
are more common in the United States today.[27]

Adding to the confusion about what lynching is, is the fact that it
has both a literal and a metaphorical meaning. The literal contemporary
definition of a lynching is limited to the illegal violent killings carried
out by a vigilante group, mob, or individual to enforce what the killers
consider to be an appropriate code of conduct. Contrary to the popular
images of who is lynched and of lynching requiring a rope and a tree,
that denotation of the term suggests that anyone can be killed, using any

means. However, the word "lynching" has another, much larger meaning, one which Jonathan Markovitz argues is nothing less than "a metaphor for, or a way to understand, race relations."[28]

Because vigilantism and lynching are two closely related phenomena, I cover them together. A quick glance at the two might suggest that lynching is simply group vigilantism in action, where the act is so violent that, unlike a killing carried out by a single vigilante (e.g., a fatal shooting), it entails a slow death—often accompanied by torture and mutilation—such that its execution usually requires a group or mob, worked up into an emotional frenzy. But that is a gross simplification. In his study of lynching vigilantism in the United States, Norton Moses begins by acknowledging the similarities between the two (e.g., both originated in the 1760s and 1770s and both entail the punishment of socially wayward behavior of people by "nongovernmental groups"). He then notes, however, that although vigilante groups often lynched people, most lynchings were not done by vigilante groups and "vigilantes did not always engage in lynching." This suggests that racial vigilantism and lynching can best be viewed as two overlapping circles, which share at their core a justification based on the criminalization of African Americans. In Chapter 7 I discuss other overlapping circles, where although criminalization may exist, it is generally not required to justify such violence—these include phenomena such as the violent actions of white supremacist organizations and anti-African American riots.[29]

As is true for any social phenomenon, setting a beginning and an end point for racial lynchings is somewhat arbitrary. Lynching in what is now the United States has roots in the American Revolution as a usually non-lethal way of terrorizing those loyal to the British, and sporadic instances of racial lynching still occur today. For my purpose of examining lynching as a racial control enforcement mechanism, I focus on a time frame similar to that of the violence-centered racial control systems of peonage and Jim Crow that it helped to enforce, when lethal lynching was deemed by many, if not most, European Americans to be not only necessary and acceptable, but good. That time interval is 1877 through 1955, from the violent end of Reconstruction to the civil rights movement-era reaction of African Americans to the murder of Emmett Till, just a few years after reports of racial lynchings had seemed to come to an end. As was also true for its peonage and Jim Crow parent systems, the mechanism of lynching during this period of economic exploitation of African Americans manifested itself as dominative aversive racism that, psychoculturally, could best be characterized by physical, social, and emotional distance. And because African Americans were no longer the valuable property of often powerful plantation owners but mere criminals, there was no need for lynching to be non-lethal as it had sometimes been for other groups during earlier periods of U.S. history. A recently released study of lynchings documented nearly four thousand cases from 1877 through 1950 in just the dozen Southern states where it was most prevalent. The peak period was 1880 through 1940, a time of intense white racial hostility; the largest number of lynchings occurred in 1892, just four years prior to the *Plessy v. Ferguson* ruling by the U.S. Supreme Court that effectively put African Americans back in their "place" by confirming the legal basis for Jim Crow.[30]

As I noted earlier, unlike slavery, peonage, and Jim Crow, racially targeted vigilantism and lynching can best be viewed as a racial control enforcement *mechanism* rather than a fully developed racial control *system*. And unlike those three highly organized systems of oppression which they help to enforce, most group vigilantism and lynching can best be viewed as collective behavior; that is, the actions of a mob that comes together just long enough to engage in violent actions, and then disperses. This is not to say, however, that some vigilantism and lynching involving white supremacist organizations or vigilante committees is not more structured, nor that such actions do not often depend on—as you will see—strong normative support from local community residents who are members of the racially dominant group, as well as the acquiescence, if not direct support, of local sheriffs, judges, and other town officials.

Again, the main function of racially targeted vigilantism and lynching was to keep African Americans sufficiently terrorized that they would not even consider challenging the existing racial order. Other functions they served included maintaining the racial solidarity and boundaries of local communities, reaffirming the ideology of "black" inferiority, and providing enjoyable social gatherings and entertainment for members of the racially dominant group. Both lynchings and contemporary police and vigilante violence can also be viewed as highly symbolic rituals that are often carried out in a very public arena, be it the public square or via video spread through social other and media, that function to reaffirm white supremacy.[31]

As I mentioned earlier, although African Americans have not been the only victims of vigilantism and lynching, the intense white racial repression that followed the end of Reconstruction made them the primary targets. This was especially true in the South and its border states, where, prior to the Civil War, it was mostly European Americans who were lynched; between 1880 and 1930, however, an estimated 85 percent of lynching victims there were African Americans. And, as is true of today's disproportionate police and vigilante killings of African Americans, while some of these victims were women, the overwhelming majority were men.[32]

Lynching as an instrument of terror has two major characteristics: its extreme and sadistic violence, which often includes torture, mutilation, and burning the victim alive, and its dramatic public display, which is intended to serve as a warning to other African Americans. A powerful warning implicit in such acts is the threat of genocide against any and all African Americans who fail to accommodate themselves to white rule. As I noted earlier, it is the threat of genocide that is the ideological and emotional center of all systems of group oppression.[33]

What type of thinking and feeling enticed whole families to travel large distances to witness the burning of another being human being as they laughed, played, and enjoyed their picnic food? It was of course the racial ideology that African Americans could not be treated inhumanely, because they were not truly human. Also at the center of that racist thinking was the belief that that black beast was a threat to all that European Americans held sacred, especially "white" womanhood. Not only did the ideology that saw African Americans as non-human and dangerous justify lynchings; those lynchings, in turn, reaffirmed African Americans' lowly status and treatment. Lynching also confirmed other

American ideals. For example, just as the American Revolution established the freedom for the citizens of the new sovereign "white" nation to own slaves, lynching demonstrated their right to exercise their moral prerogative to kill those they deemed as deserving of it. And since those lynched were often accused of committing some crime against the personhood, property, and entitlements of members of the racially dominant group, lynching helped foster the ideology of black criminality that would also prove central to the other racial control mechanisms I examine, whose goal is *ostensibly* only crime control.[34]

Vigilantism and lynchings were also enforced by racial folkways and mores, including what was deemed to be appropriate racial etiquette. According to the Equal Justice Initiative study of lynching in twelve Southern states:

> Hundreds of African Americans accused of no serious crime were lynched for social grievances like speaking disrespectfully, refusing to step off the sidewalk, using profane language, using an improper title for a white person, suing a white man, arguing with a white man, bumping into a white woman, and insulting a white person. African Americans living in the South during this era were terrorized by the knowledge that they could be lynched if they intentionally or accidentally violated any social convention defined by any white person.[35]

The major negative emotions driving vigilantism and lynching are fear, anger, and hatred: fear that African Americans, who have been stereotyped as dangerous beasts, might do harm to the personhood, property, and way of life of their racial superiors; anger that they refuse to stay in their racially designated space; and hatred of them for little more than the fact that they exist. The role of the police and vigilantism in Southern racial lynchings is in no way as simple and clear as is indicated by the movies that show a good sheriff successfully or unsuccessfully trying to disperse a lynch mob. On many occasions, the local police not only looked the other way as vigilantes or other groups carried out lynchings, but were in fact active participants in the killings.[36]

Although vigilantism and lynchings are by definition illegal, they were supported by state acts and omissions at every branch and level.

As noted earlier, they sometimes began with the local police, and then there came the local and state courts who all too often accepted the local coroner's conclusion that the death had come "at the hands of parties unknown." And when civil rights and other groups sought relief at the federal level from presidents and Congress through legislation, their pleas went unanswered. Even progressive presidents were not liberal when it came to addressing the problem of racial lynching. For example, Theodore Roosevelt justified such violence by singling out African American rapists as its main cause, and later his distant cousin, President Franklin Delano Roosevelt, declined to support an anti-lynching bill for fear of upsetting Southern Democrats who claimed such legislation violated their "states' rights." And, of course, such frequent racial lynchings could not have survived for so long without the active support of the U.S. Supreme Court. For example, in its 1883 *United States v. Harris* decision, the Court gave its blessing to lynching by forbidding the federal government from prosecuting a group of European Americans who broke into a jail in Tennessee, grabbed four African American men being held there, and beat them, in one case to death.[37]

The legacy of vigilantism and lynching in American society is anything but subtle. The popular image of a lynching in American history is of an African American man hung from a tree by a vigilante group in the Deep South during the late nineteenth to the mid-twentieth century. The fact that such killings do not however require mob action, a rope, a tree, or even a man as the victim was clear in the connection many African Americans made between the fatal shooting of teenager Trayvon Martin in 2012 and the savage killing of an even younger boy, Emmett Till, in a rural Mississippi town nearly six decades earlier. In between those two events came the 1984 shooting by Bernhard Goetz which seriously injured four African American teenagers on a New York City subway train after one of them reportedly demanded money from him, and the 1998 killing of James Byrd, Jr., who was beaten, chained, and dragged behind a truck by three European American men until his head and an arm were severed from the rest of his body, in rural Jasper, Texas, a town known for its Klan activity.[38]

The legacy of vigilantism and lynching has left a profound social and psychological mark on race relations both nationally and, especially, within those local communities in which it has occurred. This is especially true when it comes to the operation of criminal justice. As the Equal Justice Initiative concludes in its study of lynching and its impact: "Mass incarceration, excessive penal punishment, disproportionate sentencing of racial minorities, and police abuse of people of color reveal problems in American society that were framed in the terror era. The narrative of racial difference that lynching dramatized continues to haunt us."[39]

As I noted earlier, the word "lynching" has both a literal and a metaphorical meaning. Few words occupy as profound a place within the African American psyche, culture, and politics as this one. Not surprisingly, then, as an African American raised in the Jim Crow South, as I began to think of historical parallels to what is happening today with the pervasive, disproportionate, and highly publicized police and vigilante killings of African Americans, it was that awful word that came to my mind, as it has done to the minds of many other concerned African Americans; a word that sends shivers throughout our collective consciousness and memory as an oppressed people. This conceptualization of today's police and vigilante killings as "twenty-first-century lynchings" is not surprising given the many parallels between the two—not the least of which is their power as highly dramatic and intensely emotional acts of terrorism that send the powerful message to African Americans: "Stay in your place!" This perspective has become so popular that not only have social scientists come to understand lynchings as a form of racial control rather than as a matter of sporadic and isolated anomalies, but a recent *New York Times* editorial, titled "Lynching as Racial Terrorism," highlighted the release of the aforementioned Equal Justice Initiative study, and from it concluded that lynching is "the precursor of modern-day racial bias in the criminal justice system."[40]

Among the striking similarities between group vigilantism and lynchings and today's police and vigilante killings of African Americans are: their power as acts of terror; the perpetrators' impunity (e.g., it has been estimated that 99 percent of mob members escaped arrest or any other type of accountability); the demeaning racial etiquette such actions enforce; and the role of technological advances in reducing the social isolation that allows such atrocities to remain largely invisible outside of the local communities in which they occur. They are also similar in that they are both *lethal* racial control mechanisms. And while group vigilantism and lynchings are no longer major issues impacting African Americans, I will now show that their more institutionalized, lethal cousin, the highly racialized administration of the death penalty, is.[41]

The Death Penalty (1877–Present)

The death penalty is also known as capital punishment and legal execution. All three terms refer to a government's authority to kill someone who has been convicted of a crime (e.g., murder or treason) deemed by law to be so heinous as to merit being sentenced to death. The general term "death penalty" may refer to either the imposition of a death penalty sentence by a judge in a court of law, the implementation of that sentence—usually within prison walls—or both. It is important to distinguish between the two because for various reasons, including successful court appeals and the granting of executive clemency, many people who are sentenced to death are not actually executed.

Although, as I noted earlier, slave owners had a financial incentive not to kill their slaves because they were valuable property, that did not stop some slaves from being executed. Such executions happened when the economic interests of slave owners were overridden by the responsibility and right of various levels of government "to execute slaves to safeguard slavery." That safeguard was used when a slave engaged in an act, such as murder or subversion, that was deemed to be threatening to the entire racial order. While 1636 is recorded as the beginning of the ten-year period during which, according to records, a person of African descent was first executed in what was to become the United States, for the purpose of this study, which is concerned with the use of the death penalty as a racial control enforcement mechanism, I begin once again with the end of Reconstruction in 1877—when the increasingly hostile racial climate in the United States allowed white supremacists to regain control not only of the South, but also other places where the racial status quo was perceived as being threatened. It was then that the death penalty became a particularly important means of maintaining racial control. Another reason why it makes sense to discuss the death penalty after vigilantism and lynching is that there is analytical value in conceptualizing the death penalty as a more highly institutionalized and legitimized form of lynching. Unfortunately, unlike those racial control systems and mechanisms, it is still prevalent today.[42]

As is true of highly racialized lynchings and police and vigilante killings of African Americans, the fatal violence of the death penalty is a lethal form of racial terrorism and control. In brief, its main social function is the maintenance of America's racial hierarchy. In a test of their social dominance theory hypothesis that, in a society, "the greater the degree of group-based hierarchy, the more terror one should find," psychologists Jim Sidanius and Felicia Pratto found that, after controlling for other potentially relevant factors, in the United States "there was a positive association between the degree to which a state was hierarchically structured and that state's propensity to put its citizens to death." Like other forms of highly racialized lethal terrorism, executions of African Americans also serve important cultural functions for society as a morality play of black evil versus the morally righteous and avenging white good. Such highly emotive drama also achieves an important emotional function for members of the racially dominant group in allowing them to channel and act on their racial hatred and fear in a socially acceptable way. And because death penalty-based executions are administered legally by the state against convicted criminals, this also affirms and thus reinforces the stereotype of the dangerous black criminal. Fitting that "black criminal" profile, those executed have been overwhelmingly, although not exclusively, men, and they are disproportionately poor.[43]

By the end of 2015, 2,881 Federal Bureau of Prisons inmates were held under a death sentence in the United States across thirty-three states. The most striking aspect of both who receives a death penalty sentence and who is actually executed is the huge racial disparity. Although African Americans comprise only 13 percent of the population of the United States, they constitute 42 percent of death-sentence prisoners. That percentage is not very different from what has been the case historically. There were nearly 16,000 executions between 1608 and 2016 in the United States with a disproportionate number of these—more than 7,500, or nearly half (48 percent)—being African Americans. The racial nature of the death penalty in the United States is also evident by the fact that as of November 9, 2016, all of the Confederate states that fought to preserve slavery in the Civil War, and later Jim Crow, had death penalty statutes.[44]

Racial disparities in the death penalty are due to two factors: the racism, and resulting poverty, that places a disproportionate number of African Americans in situations where they commit violent crime, and racial discrimination in the administration of the death penalty.

To understand the workings of systemic racism, which are increasingly covert (what some scholars have referred to as meta-racism), on the death penalty in the United States, it is essential to examine the link between racism, poverty, crime, and the imposition and execution of the death penalty. When people are denied access to jobs and socially and economically resourceful neighborhoods due to racial discrimination, their children are deprived of the opportunity to attend good schools and remain trapped in racially segregated ghettoes with poor schools and few job opportunities. In this way, the vicious cycle of racism and poverty passes on cumulative negative effects as it intensifies across generations. But that is not all: a third phase of that cycle is disproportionately high rates of crime, alienation, hopelessness, frustration, violence, and all of the other social problems bred by poverty, which for some will lead to a fourth phase: imposition of the death penalty. Because the poor are more likely to commit violent and other crimes, they are more likely to get caught up in the web of the criminal justice system, which further deepens their levels of impoverishment, crime, and other social problems used to confirm racist stereotypes that are deployed to justify more discrimination as that intergenerational cycle of racism, poverty, crime, and the death penalty strengthens. As will be seen later, the same vicious cycle works to make African Americans more vulnerable to mass incarceration and to being killed by police and vigilantes.[45]

Racial disparities in the administration of the death penalty are also due to more overt and direct forms of racism. That fact is evident from a video of a rally celebrating the execution of Linwood Briley in 1984, in which a sign carried by a European American read "Fry Coon Fry. Kill Him. Burn. Bar-B-Q Him." An Amnesty International report has documented in great detail that while "historically, the death penalty was applied in a manner that was openly and unashamedly biased against people of colour," reflecting the often unconscious "prejudices of police, jurors, judges, and prosecutors," "racial discrimination in the contemporary US legal system remains deeply engrained: more subtle than in the past, but equally deadly." The Amnesty International report documented racism in the administration of the death penalty throughout American history at various points in the criminal justice system, including prosecutorial discretion as to whom the death penalty should be used for; the exclusion of African Americans and other people of color from juries; racist comments and actions by jurors; representation by bigoted public defenders; the racial bigotry of judges; and the U.S. Supreme Court's refusal to see such systemic racism, and its imposition of an nearly impossible burden of proof of racist intent.[46]

One of the major factors in determining whether someone gets the death penalty is who, racially, kills whom; the death penalty verdict and execution are most likely when the victim is European American and least likely when they are African American. This is how a sheriff in the state of Mississippi during the Jim Crow era explained the logic behind such actions: "We have three classes of homicide. If a nigger kills a white man, that's murder. If a white man kills a nigger, that's justifiable homicide. And if a nigger kills another nigger, that's one less nigger." Unfortunately, the legacy of such racist logic is still evident. For example, a 2016 *New York Times* editorial noted that "the last time a white person in Louisiana was executed for a crime against a black person was in 1752." Gender is also an important factor. Consistent with the racist fear of black violation of white womanhood that motivated so many southern lynchings as a defense of Jim Crow, that editorial also indicated that today in that same state "a black man is 30 times as likely to be sentenced to death for killing a white woman as for killing a black man" and that "regardless of the offender's race, death sentences are six times as likely—and executions 14 times as likely—when the victim is white than black." Finally, the same editorial pointed out that Louisiana's death sentences were not only "consistently racist" but also often—if not usually—erroneous, as indicated by the fact that 127 of the 155 death sentences (82 percent) rendered since 1976 were reversed upon appeal. Those reversals were usually made after the discovery of "major errors at trial that violate the defendant's constitutional rights, such as prosecutorial misconduct, improper jury instructions and incompetent lawyering."[47]

We do not need to look far today to find examples of the racial politics of the death penalty in the United States. Its highly racialized character and the racial tensions it causes were evident in the fall of 2011 when Georgia executed Troy Davis. That former Confederate state, which fought long and hard against equality for African Americans, acted quickly following a one-sentence rejection from the U.S. Supreme Court after two decades of various legal appeals in a case which, according to the *New York Times*, "had become an international symbol of the battle over the death penalty and racial imbalance in the justice system." Davis' conviction was based on little evidence other than the testimony of witnesses, most of whom later recanted their stories. The NAACP unsuccessfully sought the intervention of the U.S. Justice Department by arguing that irregularities in the investigation and trial constituted a violation of Davis' civil rights, as the state rejected a request by his lawyers to allow him to take a lie-detector test. Among the notables who joined 630,000 petition-signers in seeking clemency for Troy Davis were Pope Benedict XVI and "former President Jimmy Carter, Archbishop Desmond Tutu, 51 members of Congress, entertainment figures like Cee Lo Green and even some death penalty supporters, including William S. Sessions, a former F.B.I. director." As he was readied for his execution, Davis looked into the faces of family members of the police officer he was accused of killing and proclaimed his innocence.[48]

Why were the governor and other politicians and state officials so determined to execute Troy Davis despite evidence that he may not have received a fair trial and may indeed have been innocent, as well as worldwide appeals for clemency? The best guess is that their actions were politically motivated. They believed that their most important constituent group, the racially and politically conservative European American Georgia residents who were most inclined to vote for them, wanted Davis executed. The role of politics in such executions was blatantly evident in both national politics and in the politics of another Southern state two decades earlier when then Governor Bill Clinton briefly interrupted his previously scheduled presidential campaign events to return to Arkansas to oversee the execution of Rickey Ray Rector, a man whose mental capacity was so limited that, having eaten his last meal before being taken to the execution chamber, he asked that his dessert be saved for the following day.[49]

The death penalty retains strong support among American politicians who aspire to the presidency. Donald Trump expressed support for the death penalty not only in his successful 2016 election campaign but also back in 1989 when, after five young African American and Latino teenagers were arrested for the murder of a European American woman while she was jogging in Central Park, he placed full-page ads in four New York City newspapers with the headline "Bring Back the Death Penalty! Bring Back the Police!" In response to then Mayor Koch's plea not to allow the incident to cause people to hate, Trump responded: "I do not think so. I want to hate these muggers and murderers. They should be forced to suffer and, when they kill, should be executed for their crimes . . . I want them to understand our anger. I want them to be afraid." The fact that the boys' convictions were eventually overturned did not seem to faze Mr. Trump at all. He later referred to a cash settlement the boys received from the city as "a disgrace," in a 2014 op-ed essay he wrote for the *New York Daily News* in which he continued to disparage their reputations. And in a position contrary to her party's platform, Hillary Clinton, his Democratic opponent in 2016, also expressed support for the death penalty.[50]

The police are, of course, ground zero when it comes to racially targeted death penalties, because it is their assessment of an action—and the person they deem responsible for it—that typically determines what charges are brought, if any. As I noted earlier, while a local sheriff might simply choose to look away if the victim is an African American killed by a European American, or bring lesser charges if that person is killed by another African American, when a European American is killed and it is suspected that an African American is responsible, it is likely that some African American, guilty or not, will be arrested, charged, and given the death penalty.

As will be seen next, the use of racist ideologies and images of black criminals so common in relation to the racial targeting of the death penalty persists today in highly racialized mass incarceration, as it does in the police and vigilante killings of African Americans.

Mass Incarceration (1968–Present)

Narrowly defined, mass incarceration refers to a society's laws, policies, and practices that result in the imprisonment of an extraordinarily large number of its overall population and/or of a particular segment of its population. As Michelle Alexander stresses, however, mass incarceration includes much more than time spent in an actual prison system, because it also entails "the larger web of laws, rules, policies, and customs that control those labeled criminals" once they have been released that makes and keeps them second-class citizens. With more than two million people locked up in prisons and jails, the United States leads the world in incarceration rates. It is also important to note that what is happening here is a relatively new phenomenon, with incarcerations having increased by 500 percent over the past four decades—roughly the period since the end of the civil rights movement, which, as we will see, provoked a huge white backlash that was institutionalized into American politics and its criminal justice policies. The racial nature of the fact that mass incarceration in the United States has increased dramatically since the end of the civil rights movement is confirmed by the fact that the majority of the males incarcerated in state or federal prisons in the United States in 2015 were African American (37 percent) or Latino (22 percent).[51]

In 2010 Michelle Alexander published *The New Jim Crow: Mass Incarceration in the Age of Colorblindness*, a book that quickly became a manifesto for many young African American activists concerned about both highly racialized mass incarceration in the United States and the related pervasive and disproportionate police and vigilante killings of

African Americans. One of the reasons why *The New Jim Crow* strikes such a chord with African Americans is the fact that it places the current oppression we face within the criminal justice system within a larger socio-historical context that is consistent with what we have come to realize through our own collective experiences, consciousness, and memory. That is, Alexander's book recognizes the fact that African Americans not only were, but *are*, an oppressed people—with changes occurring more in *how* that oppression manifests itself at a particular point in time than in the fact of its existence. To paraphrase Frederick Douglass, mass incarceration is just another word for the new skin taken by an old and familiar snake. Indeed, Alexander acknowledges the influence of grassroots African Americans on her own thinking when she informs the reader that she got the idea for her book's "mass incarceration as the new Jim Crow thesis" from a sign she saw nailed to a telephone poll that read: "THE DRUG WAR IS THE NEW JIM CROW."[52]

In the preface to *The New Jim Crow*, Alexander expresses a sentiment that seems to be shared by many, if not most, African Americans: "something is eerily familiar about the way our criminal justice system operates, something that looks and feels a lot like an era we supposedly left behind." And in the book's introduction, she argues that while "the arguments and rationalizations that have been trotted out in support of racial exclusion and discrimination in its various forms have changed and evolved . . . the outcome has remained largely the same." That is, mass incarceration is just the latest manifestation of the racial oppression African Americans have faced throughout their history. It is with her emphasis on its reduction of the rights and opportunities for those convicted of crime, both inside and outside of prison, that Alexander compares mass incarceration to Jim Crow—the nation's system of racial control that immediately preceded today's less overt systemic racism.[53]

In tracing the origins of what she refers to as the *new* Jim Crow, Alexander focuses largely on President Ronald Reagan's highly racialized War on Drugs in the 1980s, which was built on the earlier anti-drug initiative pushed by Richard Nixon. John Ehrlichman, Nixon's domestic policy chief, was reported elsewhere to have said the following about how the Nixon administration crafted anti-drug initiatives to target two groups they considered to be their political enemies—left-wing, anti-war activists, and African Americans:

> We knew we couldn't make it illegal to be either against the war or black, but by getting the public to associate the hippies with marijuana and blacks with heroin. And then criminalizing both heavily, we could disrupt those communities . . . We could arrest their leaders, raid their homes, break up their meetings, and vilify them night after night on the evening news.

And if that was not enough, that Nixon aide concludes by saying: "Did we know we were lying about the drugs? Of course we did." In the 1980s, President Reagan exploited the national frenzy created by his administration over what it depicted as a dangerous crack cocaine epidemic to launch his full-fledged War on Drugs. Subsequent presidents, up to and including Donald Trump, have carried out anti-drug and crime policies and practices that have targeted largely African American communities, and resulted in the mass incarceration of tens of thousands of low-income African Americans.[54]

When we examine how, over the past four decades or so, the United States became the world's leading nation in terms of imprisonment of its citizens, two main culprits are evident: the white racial backlash to the civil rights movement and the economically exploitative neoliberal government policies that were put in place as the nation shifted from a manufacturing to a service-based economy. To understand the rise of mass incarceration, therefore, the best place to begin is not with the Nixon and Reagan administrations' anti-drug policies but, as historian Naomi Murakawa suggests, decades earlier, in the post-World War II years, with the convergence of a number of factors that racialized crime in the eyes of European Americans—the most important of which was the simmering white resentment of changing race relations.[55]

The impact of that emerging white backlash was quite evident in the 1964 presidential campaign when Republican candidate Barry Goldwater made a strong law-and-order link between the civil rights movement—especially civil disobedience—and crime. By the late 1960s, even liberal

Democrats had climbed aboard the law-and-order bandwagon. In response to the white backlash to the increasingly militant civil rights movement and its hijacking of his War on Poverty as an arsenal for militant community organizing, President Johnson shifted his focus to a War on Crime. In *From the War on Poverty to The War on Crime*, historian Elizabeth Hinton documents how in March 1968 President Johnson initiated his War on Crime, following a long, hot summer of urban unrest in American cities, by sending to Congress his Law Enforcement Assistance Act. That bill responded "to the threat of future disorder by establishing a direct role for the federal government in local police operations, court systems, and state prisons for the first time in American history." In brief, Hinton argues that when the War on Poverty programs failed to prevent more racial unrest, the Johnson administration turned to more repressive police measures to reestablish law and order. Later, when Richard Nixon was elected under a campaign theme of restoring "law and order" after the civil rights movement had entered its most militant Black Power phase, he, along with (especially Southern) governors and members of Congress, was able to convince many European American voters that civil rights activism was itself criminal behavior.[56]

And there is more. John Dillon Davey notes that by the early 1970s "an estimated half million protestors had participated in 500 riots with 240 deaths," and that even if all of the jails in the United States had been empty at that time rather than at near capacity, as was actually the case, they would not have had the capacity to handle much more than half of those who engaged in urban unrest. One concrete result of the move toward mass incarceration is that the various levels of the judicial racial state now have ample prison space to house the young African American males who are most likely to engage in urban rebellions or join militant organizations such as the Black Panther Party. No longer is there the need to use anti-poverty agencies to provide summer jobs to African American youth to avoid "long hot summers."[57]

The power of Johnson's War on Crime approach in addressing what was seen as a racial threat was that his bill, and many subsequent tough crime laws enacted under other administrations, both Democratic and

Republican—and liberal, moderate, and conservative—fit the emerging colorblind ideology. Such racism camouflage makes it easy to deny the existence of systemic racism, which works so well in the meta-racism stage of racism, with its psychocultural characteristics of fear, anxiety, and hostility toward African Americans, who are deemed to be people who, at best, just so happen to be poor and inclined to crime. As Hinton put it, "the seemingly neutral statistical and sociological 'truth' of black criminality concealed the racist thinking that guided the strategies federal policymakers developed for the War on Crime, first in the 1960s, and then through the 1970s and beyond." When combined with dramatic neoliberal cuts in federal aid to provide social services for inner-city areas and major job losses due to automation, globalization, and other factors, many of the those trapped in the nation's resource-depleted racial ghettoes saw few options other than to engage in the illegal activities of the undergrown economy.[58]

As I stated earlier, a major reason why African Americans are the targets of police and vigilante killings is that they are racially profiled as dangerous black criminals. And as I have also stressed, such stereotyping is not simply a result of racist ideology. Instead, there is a reciprocal relationship between the two; not only does racist ideology lead to racist policies and practices, racist policies and practices in turn reinforce racist stereotypes as that vicious cycle intensifies. It is the criminalization of African Americans through laws, policies, and practices that target them and their communities, such as the highly racialized War on Drugs, that have placed so many in the sights of police and vigilantes. While some are killed, many more are captured and imprisoned. Such individuals suffer a fate akin to that of slavery while they are imprisoned and to that of Jim Crow once they are released. That fate is mass incarceration.

As noted earlier, the police play an important role in deciding who goes to prison. For example, Alexander notes that in enforcing the nation's anti-drug policies, police and other law enforcement officials have been given "extraordinary discretion regarding whom to stop, search, arrest, and charge." And as Hinton has pointed out, and as I will examine in greater detail presently, an important factor in the increase in the highly racialized mass incarceration and police and vigilante shootings in the United States is changes in police practices brought about by the increased federal role in local policing through the War on Drugs and their militarization. Today as in the past, by definition, vigilantes are more likely to administer their notion of "justice" on the spot rather than to work through the criminal justice system.[59]

Not only does mass incarceration, like the death penalty, persist as a racial control enforcement mechanism that further fuels the racist ideology of African Americans as criminals, but the laws, policies, and practices upon which it is built place many of them at risk of police and vigilante killings.

Conclusion: Lessons Learned

What lessons about today's police and vigilante killings of African Americans can we learn from this chapter's historical review of important characteristics of three violence-centered racial control systems and three violence-centered racial control mechanisms?

As has been seen, the three earliest, most highly organized, and encompassing forms of racial oppression analyzed—slavery, peonage, and Jim Crow—were all racial control *systems*. They began not long after European colonization of what was to become the United States started, and continued through the modern civil rights movement. They entailed either the raw physical brutality of dominative racism, as was true for slavery, or dominative aversive racism—which also emphasized physical and emotional segregation—as was the case for peonage and Jim Crow. For their victims, they were near total institutions, with slavery and Jim Crow expected to last for their entire lifetimes, and with the lives of those under peonage all too often coming to an end relatively quickly due to their harsh working and living conditions. They all served the major function of economic and other social exploitation, with slavery and peonage focused specifically on labor exploitation. While slavery and Jim Crow targeted most African Americans who lived where they were in practice, peonage was more likely to be aimed specifically at African American men. They all employed a broad range of both legal and extralegal violence and terror. Whereas a general notion of racial inferiority was used to justify the inhumane treatment of slaves and second-class citizenship under Jim Crow, that ideology was refined under peonage to include the notion that African American peons were irresponsible and immoral criminals. The racial etiquette required of African Americans under slavery and Jim Crow was similar, but differed largely in the degree to which African Americans were in this case required to debase themselves as they demonstrated their acceptance of their subservient status, whereas under peonage they were expected to also accept criminal status even when they knew they had done nothing wrong.

Hatred and fear were negative emotions at the center of all three violence-centered systems of oppression, with aversion also being important for peonage and Jim Crow. Police and vigilante violence, both legally sanctioned and otherwise, were used to enforce the laws and customs of all three systems. Every branch and level of the state, in its racial state capacity, played a key role in legitimizing and protecting slavery, peonage, and Jim Crow; the roles of the individual-level state legislatures and the U.S. Supreme Court were especially important. African Americans used every means at their disposal to individually and collectively challenge those three systems of oppression, with the civil rights movement being most responsible for the dismantling of peonage and Jim Crow. The institutionalized legacies of all three racial control systems can be seen today in the nation's racial attitudes that are embedded in the operation of every social institution, widespread residential segregation and the de facto school segregation that results from it, various exploitative practices that disproportionately target African Americans, and of course police and vigilante violence.

As you have seen, it was peonage that introduced the criminalization of African Americans which also became the chief justification of the three violence-centered racial control enforcement mechanisms I examined in this chapter: vigilantism and lynching, the death penalty, and mass incarceration. Unlike vigilantism and lynching, the death penalty and mass incarceration, like the violence-centered racial control systems of slavery, peonage, and Jim Crow, are defined in such a way that makes clear that they are deemed legal and appropriate by the larger society. And unlike the three racial control systems I discussed, the racial control mechanisms of vigilantism and lynching, the death penalty, and mass incarceration still persist today—although occurrences of lynching are relatively rare. All three increased at times when European Americans felt they were on the verge of losing control of African Americans, with the demise of slavery, peonage, and Jim Crow as systems of racial control. While group vigilantism and lynching were, for the most part, loosely organized racial control mechanisms, the death penalty and mass incarceration are highly institutionalized. And whereas the primary racial function of vigilantism and lynching, the death penalty, and mass incarceration is to keep African Americans in check and reinforce racist stereotypes and controlling images, mass incarceration has the additional function of the establishment of highly coordinated and nationwide policing policies and practices that protect the lives, property, and other interests of those who have benefited from rising economic inequality by regulating and controlling the behavior of those who are deemed both economically expendable and politically and socially dangerous because their labor is no longer needed.

As with the racial control system of peonage, the primary targets of vigilantism and lynching, the death penalty, and mass incarceration have been African Americans, and especially African American men. The racial control mechanisms of vigilantism and lynching, the death penalty, and mass incarceration have involved extreme terroristic violence such as torture, mutilation, rape, solitary confinement, and excruciatingly painful death. Such inhumane actions are justified by the racist ideology that they are necessary to protect good "white" people from dangerous "black" criminals. Those lynched or facing the death penalty or mass incarceration, as well as their loved ones—and African Americans generally—are expected to humbly accept and conform to the racial etiquette of their lowly and highly stigmatized status as criminals who have few if any rights and who, under threat of violence, must do as they are told. The emotional fuel driving highly racialized lynchings and vigilantism, the death penalty, and mass incarceration includes hatred, anxiety, anger, fear, moral rectitude, and indifference. In all three violence-centered mechanisms of racial control it is the police or vigilantes who, by their actions or inaction, decide a wide range of violent actions that can be taken. Whereas with vigilantes and lynchings, different branches and levels of the state—from the local police up to the Supreme Court—have condoned such actions, largely by their refusal to take actions to stop them, with the death penalty and mass incarceration they play a more direct role by enacting, enforcing, and upholding the laws that authorize them.

In Chapter 4 I place the police and vigilante killings of African Americans within the larger context of police and vigilante violence more generally, and then identify their specific racial control functions in contemporary American society.

Notes

1. Philip S. Foner, ed., *Frederick Douglass: Selected Speeches and Writings* (Chicago, IL: Lawrence Hill Books, 1999), 579.
2. Michelle Alexander, *The New Jim Crow: Mass Incarceration in the Age of Colorblindness* (New York: The New Press, 2010), 21–22.
3. Vesla M. Weaver, "Frontlash: Race and the Development of Punitive Crime Policy," *Studies in American Political Development*, 2007, Fall (21), 230, 238.
4. Steven V. Roberts, "Reagan Signs Bill Ratifying U.N. Genocide Pact," *New York Times*, November 5, 1988, www.nytimes.com/1988/11/05/opinion/reagan-signs-bill-ratifying-un-genocide-pact.html, Accessed June 27, 2016; William L. Patterson, ed., *We Charge Genocide: The Historic Petition to the United Nations for Relief from a Crime of the United States Government against the Negro People* (New York: International Publishers, 1970, first published in 1951), vii, xiv.
5. Patterson, ed., *We Charge Genocide*, v–vi.
6. Alexander, *The New Jim Crow*, 197; Allen D. Grimshaw, "Lawlessness and Violence in America and Their Special Manifestations in Changing Negro-White Relationships," *The Journal of Negro History*, 1959, 44 (1), 56.
7. Allen E. Liska, "Introduction to the Study of Social Control," in Allen E. Liska, ed., *Social Threat and Social Control* (Albany, NY: State University of New York, 1992), 29.
8. George S. Bridges and Martha A. Myers, "Problems and Prospects in the Study of Inequality, Crime, and Social Control," in George S. Bridges and Martha A. Myers, eds., *Inequality, Crime, and Social Control* (Boulder, CO: Westview Press, 1994), 3.
9. Lerone Bennett, Jr., *The Shaping of Black America* (Chicago, IL: Johnson Publishing Company, 1975), 146; "Slavery Begins in America," *History*, no date, 2, www.history.co.uk/study-topics/history-of-america/slavery-begins-in-america, Accessed September 7, 2016; U.S. Bureau of the Census, *The Social and Economic Status of the Black Population in the United States: An Historical View, 1790–1978*, U.S. Department of Commerce, Current Population Reports, Special Studies, Series P-23, No. 80 (Washington, DC: U.S. Government Printing Office, 1979), 11, Table 3; Joel Kovel, *White Racism: A Psychohistory* (New York: Columbia University Press, 1984), xi, Italics in original.
10. Noel A. Cazenave, *Conceptualizing Racism: Breaking the Chains of Racially Accommodative Language* (Lanham, MD: Rowman and Littlefield, 2016), 69–70, 136; Pierre L. van den Berghe, *Race and Racism: A Comparative Perspective* (New York: John Wiley and Sons, 1967), 17–18.
11. Kristian Williams, *Our Enemies in Blue: Police and Power in America* (Oakland, CA: AK Press, 2015), 63–75; W.E.B. DuBois, *Black Reconstruction in America: 1860–1880*

(New York: Touchstone, 1995), 12; John Hope Franklin and Alfred A. Moss, Jr., *From Slavery to Freedom: A History of African Americans* (New York: Alfred A. Knopf, 1994), 126.

12. Lerone Bennett, Jr., *Before the Mayflower: A History of Black America* (New York: Penguin Books, 1982), 109; Gerald Horne, *The Counter-Revolution of 1776: Slave Resistance and the Origins of the United States of America* (New York: New York University Press, 2014), x–xi, 1.

13. Ida B. Wells-Barnett, *On Lynchings: Southern Horrors, A Red Record, Mob Rule in New Orleans* (New York: Arno Press and the New York Times, 1969), 7.

14. "Slavery by Another Name," PBS, no date, www.pbs.org/tpt/slavery-by-another-name/ themes/peonage/, Accessed September 9, 2016; Douglas A. Blackmon, *Slavery by Another Name: The Re-Enslavement of Black Americans from the Civil War to World War II* (New York: Anchor Books, 2008), 6–7, 9; David M. Oshinsky, *"Worse than Slavery": Parchman Farm and the Ordeal of Jim Crow Justice* (New York: Free Press Paperbacks, 1997), 16, 20–21; Carter A. Wilson, *Racism: From Slavery to Advanced Capitalism* (Thousand Oaks, CA: Sage, 1996), 79, 90, 116–17.

15. Joe R. Feagin, *Systemic Racism: A Theory of Oppression* (New York: Routledge, 2006), 123–24; Oshinsky, *Worse than Slavery*, 20–21.

16. Richard Wormser, *The Rise and Fall of Jim Crow* (New York: St. Martin's Press, 2003), 8.

17. Wormser, *The Rise and Fall of Jim Crow*, 8.

18. Wilson, *Racism*, 86–89.

19. Department of Justice, Office of Public Affairs, "Justice Department and City of Ferguson, Missouri, Resolve Lawsuit with Agreement to Reform Ferguson Police Department and Municipal Court to Ensure Constitutional Policing," March 17, 2016, www.justice.gov/opa/pr/justice-department-and-city-ferguson-missouri-resolve-lawsuit-agreement-reform-ferguson, Accessed July 25, 2016; Campbell Robertson, "Missouri City to Pay $4.7 Million to Settle Suit Over Jailing Practices," *New York Times*, July 15, 2016, www.nytimes.com/2016/07/16/us/missouri-city-to-pay-4-7-million-to-settle-suit-over-jailing-practices.html, Accessed July 7, 2017.

20. Eyder Peralta and Cheryl Corley, "The Driving Life and Death of Philando Castile," Morning Edition, NPR, July 15, 2016, www.npr.org/sections/thetwo-way/2016/07/15/485835272/the-driving-life-and-death-of-philando-castile, Accessed July 25, 2016; Jesse J. Holland, "Black, Licensed to Carry, but No Safety," *Hartford Courant*, June 19, 2017, A7.

21. Leslie Brown, "Jim Crow," in Waldo E. Martin, Jr. and Patricia Sullivan, eds., *Civil Rights in the United States, Volume 1* (New York: Macmillan Reference USA, 2000), 392; Tsahai Tafari, "The Rise and Fall of Jim Crow," PBS, 2002, www.pbs.org/wnet/jimcrow/struggle_court.htm, Accessed September 26, 2016.

22. Brown, "Jim Crow," 392; Wormser, *The Rise and Fall of Jim Crow*, xi; Wilson, *Racism*, 78–79, 116–17.

23. C. Vann Woodward, *The Strange Career of Jim Crow* (London: Oxford University Press, 1974), 12; Bennett, Jr., *Before the Mayflower*, 259.

24. Jerrold M. Packard, *American Nightmare: The History of Jim Crow* (New York: St Martin's Press, 2002), 63.

25. Brown, "Jim Crow," 393; Packard, *American Nightmare*, viii; Bennett, Jr., *Before the Mayflower*, 258.

26. Manning Marable, *Race, Reform, and Rebellion: The Second Reconstruction and Beyond in Black America, 1945–2006* (Jackson, MS: University Press of Mississippi, 2007), 9, 38, 79; Harvard Sitkoff, *The Struggle for Black Equality* (New York: Hill and Wang, 2008), 21–22, 154, 221.

27. "Vigilantism," no date, thefreedictionary.com, legaldictionary.thefreedictionary.com/ Vigilantism, Accessed August 3, 2016; H. Jon Rosenbaum and Peter C. Sederberg,

"Vigilantism: An Analysis of Establishment Violence," in H. Jon Rosenbaum and Peter C. Sederberg, eds., *Vigilante Politics* (Philadelphia, PA: University of Pennsylvania Press, 1976), 3–4.

28. W. Fitzhugh Brundage, "Lynching," in Waldo E. Martin and Patricia Sullivan, eds. *Civil Rights in the United States, Volume 2* (New York: Macmillan, 2000), 443; Jonathan Markovitz, *Legacies of Lynching: Racial Violence and Memory* (Minneapolis, MN: University of Minnesota Press, 2004), xvi.

29. Norton H. Moses, *Lynching and Vigilantism in the United States: An Annotated Bibliography* (Westport, CT: Greenwood Press, 1997),xi.

30. Brundage, "Lynching," 443; Wilson, *Racism*, 79, 116–17; Equal Justice Initiative, *Lynching in America: Confronting the Legacy of Racial Terror, Report Summary* (Montgomery, AL: Equal Justice Initiative, 2015), 3–5, www.eji.org/files/EJI%20Lynching%20in%20America%20SUMMARY.pdf, Accessed August 4, 2016; Andrew S. Buckler, "Lynching as Ritual in the American South," *Berkeley Journal of Sociology*, 1992, 37, 13.

31. Grimshaw, "Lawlessness and Violence in America and their Special Manifestation in Changing Negro-White Relationships," 55–56; Buckler, "Lynching as Ritual in the American South," 11; Orlando Patterson, *Rituals of Blood: Consequences of Slavery in Two American Centuries* (Washington, DC: Civitas Counterpoint, 1998), 173.

32. W. Fitzhugh Brundage, *Lynching in the New South: Georgia and Virginia, 1880–1930* (Urbana, IL: University of Illinois Press, 1993), 5; Brundage, "Lynching," 443.

33. Patterson, ed., *We Charge Genocide*, v.

34. Ahsraf H. A. Rushdy, *American Lynching* (New Haven, CT: Yale University Press, 2012), xi; Equal Justice Initiative, *Lynching in America*, 20.

35. Equal Justice Initiative, *Lynching in America*, 10.

36. Grimshaw, "Lawlessness and Violence in America and Their Special Manifestations in Changing Negro-White Relationships," 56.

37. Robert L. Zangrando, *The NAACP Crusade against Lynching, 1909–1950* (Philadelphia, PA: Temple University Press, 1980), 8; Rushdy, *American Lynching*, ix; Equal Justice Initiative, *Lynching in America*, 18; Robert Whitaker, *On the Laps of Gods: The Red Summer of 1919 and the Struggle for Justice that Remade a Nation* (New York: Crown, 2009), 28.

38. Max Kutner, "30 Years after Bernhard Goetz, A Subway Shooting Evokes Comparisons," *Newsweek*, March 13, 2015, www.newsweek.com/30-years-after-bernhard-goetz-subway-shooting-evokes-comparisons-313689, Accessed August 2, 2016; Carol Marie Cropper, "Black Man Fatally Dragged in a Possible Racial Killing," *New York Times*, June 10, 1998, www.nytimes.com/1998/06/10/us/black-man-fatally-dragged-in-a-possible-racial-killing.html, Accessed August 2, 2016.

39. Equal Justice Initiative, *Lynching in America*, 3.

40. Karlos K. Hill, "21st Century Lynchings?," Fifteen Eighty Four, Academic Perspectives from Cambridge University Press, February 29, 2016, www.cambridgeblog.org/2016/02/21st-century-lynchings/, Accessed August 2, 2016; Philip Dray, *At the Hands of Persons Unknown: The Lynching of Black America* (New York: Random House, 2002), xi; "Lynching as Racial Terrorism," *New York Times*, Editorial, February 11, 2015, A26.

41. Equal Justice Initiative, *Lynching in America*, 3, 6; Zangrando, *The NAACP Crusade against Lynching, 1909–1950*, 8, 11; Stewart E. Tolnay and E.M. Beck, "Lethal Social Control in the South: Lynchings and Executions between 1880 and 1930," in Bridges and Myers, eds., *Inequality, Crime, and Social Control*, 179.

42. Adalberto Aguirre, Jr. and David V. Baker, "Slave Executions in the United States: A Descriptive Analysis of Social and Historical Factors," *Social Science Journal*, 1999, 36 (1), 2; Howard W. Allen and Jerome M. Clubb, *Race, Class, and the Death Penalty: Capital Punishment in American History* (Albany, NY: SUNY Press, 2008), 13.

43. Jim Sidanius and Felicia Pratto, *Social Dominance: An Intergroup Theory of Hierarchy and Oppression* (Cambridge: Cambridge University Press, 1999), 220; David Garland, *Peculiar Institution: America's Death Penalty in an Age of Abolition* (Cambridge, MA: Belknap Press, 2010), 6–7.

44. Tracy L. Snell, *Capital Punishment, 2014–2015* (Washington, DC: Bureau of Justice Statistics, U.S. Department of Justice, May 2017), 1, www.bjs.gov/content/pub/pdf/cp1415sb.pdf, Assessed June 6, 2017; U.S. Census Bureau, *Quick Facts, United States* (Washington, DC:, U.S. Census Bureau, U.S. Department of Commerce, 2015) www.census.gov/quickfacts/table/PST045215/00, Assessed August 12, 2016; Death Penalty Information Center, "Facts about the Death Penalty," "Death Row Inmates by Race," August 17, 2017, 2, deathpenaltyinfo.org/documents/FactSheet.pdf, Accessed August 19, 2017; Death Penalty Information Center, "Executions in the U.S. 1608–2002: The Espy File," 1, "Executions by Race of Defendants: 1608–2016," no date, 2, www.deathpenaltyinfo.org/executions-us-1608-2002-espy-file, Accessed August 19, 2017; Death Penalty Information Center, "States with and without the Death Penalty as of November 9, 2016," 1, deathpenaltyinfo.org/states-and-without-death-penalty, Accessed August 19, 2017; Equal Justice Initiative, "The Death Penalty," no date, 1, www.eji.org/death-penalty, Accessed August 16, 2016.

45. William J. Bowers, *Executions in America* (Lexington, MA: Lexington Books, 1974), 72.

46. Matthew Cipolla, "The Killing of Linwood Briley," YouTube, August 10, 2017, www.youtube.com/watch?v=d2n1ouK6vrI&oref=https%3A%2F%2Fwww.youtube.com%2Fwatch%3Fv%3Dd2n1ouK6vrI&has_verified=1, Accessed August 22, 2017; Amnesty International USA, *Killing with Prejudice: Race and the Death Penalty in the USA* (New York: Amnesty International, USA, 1999), 1, 10–25, www.amnesty.org/en/documents/AMR51/052/1999/en/, Accessed July 17, 2017.

47. Robert Whitaker, *On the Laps of Gods: The Red Summer of 1919 and the Struggle for Justice that Remade a Nation* (New York: Crown, 2009), 31; The Editorial Board, "Louisiana's Color-Coded Death Penalty," *New York Times*, May 9, 2016, A18.

48. Kim Severson, "Davis Is Executed in Georgia," *New York Times*, September 21, 2011, www.nytimes.com/2011/09/22/us/final-pleas-and-vigils-in-troy-davis-execution.html?_r=0, Assessed August 12, 2016; CNN Wire Staff, "Advocates for Troy Davis Promise Last-Minute Push," CNN, September 20, 2011, www.cnn.com/2011/09/20/justice/georgia-davis-execution/, Assessed August 12, 2016.

49. Peter Applebome, "The 1992 Campaign: Death Penalty; Arkansas Execution Raises Questions on Governor's Politics," *New York Times*, January 25, 1992, www.nytimes.com/1992/01/25/us/1992-campaign-death-penalty-arkansas-execution-raises-questions-governor-s.html, Assessed August 14, 2016; "Capital Punishment: Death for the Mentally Disabled," *The Economist*, March 8, 2014, www.economist.com/news/united-states/21598681-can-you-execute-man-whose-iq-71-death-mentally-disabled, Accessed July 17, 2017.

50. Matt Ford, "Donald Trump's Racially Charged Advocacy of the Death Penalty," *The Atlantic*, December 18, 2015, www.theatlantic.com/politics/archive/2015/12/donald-trump-death-penalty/420069/, Accessed August 26, 2016; Amy Chozick, "Hillary Clinton Comes Out Against Abolishing the Death Penalty," *New York Times*, October 28, 2015, www.nytimes.com/politics/first-draft/2015/10/28/hillary-clinton-comes-out-against-abolishing-the-death-penalty/, Accessed August 26, 2016; Amanda Terkel, "Democratic Party Endorses Abolishing the Death Penalty—Breaking with Hillary Clinton," *Huffington Post* July 1, 2016, www.huffingtonpost.com/entry/democratic-platform-death-penalty_us_5776d56de4b0a629c1aa0984, Accessed August 26, 2016.

51. Alexander, *The New Jim Crow*, 13; The Sentencing Project, "Trends in U.S. Corrections," no date, 1–2, sentencingproject.org/wp-content/uploads/2016/01/Trends-in-US-Corrections.pdf, Accessed August 24, 2016; Equal Justice Initiative, "Mass Incarceration," no date, 1–2, www.eji.org/tion, Accessed August 24, 2016; E. Ann Carson and Elizabeth Anderson, "Prisoners in 2015," Bureau of Justice Statistics, U.S. Department of Justice, December 2016, 1, 30, www.bjs.gov/content/pub/pdf/p15.pdf#page=3 &zoom=auto,-304,792, Accessed August 22, 2017.
52. Alexander, *The New Jim Crow*, 3.
53. Alexander, *The New Jim Crow*, xiii, 1.
54. Alexander, *The New Jim Crow*, 5; Tom LoBianco, "Report: Aide Says Nixon's War on Drugs Targeted Blacks, Hippies," CNN, March 24, 2016, www.cnn.com/2016/03/23/politics/john-ehrlichman-richard-nixon-drug-war-blacks-hippie/, Accessed August 25, 2016; Sari Horwitz, "How Jeff Sessions Wants to Bring Back the War on Drugs," *Washington Post*, April 8, 2017, www.washingtonpost.com/world/national-security/how-jeff-sessions-wants-to-bring-back-the-war-on-drugs/2017/04/08/414ce6be-132b-11e7-ada0-1489b735b3a3_story.html?utm_term=.59d1a970f18f, Accessed May 18, 2017.
55. Naomi Murakawa, "The Origins of the Carceral Crisis: Racial Order as 'Law and Order' in Postwar American Politics," in Joseph Lowndes, Julie Novkov, and Dorian T. Warren, eds., *Race and American Political Development* (New York: Routledge, 2008), 236–37.
56. Murakawa, "The Origins of the Carceral Crisis," 234–36; Elizabeth Hinton, *From the War on Poverty to the War on Crime* (Cambridge, MA: Harvard University Press, 2016), 1–3, 10–11, 139–40.
57. Joseph Dillon Davey, *The New Social Contract: America's Journey from Welfare State to Police State* (Westport, CT: Praeger, 1995), xvii.
58. Hinton, *From the War on Poverty to the War on Crime*, 3; Wilson, *Racism*, 172, 219.
59. Alexander, *The New Jim Crow*, 103; Hinton, *From the War on Poverty to the War on Crime*, 10.

4

POLICE AND VIGILANTE KILLINGS OF AFRICAN AMERICANS AS A RACIAL CONTROL MECHANISM

Although racial and other forms of social oppression are routinely maintained through the widely disseminated ideas that justify them, ultimately it is force, based on the threat or actual use of physical violence, that keeps such hierarchies in place. Building on that premise is this study's assumption that political violence is an essential mechanism of racial control, and that such violence is often lethal. As Michael Eric Dyson put it,

> *to be black* in America is to live in terror ... It is glimpsed in cops giving chase to black men and shooting them in their backs without cause ... Our skin, our bodies, are relentlessly monitored and policed ... the way we feel about cops is how many of you feel in the face of terror. And yet, long before 9/11, long before Al-Qaeda, long before ISIS, we felt that too, at your hands, at the hands of your ancestors, at the hands of your kin who are our cops.[1]

In this chapter, I focus specifically on this book's main thesis—Proposition # 2—that *the pervasive and disproportionate police and vigilante killings of African Americans can best be understood as a violence-centered racial control mechanism.*

To that end, I build on the ideas, concepts, and historical lessons discussed in the three previous chapters, with some additional specification of racial control-related theories, concepts, and other ideas. Then I place the disproportionate police and vigilante killings of African Americans within the larger racial control context of the more routine police harassment and mistreatment of African Americans. Next, I list and describe the economic, social status, and political racial control functions those killings serve. Finally, I conclude with a brief overview of the major findings and their relevance to the next chapter, in which I view such killings through an economic lens.

More on Racial Control

As I stressed in previous chapters, this book's racial control argument is rooted in the conceptualization of social control—a major concern of sociology since its inception. You may also recall that the idea of social control is implicit in the interdisciplinary literature I reviewed on social domination. Finally, as has been seen, the social control concept has proven especially useful in explaining two phenomena central to this study: criminal justice and race relations. The form of social control that is most relevant to this study is, of course, racial control.

A Quick Review of My Racial Control Conceptual Framework

Because of its centrality to this study, and especially this chapter, I begin this section with a quick review of some of this study's basic assumptions about the concept of racial control. In Chapters 2 and 3 I distinguished between racial control systems and their mechanisms. I stated that social *systems* are large, highly institutionalized, and enduring social structures and processes, such as slavery, peonage, Jim Crow, and contemporary systemic racism, that encompass smaller, less institutionalized, and less durable violence-centered and criminalization-justified structures and processes that serve as their operational *mechanisms* (e.g., lynchings, the death penalty, mass incarceration, and police and vigilante killings). And I noted that such racial control mechanisms function to keep African Americans in what is deemed to be their proper place during different periods of American racial history.

I also stressed that while intentionality is sometimes involved, as was the case under slavery, debt peonage, and Jim Crow, it is not required.

This is especially true today with the more covert, and often indirect, forms of institutionalized racism that, on the surface at least, appear to be colorblind. There is no need, therefore, for this study of the workings of the racial control mechanism of the police and vigilante killings of African Americans to prove intent or the existence of a racial conspiracy. It is sufficient to demonstrate how such killings function in sustaining ostensibly colorblind systemic racism and the various privileges it affords members of the racially dominant group.

A Closer Look at Racial Control-Related Theories

In his introduction to the social control concept, Allen Liska notes that since the turbulent 1960s, the conflict theory perspective has dominated the sociological literature on that topic. Such a perspective assumes that a society's legal system serves powerful individuals and groups by criminalizing and punishing those who threaten their interests. As Ronald Weitzer and Steven A. Tuch put it in their study of racial- and class-based discrimination by the police, "Conflict theory links criminal justice institutions to the structure of inequality in society. The police and other criminal justice agencies are portrayed as key mechanisms in the control of subordinate groups and in the protection of dominant group interests." With that conflict-theoretical perspective in hand, Allen Liska concludes that the level of "crime control" is assumed to vary in response to "the number of acts and people" deemed to pose such a threat, and that the most severe form of social control is "fatal control," during which "the threatening population is killed."[2]

Liska has identified two sociological theories that explain race relations from a social or, more specifically, a racial control perspective, which are especially useful for this study: Herbert Blumer's group position theory and Hubert Blalock's group threat theory (also known as threat theory or racial threat theory). Both assume that prejudice and discrimination increase as a reaction to challenges to the racial status quo on the part of the racially oppressed group. As has been seen, in the United States such white racial backlashes are often justified through the crafting of ideologies and policies that racialize African Americans as dangerous criminals. Let's take another look at both of these theories and what they help us understand about police and vigilante killings of African Americans as a racial control mechanism.[3]

Racial threat theory is the theory which has been applied most often to studies of police and group vigilante (i.e., lynching) violence against African Americans, and to which I have made most reference thus far in this book. As you may recall, Blalock hypothesized that there are two "psychological mechanisms" that link the demographic factor of "minority percentage with discriminatory behavior": "a fear of economic competition" and "a power threat based on the fear that the minority might gain political dominance." As you will see, racial threat theory seems to build on the core assumptions of Blumer's work, which was published nearly a decade earlier, but focuses more attention on more objective and macro-level factors. It also operationalizes its hypotheses and concepts in such a way that they are testable through the use of sophisticated quantitative research methods, using statistical data that are largely already available. It is for those reasons that Hubert Blalock's racial threat hypothesis has served as the theoretical foundation of numerous studies on the correlates of political violence against African Americans, such as lynchings and fatal police shootings. Over decades, the racial threat theory has achieved greater validity and reliability though the refinement of its methods (e.g., including combining both objective, macro-level demographic and economic data with subjective, micro-level, attitudinal measures).[4]

For my purposes in this qualitative historical sociology study, I find Blumer's work of sufficient heuristic value for me to take more time here to flesh out some of its useful insights for improving our understanding of the police and vigilante killings of African Americans as a violence-centered racial control mechanism. From a sociology of knowledge perspective, not much analysis is required to appreciate why Blumer's group position theory proved to be so relevant. It was developed in the late 1950s as African Americans challenged the Jim Crow system of racial control in Montgomery, Alabama; Little Rock, Arkansas; and elsewhere in the South in ways that evoked an intense white racist and often violent reaction. By that time it was evident that, because the then dominant social psychological theories that focused on prejudiced individuals had proven themselves inadequate in explaining this new tumultuous era of race relations, new, more sociological theory work was needed. Such conceptualizations, like the sociological theories of race relations published decades earlier, should focus more on race *group relations*. In line with some of those older sociological theories of race relations, in his conceptualization of prejudice as a "sense of group position", Blumer stressed that challenges to the existing racial order are likely to lead to increased racial animus by members of the racially dominant group.[5]

Although Blumer's theory, with its focus on racial meanings, is largely social-psychological, its key assumption is that racial subjectivity, as it manifests itself in prejudice, is "fundamentally a matter of relationship between racial groups." Consistent with the key role that criminalization has played in various violence-centered racial control mechanisms throughout American history, Blumer asserts that "a basic understanding of race prejudice must be sought in the process by which racial groups form images of themselves and of others" and that "this process . . . is fundamentally *a collective process*." From Blumer's racial meanings perspective, one might say this is a dynamic process of making and remaking the contours of the race concept to meet changing racial control needs, while maintaining the basic notion of "white" racial superiority and "black" racial inferiority. This hierarchy-sustaining process is reinforced as African Americans who are perceived as threatening the racial status quo are criminalized in ways that fit new racial state politics, policies, and practices. Finally, when such actions are enforced through the police or vigilante killings of "dangerous black criminals" they affirm and strengthen that current conceptualization of race as well as more state-punitive actions that, in turn, justify more killings, with the cycle strengthening as it repeats itself.[6]

In accounting for that important subjective component of racial control, Blumer provides emotions with a prominent seat at his analytical table by delineating four types of feelings which members of the dominant racial group experience alongside their prejudice. Consistent with the discipline's long-time focus on social control, and this study's more specific interest in racial control, Blumer describes one of those types of emotion as "a fear and suspicion that the subordinate race harbors designs on the prerogatives of the dominant race." Such fear is evoked by acts that those who are racially privileged take to mean that members of the racially subordinated group are, as Blumer put it, "getting out of place." Blumer also stresses that the "place" or "sense of group position" that members of the racially dominant group are concerned about upholding "is not a mere reflection of the objective relations between racial groups. Rather, it stands for 'what ought to be' rather than for 'what is.' It is a sense of where the two racial groups *belong*." Finally, he states that it is the highly emotional "norm and imperative" of this "sense of group position" that gives it its power. In brief, Blumer suggests that we view racial reactions, such as increased prejudice, as "a protective device"; one that "functions, however shortsightedly, to preserve the integrity and the position of the dominant group."[7]

In this book, I stress the importance of highly publicized police and vigilante killings of African Americans—especially those done with impunity, like those of Trayvon Martin, Michael Brown, Eric Garner, and Tamir Rice—as powerful acts of terror that reinforce the racial status quo. This is what Blumer had to say about the impact of what he refers to as "the 'big event' in developing a conception of the subordinate racial group":

> The happening that seems momentous, that touches deep sentiments, that seems to raise fundamental questions about relations, and that awakens strong feelings of identification with one's racial group is the kind of event that is central in the formation of the racial image . . . When this public discussion takes the form of a denunciation of the subordinate racial group, signifying that it is unfit and a threat, the discussion becomes particularly potent in shaping the sense of social position.[8]

Although smartphones, twenty-four-hour cable television news programs, and the internet were not around to make police and vigilante killings national spectacles at that time, there were lynchings, which often did manage to capture widespread newspaper, and even some television, coverage. It is important enough for me to state again the irony that the same technological advances that have brought the police and vigilante killings of African Americans so much national, and indeed worldwide, attention in recent years have made them more effective instruments of terror.

Of course, sociology is not the only academic discipline that offers useful theories and concepts for our better understanding of the police and vigilante killings of African Americans. As has been seen, I have been particularly impressed with the insightful and empirically tested interdisciplinary scholarship of psychologists Jim Sidanius and Felicia Pratto. One need not move very far analytically from the racial control concept as referring to a form of social control to Sidanius and Pratto's focus on what they refer to as social dominance. Indeed, the authors explicitly state that their theoretical synthesis draws heavily from Blumer's group position theory. That influence is evident in the foundational assumption of social dominance theory that "all human societies tend to be structured as systems of *group-based social hierarchies.*" And, especially relevant to this study of police and vigilante violence as a racial control mechanism, social dominance theory seeks to "identify the various mechanisms that produce and maintain" such oppressive systems.[9]

Sidanius and Pratto emphasize the role of a society's legal and criminal justice systems in the building and sustenance of oppressive systems. For example, in explaining the actual, as opposed to the ideal, workings of "law and order," they note that "*law* is often written and enforced so as to favor the interests of dominants, and *order* is often defined as those social conditions that disproportionately protect and maintain the interests of dominants." It may also be recalled that one of the most important mechanisms used in the construction and maintenance of oppressive systems is what Sidanius and Pratto refer to as "systematic terror," which they define as "the use of violence or threats of violence disproportionately directed against subordinates." Such terror, which is often institutionalized within the legal and criminal justice systems, functions to "enforce the continued deference of subordinates toward dominants." Well-publicized police and vigilante killing spectacles, which fit both Sidanius and Pratto's conceptualization of systematic terror and Blumer's "big event," and which are done with impunity, reinforce the racial status quo. To fully understand how such fatal encounters help keep African Americans in their racially subordinated place, it is necessary to broaden our scope to include the larger context of the racially targeted police violence in which they operate.[10]

The Racial Control Context of Police Killings: Targeting African Americans for Harassment and Brutality

In this section I examine the pervasive, disproportionate, and persistent police killings of African Americans as a racial control enforcement mechanism both within their larger social and policing context and, more specifically, as but one point along a continuum of police violence.

The Larger Social Context

As Figure 4.1 illustrates, as a violence-centered racial control mechanism, the police killings of African Americans can best be understood as but one manifestation of the highly racialized culture of police harassment and brutality more generally, and of the much larger society-wide system of racial oppression, which not only tolerates but encourages such violence.

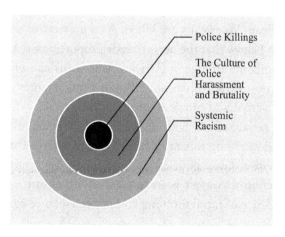

Police Killings

The Culture of
Police
Harassment
and Brutality

Systemic
Racism

Figure 4.1 The Larger Policing and Societal Context of the Police Killings of African Americans as a Violence-Centered Racial Control Mechanism

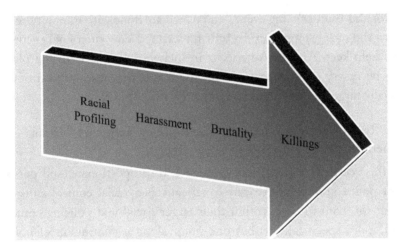

Figure 4.2 Continuum of Police Violence as a Racial Control Mechanism

Police Misconduct: Racial Profiling, Harassment, Brutality, and Killings

As Figure 4.2 illustrates, another way to conceptualize police violence as a violence-centered racial control mechanism is by placing it along a continuum that ranges from violence broadly defined as the violation of basic human rights through fatal physical violence.

In Chapter 6 I stress the importance of examining how police attitudes, culture, and violence set the stage for fatal dominative encounters in which African Americans are killed. As a preview of those insights, in this section I show that the pervasive, disproportionate, and persistent police and vigilante killings of African Americans can best be understood as the most extreme manifestation of a much larger phenomenon of the use of verbal and physical intimidation to keep African Americans in their racialized place as "dangerous black criminals"—practices not only condoned but *mandated* by the larger society through highly racialized politics, laws, policies, and practices. The contours of this larger racial control context become clear as we examine some of the extensive evidence of racial profiling and police violence against African Americans.[11]

Racial profiling in traffic stops. In the previous chapter I placed the contemporary police and vigilante treatment of African Americans in historical context. I noted, for example, that policing in the United States has deep roots in the slave patrols that were established to catch and punish runaway slaves. In her analysis of the origins and social control functions of present-day American policing, Sandra Bass places particular emphasis on the influence of those slave patrols that often engaged in what John Hope Franklin and Loren Schweninger refer to as "the hunt"—a practice that today seems eerily familiar to many African Americans, who perceive something akin to an open season of hunting, especially on their young males. Today "the hunt" usually begins with racial profiling.[12]

The police are powerful agents of racial control not only because they are legally authorized to use deadly force, but also because they have a great deal of discretion in crucial decision-making as to who should be detained and how they should be treated, with much less accountability for their actions than is the case for civilians. At the interpersonal level, racially targeted police and vigilante harassment and intimidation often begins with racial profiling, the first step in many of the unwarranted killings of African Americans—for example, Walter Scott and Philando Castile. One form of such racial profiling has received so much attention that it has been given its own name: "driving while black." That expression refers to African Americans being pulled over by the police for no legitimate reason: being suspected drug dealers, driving a nice car which it is assumed they could not possess legally, being in what the officer deems to be "the wrong neighborhood," or some minor offense for which European Americans are not usually stopped. Ronald Weitzer and Steven Tuch explain the link between the considerable leeway police have in their use of their discretionary powers and racial profiling by pointing out that "because all drivers engage in petty traffic violations, it does not take officers long to observe grounds for a stop, which may be motivated by a driver's race." Not surprisingly, a 2004 Gallup poll found that two-thirds (67 per cent) of African Americans reported that racial profiling was widespread in traffic stops, and an earlier (1999) Gallup poll cited by Weitzer and Tuch found that 40 percent of African Americans responded yes—compared to only 5 percent of European Americans—when asked "Have you ever felt that you were stopped by the police because of your race or ethnic background?" Finally, when asked "are blacks in your community treated less fairly than whites in dealings with the police, such as traffic incidents," 70 percent of African Americans responded yes, compared to only 36 percent of European Americans. Of course, the abuse of police discretion to engage in racial profiling is not limited to traffic stops.[13]

Racial profiling and stop-and-frisk. A revealing example of racially targeted policing, deployed as a racial control mechanism to keep the assumed criminality of African Americans in check, is the stop-and-frisk policies of many U.S. cities, which not only encourage but go so far as to pressure local police officers to detain and search those whom they have been taught to racially profile as potential lawbreakers. Such detentions and searches have been widely applied in a way that resembles the actions of an occupying army determined to keep people in the occupied territory both contained within the physical space reserved for them and under control within that space.

The use of stop-and-frisk policies and practices as a mechanism to enforce the racist stereotype of African Americans as dangerous black criminals has been well documented in this nation's largest city, New York. In Chapter 5, I discuss how stop-and-frisk was widely used by the Rudolph Giuliani administration as part of its neoliberal "broken windows" policy of hyperaggressive policing based on strict enforcement, for the racially targeted population, of every minor infraction, no matter how trivial (e.g., jaywalking, littering, the possession of small quantities of marijuana)—a policy that helped set the stage for highly publicized police killings such as that of Amadou Diallo in 1999. Unfortunately, since that time, the practice has continued under the politically and racially more moderate mayoral administration of Mayor Michael Bloomberg, a very successful businessman, a multibillionaire, and a proponent of neoliberalism, and to a lesser extent under the more liberal administration of Mayor Bill de Blasio, who won election with significant support from African Americans and other people of color, largely on his promise to bring stop-and-frisk under control. Based on its analysis of stop-and-frisk actions from 2002 through 2016, the New York Civil Liberties Union found that: residents of that city were stopped and interrogated more than five million times; nine of out of ten were found to be innocent of any wrongdoing; and the overwhelming number of those stopped were African American or Latino. The number of stops peaked in 2011 at 685,724 for that one year alone, with 87 percent of those stops being either African American (53 percent) or Latino (34 percent), compared with only 9 percent for those who were racially designated as being "white."[14]

The evidence supporting my racial control argument goes way beyond statistics, however. Much of the most damning testimony comes from those inside the New York Police Department (NYPD) itself. New York State Senator Eric Adams, a former captain in the NYPD, testified in court, as part of a class action suit against the policy, that at a meeting attended by himself and other African American elected officials, during which he complained about the disproportionate impact of stop-and-frisk on African Americans and Latinos, then New York Police Commissioner Ray Kelly "stated that he targeted or focused on that group because he wanted to instill fear in them that any time they leave their homes they could be targeted by police." After Kelly's lawyer attempted to read a written declaration in which he denied that he made that comment, the judge stopped him from doing so and invited Kelly to take the witness stand to testify. However, the city government effectively blocked any testimony by the commissioner by refusing to schedule a pre-trial disposition on the grounds that he was "too busy." In explaining why the Bloomberg administration would likely attempt to block any efforts to force Commissioner Kelly to testify under oath, his lawyer stated that he would probably only give testimony that had been "scripted" by its lawyers. In previous hearings that were part of that same trial, "two serving NYPD officers testified that the department maintains a rigid quota system to ensure officers make a certain number of stops, arrests, and summons" and that they had taped instructions to that effect given by their supervisors at precinct roll calls.[15]

An officer who, in 2011—when Mayor Bloomberg and Commissioner Kelly were in charge of the NYPD—was placed in a special monitored status, denied overtime, and given undesirable work assignments due to making an insufficient number of arrests for subway fare violations taped his supervisor's criticism of him for not arresting the right kind of people: African American men. The officer's response that he had only stopped and searched two African American men in a nine-month period because he didn't see any African American men committing crimes was met with a stern lecture from his captain as to who, racially and in gender terms, commits the most crime. In a federal lawsuit, the officer sued the department for taking retaliatory action against him for failing to meet quotas that targeted teenagers and people of color. The captain charged in the suit, which was filed years later, was later promoted and Bill Bratton, the police commissioner under Mayor de Blasio at the time of the suit, defended his actions. It was Bratton who, while greatly reducing the numbers of stops-and-frisks, retained the city's aggressive "broken windows" policy, which he had put into place while serving in the same capacity under the Giuliani administration.[16]

Evidence of the NYPD racially profiling and harassing its own was unearthed in a 2012 story in *Village Voice* based on interviews with current and retired African American and Latino officers, who recounted specific incidents of racist treatment by fellow officers under the city's racially targeted stop-and-frisk program. As one of the officers put it in explaining how such racial profiling of African American officers sometimes "leads to an ugly situation": "You could be on duty in plainclothes working detail outside of your command, and you become the victim of stop-and-frisk." A retired officer lamented that "It's very frustrating and humiliating" and "You'd be surprised by how many of us get stopped by cops." Another retired officer stated that the fact that he would be stopped about ten times a year when he was on the force "gives you a sense of what the community suffers." The NYPD refused to provide any comment for the story.[17]

Those are not the only members of the NYPD who have expressed concerns about its stop-and-frisk policies and practices. Michelle Conlin, a Reuters news reporter, conducted interviews with twenty-five African American male NYPD officers for a 2014 article in which she reported that they indicated they had "experienced the same racial profiling that cost Eric Garner his life" at the hands of fellow officers just five months earlier. Of the men Conlin interviewed, of whom fifteen were retired and ten were still employed within that department, all but one indicated that they had been racially profiled while off duty. She reported that incidents of harassment and mistreatment they had encountered "included being pulled over for no reason, having their heads slammed against their cars, getting guns brandished in their faces, being thrown into prison vans and experiencing stop-and-frisks while shopping." The five men who "had had guns pulled on them" could have ended up as victims of racial profiling-driven shootings. Only a third reported the incident to a supervisor, and all but one of those who did so indicated that the supervisor either took no action at all or engaged in retaliatory action against them as a result. Both the department and the local police union declined to offer comment for the story. The NYPD also failed to respond to the reporter's request for data showing the racial breakdown of officers making complaints and how they were resolved. The fact that all of the men who had been racially profiled indicated that this had been done by European American officers is especially interesting considering the explanation provided by NYPD Police Commissioner Bratton for the department's difficulty in hiring more African American officers. Bratton, who initiated the program, rooted the problem in the "unfortunate consequences" of the dramatic increase in stop-and-frisk actions that ensnared so many young men of color in the net of the criminal justice system. Of course, there are other factors that might discourage young African Americans from applying for employment within the NYPD, including, of course, both personal and vicarious experiences of its acting like an occupying army—a racial adversary that treats even its own African American officers as dangerous black criminals.[18]

In an article published in *The Atlantic* in January 2015, in which NYPD officers shared their racial experiences within that organization, an officer reported that he taped a conversation in which a supervisor instructed him as to who to target. "Male blacks. And I told you at roll call, and I have no problem to tell you this, male blacks 14 to 21." As part of a federal lawsuit an officer brought against the department a few years earlier, one of her detective colleagues testified that a supervisor who regularly used the word "nigger" once told him "If you have to shoot a nigger, do what you gotta do." Another colleague, who was also a detective, testified that he was called "a black bastard." In that same trial, a retired NYPD officer said that a superior of his had said of people of color who were suspects: "They are fucking animals. You make sure if you have to shoot, you shoot them in the head. That way there's one story."[19]

Over time, the evidence of racially targeted police misconduct by the NYPD grew to such a point that it was impossible to ignore. In August of 2013 a federal district court judge ruled that, as currently operated, New York City's stop-and-frisk program was racially discriminatory and unconstitutional, because it targeted people of color in violation of the equal protection clause of the 14th Amendment. In her ruling, Judge Shira Scheindlin directed these words to Mayor Bloomberg, who had on numerous occasions insisted that people of color were not targeted *enough* by the police and that, indeed, it was European Americans who the police disproportionately stopped.

> The City's highest officials have turned a blind eye to the evidence that officers are conducting stops in a racially discriminatory manner. In their zeal to defend a policy that they believe to be effective, they have willfully ignored overwhelming proof that the policy of singling out "the right people" is racially discriminatory and therefore violates the United States Constitution.[20]

While she did not outlaw the use of stop-and-frisk, Judge Scheindlin mandated modifications in that policy to address the issue of its being operated in a racially discriminatory fashion. As if to confirm its racial control function, after that ruling, the many protests and other challenges that preceded it, and the election of a mayor who promised to rein in the program, the number of stop-and-frisks dropped dramatically, from more than a half million the year prior to that ruling (2012) to fewer than thirteen thousand in 2016. But still, the New York Civil Liberties Union found that even with that more selective use of stop-and-frisk, 76 percent of the stop-and-frisks for that year were of people who were "totally innocent," with most (52 percent) such action taken against African Americans, 29 percent against Latinos, and only 10 percent against European Americans.[21]

One thing I hope this section on New York's stop-and-frisk policies and practices has made clear is that, because such actions tend to be racially targeted from top to bottom, you cannot fully understand their racism by focusing on whether the individual officers—who are not only instructed but indeed pressured to enforce them aggressively—happen to be racially bigoted or not. That is not the major racism at play here. For the most part, the individual police officers in the field, regardless of their own racial attitudes, are following the orders, at various levels, of their career-ambitious supervisors, who in turn work hard to please their police commissioner, who is carrying out the racial politics the mayor crafts to gain and retain political power from voters who tend to approve of their racial control actions. In brief, the people who are largely responsible for the racism of stop-and-frisk policies and actions are not lower-middle-class police officers, who are all too often portrayed by elites as ignorant and bigoted "Archie Bunker" types, but highly educated politicians and police administrators who have every opportunity to gain awareness of the overwhelming evidence that the policing they mandate is racist in both its targeting and impact; but who nevertheless, for their own political and career purposes and due to their own neoliberal beliefs, choose to ignore that fact.[22]

The racial politics that are ultimately behind such racially targeted police aggression are evident in the fact that despite all of the controversy, protests, and legal and other challenges, stop-and-frisk policing not only continues in many American cities but was a major platform and promise in Donald Trump's successful presidential campaign, during which he touted what he claimed to be its effectiveness in New York City. In that highly racialized campaign, with its popular "law and order" slogan, Trump promised to implement stop-and-frisk nationwide. And as if to prove the lessons of history mean nothing, one of his most influential campaign surrogates, former NYC mayor Rudolph Giuliani, boasted that "What I did for New York, Donald Trump will do for America." As you will see in the next section, in the United States even support for police use of violence is highly racialized.[23]

Racial differences in the support for police violence. Consistent with this study's treatment of the excessive police and vigilante killings of African Americans as a *violence-centered* racial control mechanism, not only is how people are identified and see themselves racially a strong predictor of their attitudes toward the police, with African Americans reporting both more negative attitudes and experiences, but there are also significant racial differences in support for police violence. In their study based on data collected as part of the 2012 General Social Survey, Hadden et al examined the impact of "race" and racism on the perceptions of police violence against adult males. They found—supporting Blumer's group position theory—that not only was respondents' racial identity a significant factor, with European Americans more likely to approve of such violence, but also those who held such attitudes were more likely to hold negative stereotypes of African Americans. Elsewhere, I have suggested that violent acts such as police and vigilante killings are condoned not just because they are thought to be necessary but because, reminiscent of the function served by racial lynchings during so much of American history, they articulate and implement both a rational and a highly emotional racial control norm—one we also see embodied in Stand Your Ground laws—that includes "the right to kill."[24]

As has been seen, popular support for police violence does not happen in a political and racial vacuum. In Chapter 2, I discussed research that found regional variations in the use of lethal force by the police based on the level of racial prejudice of their European American residents. And such attitudes do not just flow upward from the European American masses: racially targeted police violence is encouraged at the very top level of the federal government, in its racial state capacity. As noted earlier, U.S. Attorney General Jeff Sessions has worked tirelessly to dismantle recent police reforms and federal government monitoring of local police departments where there has been a pattern of racial harassment and abuse—policies put in place under the Obama administration—as he pushes for an intensified War on Drugs and other more aggressive policing that target low-income African American communities. President Trump even went so far as to tell a gathering of cheering and applauding police officers at a rally on Long Island that they should not be so careful in their handling of suspects of violent crime. As he put it, in words that seemed to evoke the image of the "rough ride" that caused the death of Freddie Gray, "When you see these thugs being thrown into the back of a paddy wagon—you just see them thrown in, rough . . . 'Please don't be too nice.'" The implication was clear: in the course of making those arrests, the police should rough the suspects up a bit. Essentially, what we have here is the President of the United States encouraging police officers to use excessive force more in the manner of the uniformed thugs of a police state than as members of a professionally trained police force in a democracy where the police are expected, like everyone else, to follow the rule of law. In that same speech, Trump also condoned the use of vigilante justice. He referenced a conversation with a man who assured him that if he had the authority to do so, working with the police who would supply the names of "the bad ones," he could address the crime problem in Chicago within "a couple of days." Trump, again sounding more like a petty thug than the president of a nation that prides itself in having all its citizens abide by the rule of law, said he told the man "Give me your card" and sent it to Mayor Emanuel with the message, "You want to try using this guy."[25]

The racial differences in support for police violence just discussed both reflect and help account for the major differences in different racial groups' experiences with the police. This is especially true for the age group that most frequently has enforcement-related interactions with the police: youth.

Racial differences in youth encounters with the police. You may recall that in his instructions to a subordinate as to who should be stopped and arrested, a NYPD police supervisor said: "male blacks 14 to 21." Indeed, in New York and other American cities, it is African American male youth who are most likely to be targeted as dangerous "black" males who merit unusually rough, and often abusive, treatment by the police. That stereotype was documented in an experiment by psychologist John Paul Wilson and others which found that, when respondents were shown photographs of African American and European American male athletes aged sixteen through nineteen and of the same size, the African American males were perceived to be "taller, heavier, stronger and more dangerous," with that perception being greatest when the photos of the African American athletes contained decisively African features such as "wider noses and fuller lips." Building on that racist stereotype, the participants in that experiment also felt it was more justified for the police to use violence against young African American males than against their European American counterparts of the same age. As a real-life illustration of their findings, the authors of that study cited the example of Dontre Hamilton, a mentally ill thirty-one-year-old African American man who was five feet seven inches tall and weighed 169 pounds, who was fatally shot in Wisconsin by police officer Christopher Manney. The officer described him as a person of "muscular build" whom he feared might overpower him.[26]

Through his study of forty African American males aged thirteen to nineteen, who were interviewed between spring 1999 and spring 2000 in St Louis, Missouri, Rod K. Brunson sought to better understand the impact of both their direct and their vicarious cumulative experiences with racial discrimination by the police. The location of that study is significant because it was conducted in the city of which Ferguson, Missouri is a suburb—the same Ferguson where, fourteen years later, the police killing of eighteen-year-old Michael Brown, whose killer characterized him as large and frightening, sparked intense national protests that helped build an international movement around the basic premise that "black lives matter."[27]

Of the young men Brunson interviewed, 83 percent reported that they had been "harassed or mistreated by the police" and 93 percent indicated that they knew someone who had had that experience. Consistent with both my racial control argument and the view expressed by Chief Justice Roger B. Taney in the 1857 Dred Scott Supreme Court decision that, be they slaves or free, people of African descent "had no rights which the white man was bound to respect," the young men's reported experiences indicated that the "police were more apt to respond with violence when suspects inquired about the legality of their actions or directives." Brunson notes that not only did their innocence not protect them from such violence, but being innocent actually placed them at greater risk, because those who had not done anything wrong were more likely to question both the officers' actions and the officers' attempt to stigmatize them as criminals. In an essay I published less than two months after the killing of Michael Brown, I explored what I framed as a *rights in conflict* argument which may shed some light on that finding. I explained the conflict between American police officers and African American youth as one which "pits the right of African Americans to have their young people live with dignity against the right of angry white policemen and vigilantes with guns to kill them" when challenged. Building on that observation, I also mentioned that the killers are often provoked because, due to the civil rights and other advances made by African Americans— to put it in very crude Jim Crow-era terms—many of "today's young African Americans 'don't know their place.'" Instead, they behave as if they actually expect to be treated as fully enfranchised citizens. While it is commonplace for European Americans to ask questions and to pro- claim their constitutional and other rights during encounters with the police without being harmed, the violence Brunson found young Afri- can Americans experienced when they attempted to do so sends a clear racial control message that, consistent with what Judge Taney concluded centuries earlier, it is the racially dominant group that is "in control and that black people had best stay in our place and to behave as white men with guns would have us to behave."[28]

In another article, which makes it clear that young African American males' experiences with the police are not typical of those of European American men of the same age and socio-economic status, Brunson, with Ronald Weitzer, reported the findings of another study of St. Louis youth's perceptions of the police. This time, however, the interviews were with both African American and European American youth, aged thir- teen to nineteen, conducted between the fall of 2005 and the spring of 2006 in three different low-income neighborhoods; one largely African American, one mostly European American, and the other racially mixed. The researchers found a direct correlation between the racialized iden- tities of the forty-five young men, the racial composition of the neigh- borhood, and how the young men residing there were treated. Overall, regardless of neighborhood, the young European American men had fewer problems with the police and a more positive attitude toward them than the young African American men. And on a continuum of "least problems with the police and most positive attitudes toward them" to "most problems with the police and the most negative attitudes toward them," first came the youth who lived in largely European American neighborhoods, followed by those in the racially mixed neighborhood, and finally those in the mostly African American neighborhood.[29]

Other research suggests, however, that the link between "race," class, and neighborhood context may be more complex than generally assumed, with the latter having a much larger impact than is generally realized. For example, in their quantitative analysis of those factors with regard to satisfaction with the police, Wu, Sun, and Triplett found the significant and independent effects of "race" and class disappeared when neighborhood-context factors were included. However, as in the Brunson and Weitzer study, they found more positive attitudes toward the police in predominantly European American and racially mixed neighborhoods than in largely African American neighborhoods. They also found that African Americans in more affluent neighborhoods reported less satisfaction with the police than European American residents of such neighborhoods. In contrast to the Brunson and Weitzer study, though, Wu, Sun, and Triplett found that African Americans and European Americans in the same economically marginalized neighborhoods held similar views toward the police. For numerous reasons, such neighborhoods may be the targets of more intense policing that make all of their residents feel like they live in an occupied territory.[30]

Brunson and Weitzer's study documented four major types of police misconduct, all of which were most likely to target young African American males: unwarranted stops, verbal abuse, physical abuse, and corruption. While the majority of the young African American males indicated that they drew police attention regardless of their actions, the European American young males seemed to enjoy protection from being stopped as a result of what the authors describe as a "racial halo effect." They were more likely to be stopped if they were with African American youth, in a mostly African American neighborhood, or wore hip hop-style clothing. Most of the police harassment was aimed at African American youth. An African American youth described how he and a friend were stopped and had their mouth searched for drugs: "We had grills [decorative dental molds] in our mouth[s] and he made us take them out, we showed them to him in our hand[s] and [the officer] smacked 'em out and when they [hit] the ground, he stomped on them and laughed. But he was showing us that he had more power, authority over us at the time, so there was nothing we could do or say."[31]

Among the types of verbal abuse the African American youth encountered from the police were their being "discourteous," using "inflammatory language," engaging in "name-calling," and deploying "racial slurs." One of the youth stated that when the police drove by they would say things like "You get off the corner or we're gonna . . . whoop your asses," while another recalled hearing "Get ya'll asses off this corner. What the fuck are ya'll big stupid motherfuckers doing?" Another youth recounted the following incident: "We was [sitting] in the car; we was just sittin' in there. [Police] got us out the car, check[ed] us and said he found some drugs in the car. And [the officers] said 'One of ya'll goin' with us.' [To decide] they said "Eeny, meeny, miny, moe catch a nigga by his throat," and locked up my friend because he was the oldest."[32]

Brunson and Weitzer found that the most common forms of "excessive force" deployed by the police included "shoving, punching, kicking, and the use of mace." Some of the young men had resigned themselves to the fact that physical abuse by the police was so routine that it could not be avoided through lawful behavior. One youth recalled such an incident: "Me and my brothers was sitting out one summer just chillin'. The police came up outta nowhere and just slammed my brother face in the dirt . . . I'm like, 'Dang, what's the problem?' And [another officer] pulled out a nightstick and hit me four times in the chest."[33]

Consistent with a national survey that found nearly half of African Americans saw their local police departments as rife with corruption, the African American youth interviewed in St. Louis said they had seen "crooked cops" and little accountability for police misconduct, which included the planting of drugs and other bogus incriminating evidence. Here is what one young man had to say about a corrupt police officer, Furillo, who operated in his neighborhood.

> He's very dangerous. My friend's brother was in a gang and [Furillo] wanted to lock him up for no reason but he could never catch him 'cause he always ran from him. One day he got tired [while] runnin' and he [came to a] dead end . . . [The officer] shot

him and said [the youth] had a gun on him and he was shootin'
back but [Furillo] planted that gun on him. He a crooked cop! . . .
One day, we was comin' home from school, and [Furillo] came up
and told me, "Come to the car" and I was like "Naw, 'cause I know
what you do to people." He was like, "If you don't get over here you
know what's gonna happen." I kept walkin', so he stopped his car
and I just ran . . . He will plant crack on you or somethin' like that.
If he want you, he gonna find a way to get you.[34]

Finally, in explaining how the police stick together to cover up the
misconduct of their fellow officers, one young man indicated that "If
another officer handles [the complaint], it'd probably be his buddy and
he's trying to [cover] up for him." Another concluded that "You can't
prove anything against them unless you have a videotape, so there is
really no point in prosecuting them unless you are rich and can afford
a lawyer." It is in the deep lack of belief that they will be treated fairly
by the criminal justice system that we can get a glimpse into why such
young men so often do what the young man indicated he did when
summoned by what he described as the corrupt and homicidal Officer
Furillo: run.[35]

Why do they run? Consistent with the case example just cited, police
killings of African Americans often begin when someone runs away
after having been racially profiled. Fatal chases like those of Freddie
Gray and Walter Scott resemble what has been referred to as "the hunt"
of runaway slaves during slavery: a sometimes tragic drama experienced
by many young African American males in their routine dealings with
the police. The studies just reviewed on verbal and physical intimidation of African Americans by the police, on police corruption, and on
the lack of accountability challenge the widely held assumption in the
United States that only someone who is guilty, and who is therefore
deserving of any fate that awaits them for doing so—including death—
would run from the police. The ground-zero reality of young African
American males these studies expose suggests that this assumption merits
closer scrutiny.

You may recall that the chain of events in Baltimore that led to Freddie
Gray's death began when he saw a police officer and ran. Consistent

with the widely held supposition that "he must be guilty if he ran," the police acted as if the only reason Freddie Gray would run from them was that he had done something wrong. As it turned out, Gray had not committed a crime. So why would he run? To answer the question as to why he, and others, would run, a *New York Times* reporter interviewed young men in the Baltimore neighborhood where Gray lived. He found that such behavior was so common that it could be viewed as a normal part of everyday life for many of those young men, and one that had, indeed, taken on the characteristics of a game—a sometimes fatal contest of hide and seek. "Running from officers is a way of life with its own playbook, passed down on the streets in much the way a young girl learns double dutch by watching others on the block." As one twenty-four-year-old put it: "People been running from the police . . . People going to always run from the police." When asked if Freddie Gray's death would stop them from running, they indicated that it would not. Instead, as one of them put it, "That makes you run faster." Reasons given for running included outstanding arrest warrants, possession of drugs, and the simple thrill of it. Another major factor is, of course, fear, including fear that the police may beat them up or plant false evidence on them. As some of these reasons suggest, young, low-income African American boys and men, in Baltimore and elsewhere, who are routinely terrorized as if by an occupying army sometimes run when they, like Freddie Gray, have done nothing wrong.[36]

In 2000, American police officers received support for such racial profiling and harassment from the highest court of the judicial branch of the federal government, when, in its racial state capacity, the U.S. Supreme Court ruled (*Illinois v. Wardlow*) that the police in Chicago and elsewhere had reasonable suspicion to justify their stopping and searching a person in a high-crime area who ran after they saw an officer, as Freddie Gray later did. Since that ruling, a number of highly publicized incidents of police shooting African Americans as they fled, and the subsequent pressure placed on the criminal justice system for reform, have likely impacted a more recent lower court ruling on the subject. In a lawsuit presented to the Massachusetts Supreme Court in 2016, the American Civil Liberties Union of Massachusetts provided evidence, which included data collected two years earlier, showing that the Boston Police Department disproportionately stopped African Americans. Based on that evidence, the judge threw out the conviction of an African American man, for possessing an unlicensed firearm the police had found in a yard near where he was apprehended. The court ruled that because the police had no right to stop him in the first place, and due to the way such men are treated by police, the fact that he ran could not be held against him. The first point the judge made in his ruling was about racial profiling, in that what led the police to treat the young man as a burglary suspect was a very vague description of an African American man wearing dark clothing and a hoodie. In regard to his second point, the judge concluded that while flight could not be eliminated as a basis for police suspicion of the behavior of African American males who are stopped as part of a police investigation of a crime,

> the finding that black males in Boston are disproportionately and repeatedly targeted for FIO [Field Interrogation and Observation] encounters suggests a reason for flight totally unrelated to consciousness of guilt. Such an individual, when approached by the police, might just as easily be motivated by the desire to avoid the recurring indignity of being racially profiled as by the desire to hide criminal activity.[37]

Even though African Americans may have good reason to run from the police, it would be simplistic to assume that their actions are always based on rational calculations. Again, it is important to examine the role of emotions in such fatal encounters, with particular focus on the powerful fight-or-flight response associated with fear. This is evident from the fact that among the many negative impacts of routine police harassment and mistreatment are mental health consequences. A study of the effects of New York's stop-and-frisk practices on young men that was published in the *American Journal of Public Health* found that those who had frequent police contact suffered symptoms of trauma and anxiety, the level of which was based on how often they were stopped, how intrusive those encounters were, and how unfair they perceived those actions to be. In brief, such stops cause the type of psychological trauma that leads many targeted young men to respond emotionally by removing themselves from such terror as quickly as they can, especially when innocent. Under such circumstances, we might reasonably expect that many young men might choose to run, even though to other observers, outside of that situation, it may seem irrational for them to do so.[38]

As has been seen, there is extensive evidence that in the United States the police racially target, harass, and mistreat African Americans, as if it should be assumed that they are all dangerous criminals whose behavior, both within and outside of what all too often still amounts to racial ghettoes, must be constantly monitored and controlled. Such racial control tactics range from initial racial profiling to the most extreme form of physical violence: homicide. It is within this larger context of police behavior toward African Americans that we can more fully understand the focus of this book: the racial control functions of the police and vigilante killings of African Americans.

The Racial Control Functions of the Police and Vigilante Violence against African Americans

Before I identify those racial control functions, it may be helpful if, once again, I quickly review some of the key concepts and assumptions that are central to this book's racial control argument. *Racial control* refers to the actions of members of a racially dominant group, and their allies, that keeps the racially oppressed in a socially subordinated position. As that definition suggests, racial control exists for one reason and one reason only: to maintain systems of "race"-justified oppression. The key processes and techniques essential for the operation of such systems are their *mechanisms*. As Figure 4.3 illustrates, police and vigilante violence, which includes but is not limited to killings, is one of three major violence-centered mechanisms for the racial control system of contemporary systemic racism—from which such mechanisms originate—that are justified by the criminalization of African Americans.

While oppressive systems are typically maintained through the hegemony of the widely accepted beliefs that justify them, ultimately they are preserved through force. Within systems of racial oppression,

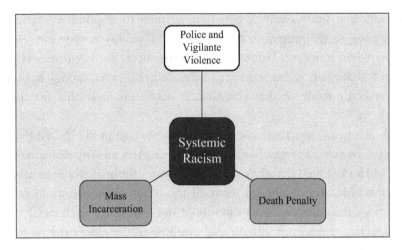

Figure 4.3 Violence-Centered Racial Control Mechanisms for Contemporary Systemic Racism

control of the subordinated group is often enforced through political violence. Finally, it is important for me to make clear, once again, that when I refer to police and vigilante violence as a racial control mechanism, *I am not suggesting that such actions are intentional or conspiratorial; only that they serve that function in the construction and sustenance of systemic racism.* In keeping with the focus of this book, in the remaining pages of this chapter I focus specifically on the racial control functions of police and vigilante killings.

These conceptualizations suggest that to understand the functions served by violence-centered racial control mechanisms, we must first specify those served by racial oppression more generally. The work of racial oppression, as organized through systemic racism, is simple; it elevates the status and wellbeing of a dominant racialized group over that of other groups deemed to be racially inferior. In explaining how racial and other forms of social dominance work, Jack Levin and William Levin refer to the various "mechanisms of control" which "dominant groups or individuals have at their disposal" as "methods for the application of their power over others." To account for the origin and persistence of prejudice and discrimination, Levin and Levin identify three major overlapping functions served by racial discrimination and prejudice for members of the dominant racial group: "(1) acquiring and maintaining economic advantages, (2) performing unpleasant or low-paying jobs, and (3) maintaining power." Similarly, in their theory of racial oppression, Jonathan H. Turner, Royce Singleton, Jr., and David Musick identify "material well-being, power, and prestige" as the scarce resources at the core of any system of oppression and conclude that "the more complete the denial of all three . . . the greater is the oppression." Building on those ideas, from a systemic racism perspective we can say, as illustrated in Figure 4.4, that racial oppression generally—and, more specifically, its violence-centered enforcement mechanisms—exists and persists because it serves the overlapping economic, social status, and political functions for members of the dominant racial group that also correspond to the key determinants of social stratification in the United States and other modern societies.[39]

The economic function entails the acquisition and maintenance of income and wealth advantage for members of the racially dominant group, for example, in reducing competition for jobs, for housing, and in business. The social status function provides a category of people all "whites" can feel superior to, for instance, by labeling "blacks" as unattractive, lazy, unintelligent, irresponsible, immoral, and violent. Finally, the political function involves obtaining and maintaining power for European American leaders, their allies, and their constituents through highly racialized ideologies, politics, policies, and practices, for example, as both Richard Nixon and Donald Trump did with their highly racialized calls for "law and order" during their successful presidential campaigns. Finally, as Figure 4.4 shows, because these three sources of socio-economic status and racial control overlap, one can be used to acquire and sustain the others. For example, the social status that comes from being designated as being racially "white" can be mobilized to obtain and sustain economic income and wealth, which can be used to gain and keep political power, which in turn can be deployed to obtain and sustain more social status. In this way, the racial control cycle strengthens as it repeats itself.

The following are economic, social status, and political functions which police and vigilante killings of African Americans serve for European Americans.

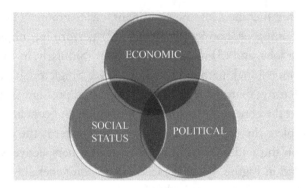

Figure 4.4 The Overlapping Sources of Socio-Economic Status and Racial Control Functions of the Police and Vigilante Killings of African Americans

Economic Functions

1. *Reduces economic competition for European Americans* by reinforcing the racist ideology of African Americans and other people of color as dangerous criminals who should be excluded from educational, employment, housing, and other opportunities.

The labeling of African Americans, especially young males, as dangerous black criminals—which is reinforced with each highly publicized killing—justifies their social segregation from the larger society and its opportunities in such a way that keeps those from impoverished backgrounds trapped in racial ghettoes and the hopelessness and crime they breed, and those in better social circumstances from achieving their full economic potential. Such killings also fuel a climate of support for the repressive laws and police practices that lead to the mass incarceration of African Americans and the numerous forms of political and social disenfranchisement that follow. By removing many African Americans from access to such scarce opportunity resources, such criminality-justified discrimination in turn provides more opportunities for European Americans, who would otherwise have to compete for them with talented African Americans. Finally, by keeping African Americans in an economically marginalized position, police and vigilante killings both reinforce the ideology of African American inferiority and help to reproduce the existing racial hierarchy of "white" on top and "black" at the bottom.

2. *Shifts tax dollars and other economic resources to the criminal justice system* that disproportionately benefit European Americans through jobs, sales, and financial investments.

As the United States continues its policy shift from what historian Elizabeth Hinton refers to as a "war on poverty" to a "war on crime," African Americans who are criminalized and pulled into the criminal justice system suffer economically, along with, of course, their families and communities. Meanwhile many European Americans benefit through jobs in the huge and growing criminal justice sector, such as police officer, security guard, or prison guard; from the sales of products and services for that industry; and through lucrative financial investments such as those in private prisons. Moreover, many African Americans are kept out of low-skilled jobs in criminal justice due to criminal records of various sorts that result from the hyperpolicing that targets their communities and those who look like them, while those with no criminal record are denied access to the higher-skilled jobs in the area due to cutbacks in funding for education and other opportunities for social mobility.[40]

It is important to note, however, that the immediate economic benefits some working-class European Americans receive from employment in low-level positions such as that of prison guard in the prison-industrial complex are more than offset by the increasing marginalization of European American and other workers who, when they can find employment, are increasingly trapped in such low-paid, low-status jobs and suffer as a result of neoliberal economic policies that include cuts in social programs and educational opportunities that make social mobility increasingly difficult for themselves and their children. Employment within the prison industry also pits those who have such jobs against those with whom they might ordinarily forge a class-based political alliance that could produce political and economic changes from which all could benefit.

3. *Supports and protects rising economic inequality* by justifying neoliberal and other hypercapitalist ideologies, politics, policies, and practices that redistribute income and wealth upward and protect their beneficiaries from crime and rebellion on the part of those who have been economically marginalized.

The fear of "black" crime is used to justify neoliberal policies that shift tax dollars from social services and programs and schools, which can assist the racially and economically oppressed and reduce crime, to pay for aggressive policing. That shift creates a vicious cycle in which the more cuts are made to social services and programs, the more crime there is; the more crime there is, the more is spent on policing; the more aggressive the policing, the more highly publicized police killings there are; and the more of such killings there are, the more justification there is for the shifting of tax dollars to fund still more aggressive policing. In that process, opportunities for upward mobility for low-income and working-class African Americans and their children are stifled, while the growing economic inequality that benefits mostly affluent European Americans is protected from threats from both crime and insurrection.

4. *Prevents the development of class-based consciousness* and solidarity across racial lines that might otherwise threaten the existing economic and class order.

Rather than supporting social policies and programs that benefit all Americans who are struggling economically, many, if not most, working-class and lower-middle-class European Americans accept both the highly racialized "law and order" ideology that targets African Americans and the benefits which some of them and their families receive from employment in the criminal justice system. While this may provide those European Americans with some social status and economic benefits, it also solidifies the class structure and growing economic inequality that harm not only African Americans but most economically marginalized European Americans—many of whom, as will be seen in the next chapter, are now being labelled by conservative intellectuals as a "white underclass" in a way that justifies greater police repression against them as they appear to present a criminal or political threat to the economic bounties of affluent European Americans. By offering European Americans what W.E.B. DuBois referred to as a "public and psychological wage" of whiteness, rather than real economic benefits, affluent European Americans are protected from threats not only from African Americans, who are disproportionately poor, but also from other

European Americans who are also economically marginalized—and, perhaps most importantly, from the threat of a potential class-based alliance of the two. I say more about the economics behind the police and vigilante killings of African Americans in the next chapter.[41]

Social Status Functions

1. *Reinforces white racial identity and solidarity* by justifying European Americans feeling morally superior to African Americans and other people of color, who are viewed as inferior races composed of dangerous criminals.

At the core of racist thinking is the notion that members of the dominant racialized group are inherently superior to those of other racialized groups. Ironically, this is especially true when it comes to issues of morality. Social scientists such as Kai Erikson have shown that one way in which a group solidifies its own identity is by juxtaposing it to who and what they are not. So, essential to the establishment and sustenance of group boundaries is the casting out, and often persecution, of those social deviants labelled as "outsiders." More specific to the focus of this study, we can say that racially there can be no superior "white" race, which is good, pure, wholesome, and wonderful, without the polar opposite and inferior "black" race, which is bad, dirty, evil, and despicable; and the creation and the prosecution or killing of dangerous black criminals affirms one's status as an upstanding and morally righteous "white" American.[42]

2. *Reinforces European Americans' belief that their superior socio-economic status is earned* and is not based on racial privilege and discrimination.

One of the reasons why it is so hard for many European Americans to accept the existence of systemic racism is that it runs counter to their preferred belief that whatever they have in life they have earned through their intelligence, talent, and strong work ethic. For European Americans to acknowledge the role of racism in significantly enhancing their life chances is unlikely because it challenges deeply ingrained American stratification beliefs about who gets what and why. It is much easier to embrace the racist stereotype of African Americans as dangerous black criminals whose laziness, lack of intelligence, and preference for welfare over work is responsible for their relatively low social status. In doing so, European Americans confirm their beliefs about the fairness of the system and thus their own superior place within it. That view of deserving "white" people and underserving "blacks" is confirmed each time an African American is killed by a police officer or vigilante who labels him or her as a dangerous criminal.

3. Provides socially demeaned groups of people to whom all "white" people can feel superior, no matter how low their own social status.

Here, good and upstanding "white" people are juxtaposed again their racial opposite, bad "black" criminals. In reference to the economic racial control function of reducing class consciousness discussed earlier, I mentioned W.E.B. DuBois' observation that, in exchange for real economic benefits, working-class European Americans settled for what has been referred to as the wages of whiteness. In his classic study of the reconstruction period of U.S. history and its aftermath, DuBois stated that as compensation for a low economic wage, European Americans received a wage of sorts that included "public deference and titles of courtesy because they were white," as well as the police being "drawn from their ranks." Self-respect was also found to be central to the work lives of the police studied by William Westley in 1950, who felt unappreciated and under constant public scrutiny. Police officers in Westley's study placed five publics along a continuum of respect, both in terms of who they respected and who they thought showed them respect. The high-respect groups were "children" and "the 'better class of people.'" Then came "the slum dwellers, the Negroes, and the criminals," who in the officer's minds were largely the same. While the police do not rank high in the relative social status pecking order, and their social status is volatile due to their occupation, it is high compared to African Americans. Westley's findings fit the observation of Herbert Blumer that

> *vis a vis* the subordinate racial group the unlettered individual with low status in the dominant racial group has a sense of group position common to that of the elite of his group. By virtue of sharing this sense of position such an individual, despite his low

status, feels that members of the subordinate group, however distinguished and accomplished, are somehow inferior.[43]

More support for the centrality of self-respect as an explanation for racially targeted police violence comes from a study by Malcolm Holmes that examines the racial threat hypothesis as an explanation of police violence. Consistent with this book's racial control mechanism argument, in his study Holmes tested the hypothesis that police brutality (i.e., the "use of excessive force") can best be viewed as "an extra-legal mechanism of control." Like Westley, Holmes found that the most immediate goal of such highly racialized social control is to enforce officers' demands that they be shown what they consider to be the proper level of respect and deference. Although European American police officers can boast their status by demonstrating their social usefulness in protecting decent "whites" from immoral "black" criminals, because of their marginalized status as an often disrespected outgroup, much of their status-seeking behavior comes from within their own group of fellow police officers—who, like a platoon of soldiers at war, matter more to them than the general public or any of the various groups they encounter. It is within this logic—a logic that also applies to vigilantes—that violence is used against African Americans to force them to show respect and to stay in their racially subordinated place. This suggests the existence of a vicious cycle. Of course, the more the police and vigilantes are violent to people, such as African Americans, whom they hold in low regard and see as relatively powerless, the more they are likely to be treated as if they are not respected; and the more they perceive disrespect from a particular group, the more likely they are to use violence to enforce their demand for respect. I say more about the social status functions of the police and vigilante killings of African Americans in Chapter 6.[44]

Political Functions

I have placed power and politics at the center of this study. That analytical focus is congruent with this book's treatment of the disproportionate police and vigilante killings of African Americans as *political* violence and its emphasis of the importance of examining racial *power* relations in understanding both their ultimate causes and solutions. Such a focus also fits my premise that it is the state, in its racial state capacity, that authorizes, sponsors, or otherwise sanctions both the formal (e.g., the police) and informal (vigilante) racial control agents who are employed, or at least protected, by its various branches and levels. Moreover, it is also the state, again in its racial state capacity, that manages the race relations surrounding such killings.

I have already discussed some of the politics of the police and vigilante killings of African Americans, and I say more about this in Chapter 5. Here I summarize some of those more important points.

1. *Reinforces the racist stereotype of African Americans and other people of color as dangerous criminals who must be kept in line by any means necessary,* including the use of fatal violence.

While it is widely known that ideology shapes a society's laws, politics, policies, and practices, not nearly as much attention has been given to the reciprocal relationship between the two. Barbara Cruikshank stresses, for example, that with regard to our understanding of the situation of women on public assistance, we must move beyond the simplistic notion that stereotypes justify practices to a recognition that "practices justify stereotypes"—or, as Dorothy Roberts makes clear, policy *is* ideology. From that perspective, we can say that not only do racist ideologies and their constituent stereotypes, such as that of the dangerous black criminal, justify criminal justice actions that target African Americans in ways that increase their risk of being killed by the police and vigilantes, but each new and highly publicized killing—especially when it happens with impunity—affirms and reinforces that racist stereotype, as that vicious cycle strengthens with repetition.[45]

Controlling images is another useful concept for understanding the reciprocal relationship between racist ideologies and stereotypes and the police and vigilante killings of African Americans. Patricia Hill Collins coined that term to help explain how stereotypes are used to control the oppressed by making "racism, sexism, poverty, and other forms of social injustice appear to be natural, normal, and inevitable parts of everyday life." An example is the widely held and enduring belief among

many European Americans that African Americans are not disproportionately targeted for police killings due to racism, but for the assumed
colorblind fact that they are more likely to engage in criminal activity.
When we combine the concept of controlling images with Philomena
Essed's conceptualization of gendered racism, which explains how racism manifests itself in gender-specific ways, we can better appreciate
how the racist stereotype of the young African American male as a dangerous black criminal is mobilized as a controlling image that justifies
violence-centered racial control mechanisms targeted against him such
as lynching, the death penalty, and police and vigilante killings. Amadou
Diallo, Timothy Thomas, Trayvon Martin, Jordan Davis, Eric Garner,
Michael Brown, Laquan McDonald, Freddie Gray, Terence Crutcher,
Philando Castile, and even twelve-year-old Tamir Rice are just a few
of the African American men and boys for whom the "dangerous black
man" label proved to be their death warrant. And once they have been
killed, the same controlling image that set the stage for their killing is
used by many members of the racially dominant group to justify it, and
other killings, and the belief that no changes are needed in the criminal
justice system and its treatment of African Americans. This amounts,
of course, to what is essentially a pat on the back for those police and
vigilantes who kill, and encouragement for them or their colleagues to
go out and kill again. In brief, the police and vigilante killings of African Americans not only provide physical, economic, social, and political
control of African Americans, but reinforce existing conceptualizations
of race, including the highly gendered and racist controlling image of
them as dangerous black criminals that justifies not only more killings
but also their subordinated status as an assumed inferior race in a myr-
iad of other ways. As seen in Chapter 3, there is nothing new about
the criminalization of African Americans and its use to justify racial
violence. As Khalil Gibran Muhammad concluded from his history of
the use of statistics in the criminalization of African Americans since
the late nineteenth century, "African American criminality became one
of the most widely accepted bases for justifying prejudicial thinking, discriminatory treatment, and/or acceptance of racial violence as an instrument of public safety."[46]

2. Reminds African Americans of their proper racial place and of what could happen to them if they attempt to challenge the racial status quo either individually or through collective action.

While systems of social oppression are typically sustained through widely disseminated ideas that justify the status quo, when all else fails they are held in place through the use of force. Throughout American history, violence has been deployed as the ultimate resource to ensure that African Americans remain in their designated racial place, both physically and socially. You may recall that among the origins of modern policing in the United States were the slave patrols that were used to capture runaway slaves and to prevent and punish slave insurrections. And as will be seen in the next chapter, with changes in the economy such that low-skilled labor is increasingly no longer needed, many African Americans are now seen as not only economically useless but also a potential threat, through either individual acts of crime or collective insurrection, to those who have benefited from those changes and the growing economic inequality they have brought. Just as throughout much of American history, big events that happen in "the public arena," such as racial lynchings, have served as warnings to African Americans who challenge the racial status quo, today highly publicized police and vigilante killing spectacles serve the same function. As you have seen, it was no accident that, in response to a white racial backlash, the United States turned away from ameliorative social programs and toward punitive crime policies just as the civil rights movement became more militant and violent unrest was seen in scores of American cities. For, as Allen Grimshaw concluded from his study of racial violence published in the late 1950s, "violence which occurs in interracial relations is an inevitable product of assaults upon the accommodative pattern."[47]

In previous chapters I noted that there is a paradoxical impact of technological advances such as smartphone videos, social media, and all-news-all-the-time cable television channels on the recording and reporting of police and vigilante killings. The good news for people concerned about the issue is that, because of the availability of that relatively new technology, incidents that would not have been known outside of the local areas where they happened now receive national twenty-four-hour/seven-days-a-week coverage. The bad news is that such intense and widespread reporting exponentially magnifies the power of their "stay in your place" message.

I also noted earlier that the ultimate threat faced by African Americans as a people is genocide. The history of Native Americans documents that such fear is far from unfounded. Native Americans were the first racialized group in what is now the United States to experience violence as a racial control mechanism. Those who refused to relinquish their lands to colonists, and later to relocate to "reservations," faced government policies and practices of genocide. Given this violence-centered racial control history, it is not surprising that according to Centers for Disease Control and Prevention statistics (1999–2015), Native Americans are killed by law enforcement officers at a rate (.21 per 100,000) similar to that of African Americans (.25 per 100,000).[48]

3. *Provides a winnable political issue for politicians* by either appealing to the racial animus of European American voters through campaigns based on highly racialized but ostensibly colorblind "law and order" and "support our police" platforms or to African Americans and other people of color based on their desire for progressive criminal justice reform.

In Chapter 3 I showed how, since peonage, the violence-centered racial control mechanisms that target African American people have been justified by the racialization of African Americans as criminals. You also saw how politics at the various branches and levels of government, acting in its racial state capacity, have been the driving force behind that process, the use of police repression, and the tolerance of vigilantism as agents of racial control.

It is also important to understand, however, that racial state actions are not simply and always racially repressive. What the state does is subject to social movement, legal, and other challenges that at times force it to be more responsive to demands of the racially oppressed. This has certainly been the case with the criminal justice policies and practices that have heavily impacted African Americans. As I stress in my urban racial state theory, depending on the current state of race relations, the various branches and levels of the racial state may shift from what I refer to as their *racially oblivious* mode, when, for example, the Eisenhower administration steered clear of addressing racial issues in the 1950s, to the *racially ameliorative* mode into which the civil rights movement pushed the Johnson administration in the racially turbulent 1960s, with its civil rights legislation and its War on Poverty and other Great Society programs. That was followed by another shift when the white backlash of the latter part of the 1960s led President Johnson to launch major anti-crime initiatives and Richard Nixon to win election under the campaign slogan of "law and order," as the federal racial state assumed its *racially repressive* mode. In the 2016 presidential election the nation had a choice between moving from, once again, a racially oblivious mode under the racism-shy Obama administration toward criminal justice reform demanded by Movement for Black Lives activists who pressured the Democratic candidates to talk explicitly about racism in the criminal justice system and to promise criminal justice reform, and Donald J. Trump, who, like Nixon, was elected with the help of the highly racialized promise to restore "law and order." In that campaign, Trump articulated his contempt for Movement for Black Lives activists and his support for the pro-police "Blue Lives Matter" backlash to the demands that "Black Lives Matter." Trump, who received endorsements from most of the major national police unions, was the only major candidate not to express the need for at least some police reform. Similar political battles have played out over the issue of the police treatment of African Americans in cities such as New York under the racially repressive policing style of Mayor Giuliani and the promise for police reform that elected Mayor de Blasio, and in the elections of reform-minded district attorneys in various cities.[49]

Unfortunately, even when African Americans have been able to pressure politicians to campaign on promises for significant reform and those candidates have won, there has been little in the way of meaningful change. Moreover, African Americans expending political capital on piecemeal and incremental criminal justice reform can serve to divert such limited resources from more fundamental challenges to the nation's racial and economic orders, as the focus is literally on trying to stay alive. Also, because it requires reacting to the framing of African Americans as criminals, this struggle keeps African Americans in a racially defensive posture. Consequently, progressive politicians need to do little more for African Americans than articulate the need for ameliorative criminal jus- tice reform, while allowing the system of racial and economic oppression to remain essentially intact. As you have seen, this has led some Afri- can American scholars, intellectuals, and activists—including myself—to conclude that piecemeal changes, through electoral politics alone, cannot end problems such as mass incarceration and the police and vigilante kill- ings of African Americans, and that meaningful change can come only through radical transformations in the nation's racial and economic order.

Conclusion

In this chapter, I applied this study's various racial control-related con- cepts and ideas in an examination of the larger context of racial intimi- dation and violence related to the police and vigilante killings of African Americans and the various functions they serve for European Ameri- cans as a racial control mechanism. With this knowledge, we can better understand not only why African Americans are targeted so dispropor- tionately, but also why such fatal encounters are so pervasive and so persistent.

Although this book is an unapologetically racism-centered analysis of contemporary police and vigilante violence against African Americans, as I have made clear, racism is not the only culprit. Another important factor, and one on which I will focus in Chapter 5, is the economic exploitation characteristic of the original form of oppression which peo- ple of African descent faced in what was to become this nation: slavery. I examine the police and vigilante killings of African Americans through a class lens as I explore the impact of neoliberalism's ideology, politics, and policies; rising economic inequality; and, intensified greatly by the election of Donald Trump as president, the growth of what in some ways amounts to a highly racialized national police state.

Notes

1. Michael Eric Dyson, *Tears We Cannot Stop: A Sermon to White America* (New York: St. Martin's Press, 2017), 177, 182.
2. Allen E. Liska, "Introduction to the Study of Social Control," in Allen E. Liska, ed., *Social Threat and Social Control* (Albany, NY: State University of New York Press, 1992), 17–19; Ronald Weitzer and Steven A. Tuch, "Race, Class, and Perceptions of Discrimi- nation by the Police," *Crime and Delinquency*, 1999, 45 (5), 495.

3. Herbert Blumer, "Race Prejudice as a Sense of Group Position," *Pacific Sociological Review*, 1958, 1 (1), 3–7; Hubert M. Blalock, Jr., *Toward a Theory of Minority-Group Relations* (New York: John Wiley and Sons, 1967).

4. Blalock, Jr. *Toward a Theory of Minority-Group Relations*, 29.

5. Blumer, "Race Prejudice as a Sense of Group Position," 3–4; Noel A. Cazenave, *Conceptualizing Racism: Breaking the Chains of Racially Accommodative Language* (Lanham, MD: Rowman and Littlefield, 2016), 51, 58.

6. Blumer, "Race Prejudice as a Sense of Group Position," 3. Italics in original.

7. Blumer, "Race Prejudice as a Sense of Group Position," 4–5. Italics in original.

8. Blumer, "Race Prejudice as a Sense of Group Position," 6.

9. Jim Sidanius and Felicia Pratto, *Social Dominance: An Intergroup Theory of Social Hierarchy and Oppression* (Cambridge: Cambridge University Press, 1999), 31–32. Italics in original.

10. Sidanius and Pratto, *Social Dominance*, 41–42. Italics in original.

11. Because there is considerable overlap in the literatures on the topics of racial profiling by the police, police harassment, police brutality, and police killings I will not attempt to present them separately and sequentially.

12. Sandra Bass, "Policing Space, Policing Race: Social Control Imperatives and Police Discretionary Decisions," *Social Justice*, 2001, 28 (1), 159; John Hope Franklin and Loren Schweninger, *Runaway Slaves: Rebels on the Plantation 1790–1860* (Oxford: Oxford University Press, 1999), 149.

13. Ronald Weitzer and Steven A. Tuch, "Perceptions of Racial Profiling: Race, Class, and Personal Experience," *Criminology*, 2002, 40 (2), 436, 442, 444; Darren K. Carlson, "Racial Profiling Seen as Pervasive, Unjust," *Gallup*, July 20, 2004, www.gallup.com/poll/12406/racial-profiling-seen-pervasive-unjust.aspx, Accessed February 27, 2017.

14. New York Civil Liberties Union, "Stop-and-Frisk Data," no date, www.nyclu.org/en/stop-and-frisk-data, Accessed August 27, 2017.

15. Bruce Golding, "Ray Kelly Admitted Cops Target Blacks, Hispanics in 'Stop-Frisk,' State Lawmaker Testifies." *New York Post*, April 1, 2013, nypost.com/2013/04/01/ray-kelly-admitted-cops-target-blacks-hispanics-in-stop-frisk-state-lawmaker-testifies/, Accessed February 28, 2017; Ryan Devereaux, "NYPD Commissioner Ray Kelly 'Wanted to Instill Fear' in Black and Latino Men," *The Guardian*, April 1, 2013, www.theguardian.com/world/2013/apr/01/nypd-ray-kelly-instil-fear, Accessed February 28, 2017.

16. John Marzulli, "NYPD Cop Claims He Was Punished for Not Busting Minorities," *New York Daily News*, January 7, 2016, www.nydailynews.com/news/politics/nypd-admits-quotas-summons-article-1.2488316, Accessed February 28, 2017; Jennifer Newton, "NYPD Captain Caught on Tape 'Pressuring Officer to Stop and Question More Black Men Because They are More Likely to be Criminals,'" *Daily Mail*, July 14, 2016, Accessed March 1, 2017; Kristian Williams, *Our Enemies in Blue: Police and Power in America* (Oakland, CA: AK Press, 2015), 346.

17. Sam Levin, "Cops by Day, Targets by Night: Stop-and Frisks Also Happen to NYPD Officers," *Village Voice*, June 6, 2012, digitalissue.villagevoice.com/article/News/1083927/114549/article.html#, Accessed March 1, 2017.

18. Michelle Conlin, "Off Duty, Black Cops in New York Feel Threat from Fellow Police," *Reuters*, December 23, 2014, www.reuters.com/article/us-usa-police-nypd-race-insight-idUSKBN0K11EV20141223, Accessed February 28, 2017; Lauren Gambino, "NYPD Chief Bratton Says Hiring Black Officers is Difficult: 'So Many Have Spent Time in Jail,'" *The Guardian*, June 9, 2015, www.theguardian.com/us-news/2015/jun/09/bratton-hiring-black-nypd-officers-criminal-records, Accessed February 28, 2017.

19. Conor Friedersdorf, "The NYPD Officers Who See Bias in the NYPD," *The Atlantic*, January 7, 2015, www.theatlantic.com/national/archive/2015/01/the-nypd-officers-who-see-racial-bias-in-the-nypd/384106/, Accessed March 1, 2017.

20. The Editorial Board, "Racial Discrimination in Stop-and Frisk," *New York Times*, August 12, 2013, www.nytimes.com/2013/08/13/opinion/racial-discrimination-in-stop-and-frisk. html, Accessed February 28, 2017; Dylan Matthews, "Here's What You Need to Know about Stop-and-Frisk—And Why the Courts Shut it Down," *Washington Post*, August 13, 2013, www.washingtonpost.com/news/wonk/wp/2013/08/13/heres-what-you-need-to-know-about-stop-and-frisk-and-why-the-courts-shut-it-down/?utm_term=.6aac985e75d4, Accessed March 1, 2017; Philip Bump, "The Facts about Stop-and-Frisk in New York City," *Washington Post*, September 26, 2016, www.washingtonpost. com/news/the-fix/wp/2016/09/21/it-looks-like-rudy-giuliani-convinced-donald-trump-that-stop-and-frisk-actually-works/?utm_term=.79b5ec6bafd4, Accessed February 28, 2017.

21. The Editorial Board, "Racial Discrimination in Stop-and Frisk"; New York Civil Liberties Union, "Stop-and-Frisk Data."

22. Archie Bunker is the name of the fictional star of "All in the Family," a 1970s television series which portrayed him as the stereotype of European American, working-class ignorance and bigotry.

23. Bump, "The Facts about Stop-and-Frisk in New York City."

24. Weitzer and Tuch, "Race, Class, and Perceptions of Discrimination by the Police," 494; Bernadette R. Hadden, Willie Tolliver, Fabienne Snowden, and Robyn Brown-Manning, "An Authentic Discourse: Recentering Race and Racism as Factors that Contribute to Police Violence against Unarmed Black or African American Men," *Journal of Human Behavior in the Social Environment*, 2016, 26 (3–4), 336, 338; Noel A. Cazenave, "Understanding Our Many Fergusons: Kill Lines—The Will, the Right and the Need to Kill," *Truthout*, September 29, 2014, www.truth-out.org/opinion/item/26484-understanding-our-many-fergusons-kill-lines-the-will-the-right-and-the-need-to-kill, Accessed March 1, 2017.

25. Eric Hehman, Jessica K. Flake, and Jimmy Calanchini, "Disproportionate Use of Lethal Force in Policing is Associated with Regional Racial Biases of Residents," *Social Psychological and Personality Science*, released online, 2017 (July 27), 1; Sari Horwitz, "How Jeff Sessions Wants to Bring Back the War on Drugs," *Washington Post*, April 8, 2017, www.washingtonpost.com/world/national-security/how-jeff-sessions-wants-to-bring-back-the-war-on-drugs/2017/04/08/414ce6be-132b-11e7-ada0-1489b735b3a3_story.html?utm_term=.59d1a970f18f, Accessed May 18, 2017; Andrew Rafferty, "Trump to Police: 'Don't Be Too Nice' To Suspects," NBC News, July 28, 2017, www.nbcnews. com/politics/politics-news/trump-police-don-t-be-too-nice-suspects-n787646, Accessed July 29, 2017; David A. Graham, "Trump's Vision of Lawless Order," *The Atlantic*, July 28, 2017, www.theatlantic.com/politics/archive/2017/07/trump-long-island-ms-13/535317/, Accessed July 29, 2017.

26. Christopher Brennan, "Black Men Viewed as Larger, More Dangerous than Same-Size Whites," *New York Daily News*, March 13, 2017, www.nydailynews.com/news/national/black-men-viewed-larger-dangerous-same-size-whites-article-1.2996949, Accessed March 14, 2017.

27. Rod K. Brunson, "'Police Don't Like Black People': African-American Young Men's Accumulated Police Experiences," *Criminology and Public Policy*, 2007, 6 (1), 71, 76.

28. Brunson, "'Police Don't Like Black People'", 81, 89, 95–96, 101; Earl E. Pollock, *Race and the Supreme Court: Defining Equality* (Sarasota, FL: Peppertree Press, 2012), 33–36; Cazenave, "Understanding Our Many Fergusons."

29. Rod K. Brunson and Ronald Weitzer, "Police Relations with Black and White Youths in Different Urban Neighborhoods," *Urban Affairs Review*, 2009, 44 (6), 858, 863–64.

30. Yuning Wu, Ivan Y. Sun, and Ruth A. Triplett, "Race, Class or Neighborhood Context: Which Matters More in Measuring Satisfaction with Police?," *Justice Quarterly*, 2009, 26 (1), 125.

31. Brunson and Weitzer, "Police Relations with Black and White Youths in Different Urban Neighborhoods," 865–67, 869, 871, 873.
32. Brunson and Weitzer, "Police Relations with Black and White Youths in Different Urban Neighborhoods," 869.
33. Brunson and Weitzer, "Police Relations with Black and White Youths in Different Urban Neighborhoods," 871.
34. Brunson and Weitzer, "Police Relations with Black and White Youths in Different Urban Neighborhoods," 873–75.
35. Brunson and Weitzer, "Police Relations with Black and White Youths in Different Urban Neighborhoods," 877–78.
36. John Eligon, "Running from Police is the Norm, Some in Baltimore Say," *New York Times*, May 10, 2015, www.nytimes.com/2015/05/11/us/running-from-police-is-the-norm-some-in-baltimore-say.html?_r=0, Accessed March 6, 2017.
37. Eligon, "Running from Police is the Norm, Some in Baltimore Say;" Zeninjor Enwemeka, "Mass. High Court Says Black Men May Have Legitimate Reason to Flee Police," WBUR News, September 20, 2016, www.wbur.org/news/2016/09/20/mass-high-court-black-men-may-have-legitimate-reason-to-flee-police, Accessed March 6, 2017. Italics in original.
38. Amanda Geller, Jeffrey Fagan, Tom Tyler, and Bruce G. Link, "Aggressive Policing and the Mental Health of Young Urban Men," *American Journal of Public Health*, 2014, 104 (12), 2321.
39. Jack Levin and William Levin, *The Functions of Discrimination and Prejudice* (New York: Harper and Row, 1982), 62, 159–60; Jonathan H. Turner, Royce Singleton, Jr., and David Musick, *Oppression: A Socio-History of Black–White Relations in America* (Chicago, IL: Nelson-Hall, 1984), 2–3.
40. Elizabeth Hinton, *From the War on Poverty to the War on Crime: The Making of Mass Incarceration in America* (Cambridge, MA: Harvard University Press, 2016).
41. W.E.B. DuBois, *Black Reconstruction in America: 1860–1880* (New York: Touchstone, 1995), 700.
42. Kai Erickson, *Wayward Puritans: A Study in the Sociology of Deviance* (Boston, MA: Pearson/Allyn and Bacon, 2005).
43. DuBois, *Black Reconstruction in America: 1860–1880*, 700; William A. Westley, *Violence and the Police: A Sociological Study of Law, Custom, and Morality* (Cambridge, MA: The MIT Press, 1970), xiv–xv, 96; Blumer, "Race Prejudice as a Sense of Group Position," 5.
44. Malcolm D. Holmes, "Minority Threat and Police Brutality: Determinants of Civil Rights Criminal Complaints in U.S. Municipalities," *Criminology*, 2000, 38 (2), 343, 345–46; Westley, *Violence and the Police*, 124; Blumer, "Race Prejudice as a Sense of Group Position," 5.
45. Barbara Cruikshank, "Welfare Queens: Policing by the Numbers," in Sanford F. Schram and Philip T. Neisser, eds., *Tales of the State: Narrative in Contemporary U.S. Politics and Public Policy* (Lanham, MD: Rowman and Littlefield, 1997), 113; Dorothy Roberts, *Killing the Black Body: Race, Reproduction, and the Meaning of Liberty* (New York: Vintage Books, 1997), 10.
46. Patricia Hill Collins, *Black Feminist Thought: Knowledge, Consciousness, and the Politics of Empowerment* (New York: Routledge, 2000), 69; Philomena Essed, *Understanding Everyday Racism: An Interdisciplinary Theory* (Newbury Park, CA: Sage, 1991), 31; Khalil Gibran Muhammad, *The Condemnation of Blackness: Race, Crime, and the Making of Modern Urban America* (Cambridge, MA: Harvard University Press, 2010), 4.
47. Blumer, "Race Prejudice as a Sense of Group Position," 6; Allen D. Grimshaw, "Lawlessness and Violence in America and their Special Manifestations in Changing Negro-White Relationships," *The Journal of Negro History* 1959, 44 (1), 55.

48. Paul Kivel, *Uprooting Racism: How White People Can Work for Racial Justice* (Gabriola Island, BC, Canada: New Society Publishers, 2011), 153–55; Sidney M. Wilhelm, *Who Needs the Negro?* (Hampton, VA: U.B. and U.S. Books, 1993), 3; Centers for Disease Control and Prevention, National Center for Health Statistics. Underlying Cause of Death 1999–2015 on CDC WONDER Online Database, released December, 2016. Data are from the Multiple Cause of Death Files, 1999–2015, as compiled from data provided by the fifty-seven vital statistics jurisdictions through the Vital Statistics Cooperative Program. Accessed at wonder.cdc.gov/ucd-icd10.html on March 8, 2017.

49. Noel A. Cazenave, *The Urban Racial State: Managing Race Relations in American Cities* (Lanham, MD: Rowman and Littlefield, 2011), 30–31.

5

VIEWING THE KILLINGS THROUGH AN ECONOMIC LENS: HYPERCAPITALISM AND THE GROWTH OF THE AMERICAN POLICE STATE

I have defined neoliberalism as both an ideology and a set of economic and political policies and practices that have helped push governments to the right by promoting an extreme form of unbridled hypercapitalism and its rampant economic inequality. Here I analyze the impact of neoliberalism's alliance with the extreme right-wing and highly racialized populism that propelled Donald Trump to the White House on the police and vigilante killings of African Americans, through an examination of Proposition # 3 of this study. That proposition reads as follows: *the extreme economic and political policies and practices of political neoliberalism that have exacerbated economic inequality and racial tensions require police and vigilante violence to control what is seen as a surplus and dangerous population.*

As you will see, I reject the simplistic assumption that Donald Trump's election as president is indicative of the political failure and defeat of neoliberalism. I argue, instead, that Trump's victory—which was indeed fueled by the failures of neoliberalism, which he exploited in a potent blend of nationalism, populism, and racism not expressed so overtly since the white backlash-driven campaign of Southern segregationist

George Wallace in the late 1960s—can best be understood as a redemption-through-adaptation of neoliberalism's core economic ideology, policies, and practices.

The elite proponents of neoliberalism were initially quite wary of a Trump presidency and many, if not most, preferred what they saw as the more Wall Street-friendly and predictable Hillary Clinton. After Trump's election, however, it did not take them long to regroup and embrace his ruthless blend of white nationalist populism and neoliberalism—the same alliance that fueled the initial emergence of political neoliberalism in the United States that began in the 1950s and crystalized in the late 1970s.

I show in this chapter how the growth of economic inequality, racial animus, and a repressive police state impacts the police and vigilante killings of African Americans, as well as attempts to use all of the powers of the racial state at every branch and level to suppress any organized resistance to such oppression and the violence which helps maintain it.[1]

In brief, this chapter examines the racial and economic implications of the rise of Trumpism and its alliance with neoliberalism, and their negative impacts on low-income and poor people of color—including, of course, police and vigilante killings. While it will take some time to ascertain their full effect, there are at least two possibilities. One is that such violence, if left unchecked, could increase exponentially with increased racial animus and the racially targeted policies of Trump's racially repressive racial state. The other is that it will remain basically the same. One explanation for that second possibility is articulated by Paul Butler, who suggests, in his study of police repression of African Americans, that because these killings have become so institutionalized, they are likely to continue at about the same level regardless of who is president. I believe a more complete explanation supporting the view that the number of such incidents will remain basically the same under the Trump administration must also include the challenges the president's racist words and actions will face from an increasingly vigilant Movement for Black Lives—which, combined with the institutionalization of such killings to which Butler referred, could force what essentially amounts to a stalemate that preserves the racial status quo.[2]

You may recall that in Chapter 2 I said that explanations of economic neoliberalism fall under neo-Marxist theories that attempt to update and refine Marxist theory to make it relevant in explaining today's capitalistic economies and their class-based exploitation. In this chapter, I focus on the role of class oppression in the pervasive, disproportionate, and persistent police and vigilante killings of African Americans, who are also largely and disproportionately from the working and lower classes. As I also noted in Chapter 2, in the early 1970s, African American intellectuals such as Samuel Yette concluded that many low-income African Americans were facing nothing short of potential genocide because, due to automation, their labor was no longer needed, making them economically obsolete. It is here that I examine how, in this era of Trumpism, social and economic policies that have their roots in neoliberalism, while disproportionately impacting African Americans, can target anyone who is deemed economically useless and socially and politically dangerous.

While I believe that economic and social class-based oppression and the subsequent need for economic elites to control the economically marginalized are important enough to occupy their own chapter in this racism-centered analysis of the disproportionate police and vigilante killings of African Americans, I should also stress again that these two systems of oppression overlap. That connection is historically evident when we examine the roots of today's racism in economically exploitative systems such as colonialism, slavery, and peonage, and it is also apparent today in the fact that it is lower-class and working-class African Americans in neighborhoods with high concentrations of racial residential segregation and poverty who are most vulnerable to the policing violence of those living in what amounts to occupied territories.

Neoliberalism: Basic Assumptions, Goals, and Justifications

In my brief overview of the literature on neoliberalism I noted that at its core is the assumption that what is good for the market is good for society, and that therefore there should be no regulation, taxes, or other limits placed on what are assumed to be "free" market forces. I also discussed the fact that with rising economic inequality, exacerbated not only by automation and globalization but also by the economic elites' ability to successfully deploy their money to control politics and politicians, there has been a radical redistribution of income and wealth upward and the enactment of criminal justice laws, policies, and practices to protect such elites' property and lives from challenges—both real and imagined—from the economically marginalized masses. I further stated that, while economic and political neoliberalism calls for little or no regulation of markets or the lives of wealthy people, it mandates that *while the safety nets that provide for those who are struggling economically are eliminated, the social control apparatus of repressive laws, police, courts, and prisons that protect the property and other interests of the economic elite are greatly expanded.* I concluded that the irony of neoliberalism, as a form of extreme capitalism, is that while it rejects any regulation of the markets that benefit the wealthy, it requires very tight regulation of nearly every facet of the lives of the those who are not affluent, and especially those who are poor. It is also important to note that while much of the impetus for neoliberal ideas and policies comes from the United States, neoliberalism and the extreme economic inequality it exacerbates are now worldwide phenomena that have spread to even former communist countries such as Russia and China. Finally, throughout the world, under neoliberalism, the ultimate form of control of the poor entails their killing by the police, other state security forces, and vigilantes.[3]

In explaining the rise of neoliberalism in the United States and its consequences in shifting government policy away from a *social contract* that benefited not only the nation's rich but also a substantial and growing middle class, as well as those who were struggling economically, John Dillon Davey argues that that contract was changed in the early 1970s as the U.S. economy faced serious challenges such as a trade deficit and rising oil prices that reduced businesses' profits. With the deregulation of international currencies, corporations reacted through economic globalization that radically reduced their labor costs by exporting millions of American jobs to countries where labor was not unionized and was therefore compliant and cheap. Such changes resulted in what Davey characterizes as a "war on labor," "growing poverty," "the threat of the disruptive poor," "the war on the poor," and the creation of "a Leviathan" of government control as the criminal justice system was bolstered to address "the problem of falling corporate profits and the threat of social turmoil." To justify the building of a prison infrastructure large enough to contain any threat to those ruthless economic policies, despite evidence that crime rates were actually declining, politicians created a panic over a bogus crime wave, fabricated by themselves. Quietly, justified by money pumped into right-wing think tanks, government funds were shifted from helping the poor to building prisons. Like Davey, in her analysis Keeanga-Yamahtta Taylor includes the impact of the white backlash to the civil rights movement. She notes that although "anti-Black policing and law-and-order rhetoric had a much earlier start . . . the exponential growth of imprisonment and the turn toward hyper-punitive prison terms began after the Black Power uprisings of the 1960s had ended." Once again, this time in the election of Donald Trump as president, we see another white racial backlash that has fueled yet another wave of economic and politically repressive policies. That phenomenon is Trumpism.[4]

Trumpism: The White Backlash of 2016

As the elections of Trump and extreme right-wing leaders in other largely and traditionally "white" western nations have demonstrated, one of the key resources which economic and political elites have at their disposal in keeping the white masses on board with policies that do not serve their economic interests is white racial animus and backlash, as they shift their racial states toward more racially repressive ideologies, policies, and practices. This is evident from an examination of the key roles that racism and neoliberalism played in the rise of Trumpism.

There has been much focus on the assumed economic angst of the European American working class as the driving force behind the white backlash that drove Donald Trump in office. Unfortunately, such racism-evasive analyses fail to explain why Hillary Clinton actually received the votes of those European Americans who suffered the most economically or why Trump was the choice of *most* European Americans who voted in that election, not just those who were working class. If we are to truly understand Trump's victory, we cannot ignore white racism as its main driving force. And a good place to begin that analysis is with an examination of the racial biography of a man who was born into a life of great wealth and racial and gender privilege.

The Racial Biography of Donald J. Trump

In the United States and other highly racialized countries, there is a tendency among members of the dominant racialized group to reduce racism to the prejudice of lone individuals and then to dare anyone to know what is in the head and heart of another to the degree necessary to prove that they are, indeed, a racial bigot. I argue here and elsewhere that racial bigotry can best be understood as being but one component of a highly organized system of racial oppression into which individuals are born and socialized. This runs contrary to the popular sociological catchphrase that suggests we now live in a world that is so racially sophisticated that in most arenas of social life there is somehow "racism without racists." I believe, instead, that where there is systemic racism, there is no shortage of racial bigots operating its throttles; and, dependent upon how powerful they are, their attitudes and actions—whether conscious or unconscious—can be quite consequential. If indeed a case for racial animus and bigotry can be made against anyone based on their own words and actions, then the evidence against President Trump, arguably the most powerful person in the world, is hard to ignore.[5]

In 1973, as a young man, Donald Trump and his father were sued for racial discrimination in the rental of apartments. As revealed by a set of African American and European American "testers" who expressed interest in renting apartments, African Americans were told there were no vacancies while European Americans were shown units ready to rent. More details surfaced about that discriminatory practice when a former building superintendent explained that he was instructed to code applications from African Americans with a C, for "colored." The Trumps settled, but were sued again three years later for continuing to discriminate against African Americans. And there is more, lots more.[6]

In 1989, as the mayor of New York called for racial calm after five African American and Latino youth were arrested for the rape and beating of a young European American woman jogging in Central

Park, Donald Trump instead urged the public to express its outrage, through full-page newspaper ads he bought calling for those arrested to be given the death penalty. After spending years in prison, the young men in this case were cleared of all charges. During that same decade, a worker in a Trump casino told a reporter for the *New Yorker* that "When Donald and [his wife] Ivana came to the casino, the bosses would order all the black people off the floor . . . They put us all in the back." The Trump Plaza Hotel and Casino in Atlantic City was fined $200,000 for an incident in 1991 in which it catered to an overtly racist high roller with mob connections by removing African American employees from the gambling table he was playing at. And in a book published that same year by John O'Donnell, a former president of that same hotel and casino, Trump was quoted as complaining about an African American accountant, who finally resigned after Trump spent months pressuring the casino president to fire him, saying:

> Black guys counting my money! I hate it. The only kind of people I want counting my money are short guys wearing yarmulkes every day . . . I think that the guy is lazy. And it's probably not his fault, because laziness is a trait in blacks. It really is, I believe that. It's not anything they can control.

After initially denying the allegations, in a 1997 interview in *Playboy* magazine Trump admitted that "the stuff O'Donnell wrote about me is probably true."[7]

Trump kept himself in the national news in the years prior to his successful presidential bid by fanning the white backlash to President Obama's election as the nation's first African American president. Trump questioned Obama's right to be president by suggesting he was born in Kenya, not the United States. He added more fuel to that racial fire by also speculating that Obama was admitted into Harvard, and other prestigious schools he attended, as a result of affirmative action policies.[8]

Donald Trump continued to fan the flames of racial animus when he launched his presidential campaign, saying about the Mexican immigrants whom he had promised to keep out of the United States by building a wall: "They're bringing drugs. They're bringing crime. They're rapists. And some, I assume, are good people." Later during that Republican primary, he also called for a ban on Muslim immigrants who might try to enter the country, challenged an American judge's ability to fairly handle a lawsuit against him because of the judge's Mexican ancestry, was slow in denouncing Ku Klux Klan support for his candidacy, and retweeted the bogus statistic that 81 percent of European American murder victims were killed by African Americans. Trump also effectively relaunched the highly racialized call for "law and order" made by Richard Nixon that was so successful in fueling the white racial backlash to African American social protest that helped elect Nixon president. And there are other examples of Trump's racial bigotry, too numerous to mention here.[9]

Trump's Racist Message Pays Off

All of these racist Trump words and actions, and more, were widely reported in the media, but none disqualified him as a president in the eyes of those who voted for him. In fact, it was precisely the racist attitudes and animus communicated by Trump that made his campaign so successful both in the Republican primary and the general election. The fact that he was able to tap deeply into the well of racial hatred in the United States was evident in the endorsement he received from the *Crusader*, one of the Ku Klux Klan's most influential newspapers, which devoted its entire front page to Trump and his campaign slogan, "Make America Great Again!" This suggested to many of Trump's supporters that America was great during the good old days when "white" people ruled. Trump also won the endorsement of other white supremacist organizations and leaders, including former KKK Grand Wizard David Duke.[10]

Of course, not all of the Trump supporters attracted to his racial rhetoric were overtly racist members of white supremacist organizations. During the Republican primary, there emerged evidence that Trump's appeal was part of a global movement toward xenophobia-driven white nationalism that was engulfing many Western democracies. For example, a study of Republican primary voters by Michael Tesler found that those who voted for Trump were more likely to score high on measures of racial resentment such as acceptance of the racist stereotypes that African Americans are lazy and undeserving, and to harbor prejudice against Hispanics and Muslims. Another social scientist, Philip Klinkner, found racial resentment to be a key factor in support for Trump, while the widely touted explanation of "economic anxiety" was not. Another team of researchers found that most of the "strong Trump supporters" surveyed (52 percent) held the racist view that African Americans were less racially evolved than European Americans. They were more likely to see African Americans as "lacking self-restraint, like animals" and as being "savage" and "barbaric." And in another study, political scientists Brian Schaffner, Matthew MacWilliams, and Tatishe Nteta found that even when factors like political partisanship and ideology were controlled, racial bigotry and sexist attitudes were better predictors of support for Trump than was economic dissatisfaction. Racism's impact was also confirmed by the 2016 American National Election Study and by another post-election study by the Public Religion Research Institute and *The Atlantic* magazine.[11]

To the surprise of most pundits, Trump's racial message was also quite effective in the general election. Trump won with 57 percent of the "white" vote, compared to only 21 percent of the "non-white" vote and only 8 percent of the "black" vote. And despite his very vulgar remarks about and alleged actions against women, and the fact that a Clinton victory would have been historic as the election of the first woman president in the United States, Trump received the majority (52 percent) of the votes of European American women voters. Their Trump vote stands in stark contrast to the only 4 percent of African American women voters who voted for him.[12]

Although during the campaign Donald Trump repeatedly complained that the system was rigged against him, and warned that there would be a violent revolt by his supporters if he lost, in fact it was actually rigged in favor of candidates like himself, who were skilled at exploiting white racial animus. Before the votes were counted, Trump had what would prove to be the decisive racial advantage of an electoral college system that was designed, in part, to protect slave states and their peculiar institution (where a large proportion of their population were politically disenfranchised slaves) from what their leaders considered to be the tyranny of electing the nation's presidents by the popular vote. Today the electoral college makes the votes of the residents of sparsely populated, rural, overwhelmingly European American, socially and racially conservative states count significantly more than those of more urban, liberal, and racially diverse states. For example, the vote of a resident of Wyoming actually counts 3.6 times more than the vote of a resident of California. As a result of this bias, America's raceocracy prevailed over any pretense of democracy as Trump was elected president with the majority of the electoral college votes, even though nearly three million more Americans actually cast their ballots for Hillary Clinton.[13]

Celebrating Making America White Again

Many of Trump's supporters clearly saw his election as a victory for white supremacy and other forms of social oppression. The Southern Poverty Law Center, which monitors hate crimes in the United States, documented that during the ten days following Trump's election, there were 867 reported non-internet "hate incidents" of harassment or intimidation, with the likelihood that most such incidents went unreported. Consistent with Trump's highly racialized exploitation of anti-immigrant sentiments to fuel his campaign, of those reported hate incidents, the largest categorization of motivation was "Anti-Immigrant" (280). That was followed by "Anti-Black" (187), "Anti-Semitic" (100), "Anti-LGBT" (95), "Anti-Muslim" (49), "Trump-General" (43), "Anti-Woman" (40), and "White Nationalist" (32). Only twenty-three incidents were categorized as "Anti-Trump" and the remaining eighteen were placed under an "Other" category. Some of the incidents involved racist graffiti that made reference to Trump's election, such as an image of a swastika with "Make America White Again" written on both sides, an obvious racialized reference to Trump's campaign promise to "Make America Great Again." Mosques in California received letters that referred to Muslims as "a vile and filthy people" and called for genocide against them. A Puerto Rican family found the words "Trump" and "Go Home" scratched into their car. Some of the racist words referred specifically to the Black Lives Matter movement. For example, in Durham, North Carolina a building had scrawled on it "Black Lives Don't Matter and Neither Does Your Votes [sic]," while a flyer in Washington, D.C. read "We are organizing a new movement to rid our neighborhood of niggers. No more Black Lives Matter! Kill them all." Other incidents involved more direct confrontations. In the Queens borough of New York City, an Uber driver—an American citizen who was originally from Morocco—videotaped his being confronted by another motorist who told him, as reported by CNN, "Trump is president a******, so you can kiss your visa goodbye, scumbag. They'll deport you soon, don't worry, you f***ing terrorist." And a twelve-year-old African American girl in Colorado was reportedly told by a boy who approached her: "Now that Trump is president, I'm going to shoot you and all the blacks I can find."[14]

President Elect Trump Welcomes Aboard His Motley Crew with Lots of Their Own Racial Baggage

Trump's appointment of top aides and cabinet members did nothing to assure his non-supporters that he would heal the racial divide created by his racially charged campaign. Shortly after he was elected, Trump announced that he would appoint as one of his top White House aides Steve Bannon, his campaign chief strategist and the chairman of Breitbart, an internet news site that Bannon referred to as the "home of the alt-right," a network of white supremacist and likeminded groups. Trump also announced the appointment of Mike Flynn, a retired general who had posted a tweet asserting that the "fear of Muslims is rational," supported Trump's temporary ban on Muslim immigration into the United States, and indicated that he would be receptive to a return to the use of waterboarding and other methods of torture. As Treasury Secretary Trump nominated Steve Mnuchin, a hedge fund manager previously accused of benefiting financially from discrimination in housing loans and foreclosures in largely African American and Latino neighborhoods. And as his Attorney General, the person who would be most responsible for matters involving civil rights and the police and vigilante killings of African Americans, Trump nominated U.S. Senator Jefferson Beauregard Sessions from Alabama, a man with a racial history so bad that the U.S. Senate refused to confirm his nomination as a federal judge by Ronald Reagan when it was brought to light that he had made racially charged comments such as that the only reason he would not join the Klan was because its members smoked marijuana.[15]

Neoliberalism Remixed with Trumpism

For some observers, the election of Donald Trump as president raised the question of whether Trumpism, with its strong populist, racist, nationalistic, emotive, and authoritarian hues, could exist alongside neoliberalism. In stark contrast to the populist façade of Trumpism, neoliberalism is run by and for economic and political elites; hides much of its racial work behind a facade of impersonal, colorblind market forces; is global in scope; seems quite rational; and, despite its ruthlessness, flaunts its apparent support of established liberal values such as personal liberty, freedom of speech, freedom of the press, constitutional rights, and the rule of law.

Can Trumpism and Neoliberalism Get Along?

Some scholars, such as Cornell West, saw the rise of Trumpism, with its populist appeal, as a reflection of the crisis and failure of neoliberalism to address the problems associated with growing economic inequality, with Trumpism, or whatever the new order might be called, replacing neoliberalism. Others, such as Wendy Brown, caution us not to underestimate the flexibility and adaptability of neoliberalism, which, she argues, while "globally ubiquitous," "has no fixed or settled coordinates," but instead shows great "temporal and geographical variety in its discursive formulations, policy entailments, and material practices" as it "takes diverse shapes and spawns diverse content and normative details." Yet another perspective comes into view if we follow the lead of David Harvey in examining neoliberalism from a political rather than an economic analytical lens. Harvey defines neoliberalism as a "political project" that arose in the late 1960s and 1970s to reduce the power of organized labor. So, if we see neoliberalism as the political arm of that particular phase of an advanced and evolving capitalism, we can expect capitalism to grow other political projects as needed while retaining its essential exploitative elements. Therefore, it may make more sense to think of the evolving nature of capitalism as a whole, rather than of how it manifests itself politically and ideologically during a particular historical era. Consistent with this view, I agree with Nancy Fraser that Trump's election signals not the end of neoliberalism, as some have suggested, but the end of the "progressive neoliberalism" of the Clintons and Obama, which had efficaciously wrapped economic neoliberal ideology and policies around concern for socially liberal ideals such as diversity, multiculturalism, and tolerance, and social movement causes such as anti-racism, feminism, and the rights of LGBTQ people.[16]

Those scholars who suggest that white nationalism and neoliberalism are incompatible have failed to include in their reflections on neoliberalism and its future during the Trump presidency the role that racism played in neoliberalism's origins here in the United States, and continues to play today. In *Race and the Origins of American Neoliberalism*, Randolph Hohle argues convincingly that such a false dichotomy is rooted in a misunderstanding of history. Indeed, Hohle traces the rise of neoliberalism, which became a powerful political force in the United States in the late 1970s, back to the 1950s, when "elite struggles to protect their white privilege" led to "the fusion of the liberal business class and segregationists." This was done through the crafting of ideologies, politics, and policies that effectively blended reactionary racial goals such as opposition to busing with conservative economic agenda items such as reducing taxes, shrinking the size of government, and deregulating businesses. Within that ideological mix, the public sector and government programs, such as the War on Poverty and public assistance, that were seen as benefiting African Americans were racialized as being "black" and bad, while the private sector, and the self-sufficiency it was said to promote, were colored as being "white" and good. Hohle goes as far as to stand Marxist and neo-Marxist analyses on their heads by concluding that the emergence of political neoliberalism and the class exploitation it fostered in the United States were ancillary to racial oppression. Following that argument, rather than being something new and different, Trumpism can best be understood as a continuation and evolution of that foundational alliance between systemic racism and political neoliberalism. Finally, in explaining its "resiliency," Hohle suggests that because of political neoliberalism's deep and sprawling roots in systemic racism, it will survive as long as racial oppression does.[17]

In brief, I believe that while analytically we can root the rise of Trumpism in the failures of neoliberalism and its political and economic elitism that politically and economically disenfranchised large segments of the population, we are now witnessing the unfolding of an alliance of Trumpism and hypercapitalism into a new, more aggressively anti-African American, racial state synthesis built on Trump's call for "law and order," repressive and highly racialized policies such as "stop and frisk," and economic and fiscal policies such as tax cuts that favor the wealthy. While Trump's campaign rhetoric has been racist, nationalistic, and populist, his extreme capitalist bent is more evident in his governing actions, which include the appointment to cabinet posts of Washington insiders with strong ties to pro-business and Wall Street lobbyists and his successful effort to pass legislation that created huge tax breaks for the wealthy. There is little evidence to suggest that Trumpism will actually replace what has been called neoliberalism. Instead, it is more likely that the current crisis of neoliberalism has been fixed, at least temporarily, by Trump and those in his inner governing circle, through their synthesis of the Trump political movement with the latest manifestation of hypercapitalism as a new and more lethal form of racial and class oppression.[18]

Under Trumpism the American racial state has become extremely right-wing, more authoritarian, and more overtly racist, with a closer resemblance to neofascism than previous forms of neoliberalism. If left unchecked, this new coalition of overwhelmingly "white" political factions could be expected to lead to an increase in the numbers of and justifications for state-sponsored and sanctioned police and vigilante killings of African Americans. Finally, while the ideology and name may change, in that it is more overtly racist and right-wing, we can also expect to see not only the continuation but the intensification of neoliberal policies and practices, under a more nationalistic facade.

Now that we know that, whatever name they may be called by, the basic tenets of neoliberalism are not going anywhere soon, it will be useful to take a closer look at the literature on the topic and its implications for police and vigilante killings of Africans which I began reviewing in Chapter 2, but this time with the necessary tweaks to accommodate the rise of Trumpism.

Neoliberalism's Impact on the American Criminal Justice System

To answer the question of what happens when a state cannot resolve the problems that accrue from the rampant economic inequality it has created, Richard Quinney offers a class-centered analysis of the state and its criminal justice system as a repressive state apparatus. To that end, he focuses on the social consequences of the crisis that emerges during the shift in advanced capitalism from social contract liberalism to neoliberalism and its struggles to deal with a "growing surplus population" of those judged to be economically expendable. His chief argument begins with the observation that "criminal justice has traditionally been one part of the policies of the welfare state" and adds that "as the liberal welfare state fails to solve its own contradictions, its demise becomes imminent, and criminal justice takes on new forms" as it shifts to a model "based explicitly on punishment." In brief, its leaders design, implement, and adjust social control policies targeted at the populations it deems most threatening.[19]

French sociologist and Marxist scholar Loic Wacquant provides important insights into the social consequences of neoliberal policies and practices through his analysis of the dramatic increase in the mass incarceration of African Americans—a form of racial targeting which is inextricably linked to the current police and vigilante killings of African Americans. In making his case that the mass incarceration of African Americans is the United States' new "peculiar institution," Wacquant places what he sees happening to African Americans within the larger political-economic context of the exploitation they have faced throughout American history. And in a later publication he stresses how such very public and highly ritualized, punitive "law and order" crackdowns serve as a form of terrorism against African Americans. As seen in the outrageous, almost theatrical case examples of police and vigilante killings of African Americans which I examined in Chapter 1, for African Americans the terror value of such killings seems to be enhanced by their performance as all-too-predictable public spectacles, with carefully scripted plots and casts of characters. The plotlines of such dramas have intensified as a result of President Trump's call for more law and order and his advocacy of repressive policing policies and practices such as stop-and-frisk.[20]

In placing such violence in what he believes to be its proper historical and economic context, Henry Giroux argues that

> rather than being viewed or forgotten as isolated, but unfortunate expressions of extremism, these incidents are part of a growing systemic pattern of violence and terror that has unapologetically emerged at a time when the politics and logic of disposability, terror and expulsion has been normalized in US society and violence has become the default position for solving all social problems.

In what he refers to as this "age of disposability," Giroux sees the "rise of the punishing state as a way to govern all of social life" such that "life becomes disposable for most, but especially for poor minorities of class and color." From this perspective, more than just individual acts of violence, police and vigilante killings serve as a warning to all of what could happen to them if they get out of line.[21]

Neoliberalism and Police and Vigilante Violence in New York City

An example of how such punitive policies toward the poor work is provided in a study of police and vigilante repression in New York City during the 1990s as it underwent an intense period of neoliberal transformation under the administration of Mayor Rudolph Giuliani. New York is not only the United States' largest city and financial hub but, as Kaplan-Lyman notes, "the quintessential neoliberal city, on which other cities model reform." Following the neoliberal playbook closely, in the 1990s its Republican mayor cut thousands of city jobs and reduced city services while dramatically increasing the size of the city's police force. Over that decade New York hired six thousand new police officers and increased its spending on public safety by 53 percent. It also launched new police initiatives, the best known of which was its Stop and Frisk program, which resulted in more than a half million people being detained in 2009 alone. The political-economic roots of such actions are evident in the facts that more than 90 percent of those stopped and frisked were found to be innocent of any crime and that the number of arrests actually increased significantly as the crime rate declined. Kaplan-Lyman also notes the irony that under neoliberal ideologies, policies, and practices that call for less government, both the size and the role of the police increase significantly.[22]

Kaplan-Lyman traces the roots of neoliberal restructuring in New York City to the 1970s, after President Nixon's cutting of aid to cities forced the nation's biggest city into bankruptcy. As part of its fiscal bailout, corporate and financial entities assumed increasing control and pushed the city into policies of extreme austerity. By the mid-1990s, as neoliberalism took shape in New York in a way that served as a prototype for urban reform in cities across the globe, the following three characteristics of neoliberalism came clearly into focus. First, it requires organizational changes that reduce police accountability to area residents while increasing it to corporations and other elite institutions. Second, it entails the adoption of a policing strategy that has as its chief goal the maintenance of social order. Such "broken windows policing" is based on the conservative social science theory that the best way to reduce crime is through heavy police enforcement of even the most minor of infractions, such as littering or jaywalking. And finally, it relies heavily on the racially targeted policy of stop-and-frisk, which Kaplan-Lyman found serves the dual functions of increasing police surveillance in targeted areas and providing the spectacle of public punishment through the intimidation and humiliation of those stopped and searched.[23]

In the United States, and in other nations, police repression has often been coupled with vigilante violence, and sometimes the lines of distinction between the police and vigilantes are blurred. For Kaplan-Lyman, that connection surfaced during his research when he found an April 14, 1995 article in the *New York Times* with the title "Ex-Outreach Workers Say They Assaulted Homeless." The reporter who wrote that article traced that violence to an initiative launched by the Grand Central Partnership (GCP), a local business improvement district with the power to levy taxes on and render services for its member businesses. While the organization prided itself on its "outreach" efforts for the homeless, the *New York Times* expose suggests that it resembled the type of protection racket commonly associated with organized crime, in that as pressure, including force, was applied to move the homeless out of the targeted area, businesses in the surrounding areas to which they relocated felt the need to join the business improvement district. The GCP was but one of sixty-four such entities in the city at that time, each of which raised serious questions about citizen accountability in that they had their own "private, quasi-police" force—which in fact served as a state-sanctioned vigilante group. The *New York Times* article reports that four homeless men were recruited by the GCP to serve as what program administrators referred to as "the goon squads." Although they were not told so explicitly, when they were instructed to "do whatever you have to do" and to "hold a nonverbal conversation," they understood their job as being to beat up homeless people to force them out of the protected area. Members of the goon squads were well aware of the police-like authority to use violence granted them. As one of them put it, "I was slapping people around with my walkie-talkie . . . That was my main weapon. I felt like a police officer." As their reputations grew, the workers obtained more contracts, including one with the GCP's largest client, Chase Manhattan Bank, which contracted for "outreach services" for its forty-seven Manhattan branches.[24]

The literature on racism and neoliberalism offers more specific insights into what might be expected in terms of the police and vigilante killings of African Americans during the current Trump era of American race relations and neoliberal economic and political policies.

The Rise of Neoliberalism, the Persistence of Racial Oppression, and the Emerging Specter of Genocide

While members of racially oppressed groups have always been more disposable than those of the dominant racial group, as sociologist Sidney Wilhelm made clear as he envisioned the coming of neoliberalism in 1970 with the publication of *Who Needs the Negro?*, the racially oppressed are especially vulnerable when they are viewed as being economically obsolete. In stating his thesis about the culmination of the historical relationship between economic value and race relations that caused African Americans to be both hated and deemed useless in the United States, Wilhelm warned, "while harboring constant antipathy toward nonwhite people, White America could not dismiss the black man until the invention of machines severed its dependency upon labor.

Now the economics of technology combines with white racism to make possible the Negro's total exclusion and possibly even extermination." Wilhelm compared the role of the police in African American ghettoes to that of "the U.S. cavalry in pacifying the plains Indian." And, taking a wide-ranging view of genocide consistent with that of the United Nations, he concluded that "genocide is likely not as a calculated scheme of gas chambers but as an indiscriminate white response to black violence which in turn responds to the poverty, dehumanization, and sense of uselessness produced by the system." Finally, in explaining how such "indefensible deeds" are justified as part of "an unabated heritage of violence toward undesirable minorities and incompatible ideas," Wilhelm pointed to the "law and order" slogan and ideology successfully deployed in the presidential campaigns of Richard Nixon at that time (and, most recently, by Donald Trump). As you may recall, in Chapter 2 I mentioned that African American journalist Samuel Yette popularized the theme of automation and genocide among African Americans in his book *The Choice*. Yette also shared Wilhelm's view that tough anti-crime rhetoric and measures were being deployed as part of white backlash-driven political campaigns. As Yette put it, the call for law and order was, in fact, "a euphemism for the total repression and possible extermination of those in the society who cry for justice where little justice can be found."[25]

A dozen years later, in *How Capitalism Underdeveloped Black America*, African American historian Manning Marable also examined the link between capitalism, racism, and violence against African Americans. After asserting his premise that "at the core of the capitalism accumulation process is coercion," and in a statement that seems to build on Louis Althusser's concepts of ideological state apparatus and repressive state apparatus, Marable asserts that "American capitalism is preserved by two essential and integral factors: fraud and force," with fraud being "the ideological and cultural hegemony of the capitalist creed," as articulated in, for example, "educational institutions, churches, media and popular culture." And about force, Marable says: "Beneath the velvet glove of fraud exists the iron fist of force. For reasons of history, Black people are more aware than whites of this delicate dichotomy between consensus and force." Finally, in explaining why African Americans are more likely to be the targets of repressive violence, Marable points to their concentration in low-skilled, low-wage labor, the fact that they comprise a large proportion of the nation's surplus labor pool, and their historical victimization as members of a racially oppressed group.[26]

More recently, radical African American scholars such as Sundiata K. Cha-Jua and Keeanga-Yamahtta Taylor have also placed systemic racism at the core of their explanation of contemporary African American exploitation under neoliberalism. Their analyses stress how racism works under today's colorblind ideology and how the growing class cleavages among African Americans make members of lower classes more vulnerable to exploitation and abuse.[27]

Like Wacquant, Alexander, and other scholars, Cha-Jua argues that racial oppression has taken different forms during different periods of American history, as it surely has now under Trumpism. Borrowing the concept of *Nadir* from historian Rayford Logan's reference to the period of intense African American repression of 1877–1917 in which African Americans also made some gains, including the rise of their bourgeoisie classes, Cha-Jua states that the current state of oppression in which African Americans find themselves can best be called "the New Nadir." A key characteristic of the New Nadir is the changing class structure and dynamics among African Americans. As Cha-Jua puts it, "Indeed, the most important factor underlying the New Nadir has been the restructuring of class in the black community"—for while there have been advances for the bourgeoisie classes, there has also been marginalization of African American workers and a widening of class divisions. This suggests that there is increasingly a class-based filtering process as to who in the African American community is most vulnerable to the new covert mechanisms of racial control—with the poor, who are most likely to be stigmatized as a criminal class, of course being the most exposed. Exacerbating that vulnerability is the fact that their cause is less likely to be championed by more affluent African Americans, who may see them as a source of embarrassment and a threat to their own insecure social status.[28]

In her analysis of neoliberalism and the police suppression of African Americans, Taylor also stresses the intersection of racial and class oppression, the new form such oppression has taken under neoliberalism and color-blind ideology, and the growing class divisions among African Americans. On the intersection of racial and class oppression, Taylor stresses:

> Racism in the United States has never been just about abusing Black and Brown people just for the sake of doing so. It has always been a means by which the most powerful white men in the country have justified their rule, made their money, and kept the rest of us at bay. To that end, racism, capitalism, and class rule have always been tangled together in such a way that it is impossible to imagine one without the other.

Building on that premise, Taylor concludes that in understanding racism among police officers in the United States, we must appreciate the fact that it "is not the product of vitriol" but "flows from their role as armed agents of the state," as "the police function to enforce the rule of the politically powerful and the economic elite."[29]

In reference to the role of colorblind ideology, which denies the existence of systemic racism in its justification of neoliberal ideology and policies, Taylor notes that the myth of America as a colorblind meritocracy is used to deny the existence of racial oppression and to dismantle welfare state policies and programs that tackle not only racial discrimination but also the growing economic inequality in the United States. It is therefore to the advantage of working-class European Americans to debunk those myths. In explaining why what was then called the Black Lives Matter movement is a threat to neoliberalism, Taylor states:

> the spotlight now shining on pervasive police abuse, including the ongoing beatings, maimings, and murders of Black people, destabilizes the idea of the United States as colorblind and thus reestablishes the basis for strengthening regulatory oversight and antidiscrimination measures. In this process, larger questions inevitably arise as to the nature of such a society that would allow police to brazenly attack and kill so many African Americans. This is why the persisting issue of police violence is so explosive, especially in this particular historical moment of supposed colorblindness and the height of Black political power.

In brief, the issue of police and vigilante violence against African Americans is a threat to the ideological hegemony of political neoliberalism. The rise of Trumpism and its more overtly racist attitudes and policies since the publication of Taylor's book has also gone a long way to debunk colorblindness and other ideologies that had previously made neoliberalism more palatable.[30]

Taylor argues that the wide and growing class divisions among African Americans are behind African American politicians' support for repressive anti-crime laws that have resulted in the mass incarceration of African Americans. She points out, for example, that the Congressional Black Caucus (CBC) co-sponsored Ronald Reagan's 1986 Anti-Drug Abuse Act, and that that act was central to the War on Drugs and the rise of the mass incarceration of African Americans. For example, it was responsible for the sentencing disparities between powder and crack cocaine users and authorized 1.7 billion dollars to fund the racially targeted War on Drugs. Later African American mayors, faced with growing concern about crime and diminished federal resources to address its root causes, pressured most of the by then weary members of the Congressional Black Caucus to support President Clinton's tough anti-crime measure, the Violent Crime Control and Law Enforcement Act of 1994. With its passage, "by the end of Clinton's term, Black incarceration rates had tripled and the United States was locking up a larger proportion of its population than any other country on earth." Taylor presents a long list of Congressional Black Caucus corporate donors, including the right-wing, neoliberal American Legislative Exchange Council (ALEC), and concludes that this "at least partially explains CBC members' reluctance to participate in responding to the murders of Mike Brown, Eric Garner, and the many other victims of police brutality." Taylor laments the fact that rarely do the "toothless hearings" of African American elected officials translate into actual proposed policy changes, and that instead their main focus tends to be on attempting to channel the outrage of their constituents into greater participation in electoral politics.[31]

The political economy of the pervasive, persistent, and disproportionate police and vigilante killings of African Americans is also evident when we look at how gun manufacturers and sellers have benefited from promoting legislation that exploits the white nightmare of being attacked by "dangerous Black criminals" or rioters. Gun manufacturers and retailers such as Walmart that sell guns and ammunition have used the National Rifle Association (NRA) and other lobbying groups they fund, such as ALEC, to promote state laws such as Stand Your Ground legislation that allows people to kill others they perceive as being threatening to them, even when they can avoid harm by simply leaving the situation. Such legislation emboldens vigilantes to engage in killings, like those of Trayvon Martin and Jordan Davis in Florida, where there is a strong Stand Your Ground law in effect. Another blatant example of the political economy of criminal justice in the United States under the rise of neoliberalism is the multibillion-dollar private prison industry, a business that incentivizes keeping prisons full to ensure the profits of stockholders and to protect the jobs of working-class European Americans in the rural, economically devastated communities where many of the prisons are located. Things have gotten so out of control with private prisons that in 2011 a county judge in Pennsylvania was sentenced to a twenty-eight-year prison term for accepting a million dollars in bribes in a "kids-for-cash" racketeering scheme that funneled largely African American youth into private, for-profit juvenile delinquency centers.[32]

Although my focus in this book is police and vigilante killings of African Americans in the United States, viewing such violence through the lens of economic and political neoliberalism and rapidly spreading highly racialized nationalism such as Trumpism allows us to place it in the global context that is needed to understand why movements against police and vigilante repression are emerging worldwide both in ethnically diverse countries such as Canada, Britain, France, and Brazil and in nations that are characterized more by racial homogeneity. In ethnically diverse Brazil, for example, its extreme economic inequality must also be taken into account in explaining its long history of police and vigilante death squads that execute, with virtual impunity, homeless children who are considered to be a nuisance. And, underscoring the fact that racism cannot be viewed as the *only* cause of such violence, smartphone videos and social media have exposed the problem of police killings by corrupt governments run by people of African descent in nations such as Nigeria, the Ivory Coast, Guinea, Cameroon, and Sierra Leone. Finally, in the Philippines, President Duterte—who, in a leaked transcript of a phone conversation, was praised by President Trump for his handling of the problem—has encouraged what seems to some observers to be genocide against drug dealers and users both by the police and by vigilante groups.[33]

In all of these countries, such police and vigilante-based repression entails the emergence of various degrees of a national police state. Let's take a closer look at what is happening here in the United States.

The Growth of the Police State and State-Sanctioned Vigilantism during the Trump Era of American Race Relations

The Re-Emergence of the Racially Repressive Federal Racial State

From a racial state-theoretical perspective, we can say that under the presidency of Donald J. Trump we are witnessing the return of all branches of the federal racial state from their ostensibly colorblind and largely racially oblivious mode under the Obama administration to the racially repressive mode of earlier eras. President Trump made himself clear on the very day of his inauguration, when—in a message that seemed to be aimed at those who protested the pervasive, disproportionate, and persistent police killings of African Americans—he posted on the White House website, under the title "Standing Up for Our Law Enforcement Community," that his would be a "law and order administration," one that would "end" "the dangerous anti-police atmosphere in America." Although there are some sites of resistance, such as sanctuary cities, and cities and towns that are overwhelmingly African American, that shift at the federal government level also provides support for similar repressive racial actions by the various branches of the racial state at the individual and local state levels.[34]

In my book *The Urban Racial State*, I developed a theory that focuses specifically on the *urban* racial state as a manager of race relations in American cities. In that book I also showed that, although the focus of urban racial state theory is explaining how racial politics works in urban areas, its basic assumptions and concepts can explain the racial workings of any branch or level of the state—which can be broadly defined as government and its various organizational appendages, be they public (e.g., public universities, commissions, and boards) or private (e.g., private universities, think tanks, and lobbying groups). In Chapter 2 of this book I explained how urban racial state theory incorporates Louis Althusser's explanation of the state's role in maintaining social oppression through his elaboration of Karl Marx's notion of *state apparatus* and Antonio Gramsci's concept of *hegemony*. According to Althusser, the state derives its power through both its ideological state apparatuses (ISA), such as a nation's dominant ideologies of who should be treated in what way and why—which are generated and disseminated throughout the culture, including the media, schools, and various government agencies and policies—and its repressive state apparatuses (RSA), such as laws, the courts, the police, the national guard and other branches of the military, and the vigilantes whose actions the state sanctions.[35]

Case examples I used to illustrate that theory at the urban level included the police killings of Anthony Baez, Amadou Diallo, and Patrick Dorismond in New York City under the administration of Mayor Giuliani, as well as the non-fatal shooting of Antoine Reid and a police officer's sodomization of Abner Louima with a broken broomstick. Like the recent killing of Eric Garner in that same city, all of those incidents involved what on the surface may appear, when viewed at the interpersonal level, to be little more than very emotional, hypermasculine actions by the members of the NYPD, but upon closer scrutiny reveal racial state policies and practices that were highly scripted as part of that city administration's very rational and racially targeted program of neoliberal police repression.[36]

In *The Urban Racial State* I identify nine points of analytical focus based on the three branches and three levels of the racial state: the executive, judicial, and legislative branches of the federal, individual state-level, and urban (or local) government and their various organizational appendages. For example, when I analyze the Trump administration's actions that relate to the police and vigilante killings of African Americans, my main focus is on the executive branch of the federal racial state, and when I examine the same issue under the Giuliani administration my attention is largely on the executive branch of the urban racial state—although, as I show, its judicial branch also played a major role as one of the mayor's most powerful allies.[37]

A basic premise of urban racial state theory is that while politicians try to skillfully manage the actions of the state in their own interests, in its racial state capacity the state's ultimate function is the maintenance of the racial status quo. Usually such management of race relations is done by ignoring serious racial issues and problems such as housing segregation, as is the case when the racial state is in its racially oblivious mode—an approach that works especially well under the ideology of colorblindness. However, when the racially oppressed are successful in forcing some, usually minor, reforms, the system shifts to its racially ameliorative mode. Finally, in response to the white backlash to such reforms, or simply the perceived advances of African Americans and other people of color, politicians can appease a European American electoral majority by shifting the various branches and levels of the racial state into their racially oppressive mode. While one can make the case that during Barack Obama's two terms the federal racial state was either in a racially oblivious mode, because of his unwillingness to confront systemic racism directly, or could be more appropriately characterized as being in a racially ameliorative mode, because of the hope and largely symbolic changes it did bring about, it is clear that with the white racism-driven election of Donald Trump, the nation and its federal racial state are clearly back in their racially oppressive mode. African Americans found the same to be true in the 1990s with the election of Rudolph Giuliani, who is now one of Trump's most influential advisers, as the mayor of New York—the nation's largest city, and its model of neoliberalism. The NYPD shootings of Antione Reid and Patrick Dorismond are particularly instructive about the intersection of racial, class, and gendered oppression, as Mayor Giuliani—who, like Trump, was elected in a racially divisive campaign with strong backing by police unions and little support from African Americans—shoved New York into the socially surrealistic and violent world of neoliberalism.[38]

In the summer of 1998, off-duty NYPD officer Michael Meyer shot Antoine Reid in the chest at point-blank range during a confrontation

after Reid attempted to engage Meyer during his daily routine of wash-
ing the windshields of cars that stopped at his intersection and soliciting money from their drivers. Meyer shot Reid less than a year after
the shocking sodomization of Haitian immigrant Abner Louima by a
macho NYPD officer bent on demonstrating his male dominance over
someone he mistakenly thought had punched him. After taking turns
with other officers to beat Louima before they took him to the station,
officer Justin Volpe beat him again before sodomizing him with a broken broomstick and then bragging "I just broke a man down" to his
fellow officers as he paraded Louima out of a precinct bathroom. The
shooting of Reid came less than eight months before NYPD officers, in
what seemed to be a follow-through on their cocky Street Crime Unit's
macho motto "We own the night," riddled West African immigrant
Amadou Diallo's body with bullets.[39]

When NYPD officers engaged in such outrageous acts of violence
against people of color, Mayor Giuliani seemed to go out of his way
to increase the racial drama and tension of such "big events"—perhaps
as a rallying cry to his European American supporters and as a kind of
victory dance in the face of the grievances of the African Americans
who overwhelmingly rejected him as a mayoral candidate. However,
the mayor's defense of his police department and one of his officers
was made more difficult by the fact that the NYPD apparently knew
they had a problem in Meyer. Prior to his shooting of Reid, Officer
Meyer had been the subject of seven complaints—most of which were
about the use of excessive force—and had been reassigned to maintain
a police precinct building. But that did not stop Mayor Giuliani, who
typically defended the NYPD through attacks on the characters of those
killed or wounded by officers. That was especially important in the Reid
case, because the police shooting of what the media deemed a "squeegee" man evoked a narrative of a highly racialized, class-based struggle,
which Mayor Giuliani pushed to frame as an issue of aggressive beggars
harassing decent citizens. The success of such a narrative was essential
for the mayor in his radical recasting of New York as the model city of
neoliberalism, as he sought to align its new racial state-ideological state
apparatus with its repressive state apparatus through his administration's

hyperaggressive "broken windows" policing policy of cracking down on any nuisance behavior by dark-skinned people. In its effort to discredit Reid, the NYPD released his "rap sheet," which listed nine arrests; all of these, his lawyer stated, were misdemeanors, and none involved violence.[40]

Of course, such arrests were not uncommon for low-income African American panhandlers in New York at that time. As you may recall, under Giuliani's extremely aggressive "broken windows" policing policy the NYPD made frequent stop-and-frisk-based arrests of African American and poor people, many of which were groundless. The Reid shooting case makes clear the vicious cycle of the NYPD criminalizing targeted populations then justifying the use of violence against them by deeming them dangerous criminals. In New York, the Giuliani administration's executive branch of the urban racial state had a strong ally in the judicial branch, where the criminal courts, at various levels, rarely rule against the police, no matter how egregious their actions. Consistent with that practice, the charge of attempted murder against Officer Meyer was dismissed by a state Supreme Court judge and he was acquitted of the charges of assault and reckless abandonment. That legal victory helped further fuel the mayor's ideological war and repressive policies against the poor. Months later he publicly expressed his impatience with "squeegee men" and others he branded as a public nuisance.[41]

Just three weeks after four members of the NYPD were acquitted in the killing of Amadou Diallo, the lethal effects of Giuliani's "broken windows" policy of cracking down on nuisance crimes once again became evident. This time it was the fatal shooting of Haitian immigrant and security guard Patrick Dorismond by an NYPD undercover detective, Anthony Vasquez. Officer Vasquez claimed that a policeman's gun went off during a scuffle over the weapon as the two men fought. As was often the case with the NYPD's actions at that time, the important question was: why did the police confront Dorismond in the first place? Why didn't they simply leave him alone as he waited for a cab after a night at a local club? In what appeared to be a hypermasculine confrontation, Dorismond took offense, and actually threatened to call the police, upon being approached by another undercover officer who attempted to purchase drugs from him as part of a drug-sting operation. It was that righteous indignation about being racially profiled as a drug dealer that went on to make Dorismond a martyr of a proud, law-abiding citizen, who refused to bow down to racial stereotyping and denigration. Mayor Giuliani once again engaged in a smear campaign against the victim of a police shooting, this time by having his police commissioner release Dorismond's sealed juvenile arrest records—documents that are normally not released because they involve a minor and refer to arrests only, not any actual conviction. In defending that action, Giuliani puzzled legal experts by claiming that he had not violated Dorismond's legal rights to have his juvenile records kept sealed because, as a dead man, Dorismond had no legal rights. Giuliani also released an autopsy report that found traces of marijuana in Dorismond's body that were so small that toxicology experts later surmised they could have come from second-hand smoke from the bar Dorismond was in before he was confronted by the police. But that was not the main self-inflicted blow to what was left of Giuliani's reputation. The mayor also defended his actions by cautioning the media that it would not want to give the impression that Dorismond was "an altar boy." When the facts were revealed they proved otherwise: Dorismond had in fact been an altar boy. As usual, the police officer was acquitted of all charges and, as is so often true, the family of the deceased received a large out-of-court financial settlement of its civil suit.[42]

While I focused on the Giuliani administration in illustrating my urban racial state theory, many of the "broken windows" police practices have continued beyond his administration, as was clearly the case with the more recent killing of Eric Garner, who was also initially confronted because, under neoliberalism's watchful eye, he was deemed to be no more than—as you will see in the next chapter—a "condition" that needed eradicating.[43]

During the 2016 presidential campaign, Rudy Giuliani was the most prominent advocate of the Trump administration's adoption of nationwide stop-and-frisk and other highly racialized policing strategies and tactics so closely linked to the police killings of African Americans in New York under his administration in the 1990s and the racial tensions they caused. Just as New York City provided an international test case of a highly racialized urban neoliberalism, its policing and vigilante pol-icies and practices offer a precursor to the lethal blend of racial animus, hypermasculinity, and neoliberalism present under the presidency of Donald Trump—a native New Yorker who, as a real estate developer, has been both a model of machismo and a strong supporter and benefi-ciary of such policies.

The Growth of the Police State under the Trump Presidency

As I have shown, the movement toward the nationalization of the police as a racially and economically repressive force in the United States began in the late 1960s as part of the white backlash against the suc-cesses of the civil rights movement. It was further fueled by the growth and spread of neoliberalism from the 1970s to the present. And as I have also mentioned, it has more recently been given another major boost by the election of a president who has expressed not only strong racial animus and support for hypercapitalism, but also inclinations toward authoritarian rule. These are, of course, all key ingredients for the emergence of a large, federal government-backed police presence in the United States, in its racially oppressive racial state mode; something that could ultimately develop into a police state. It is, of course, also an arrangement under which, if left unchallenged, police and vigilante killings of Africans Americans and low-income European Americans could be expected to flourish.

As mentioned earlier, in the 2016 campaign there was a near consen-sus among both Democratic and Republican presidential candidates that criminal justice reform was needed for a variety of reasons, including the devastating social consequences of mass incarceration, out-of-control spending on prisons and policing, and the increased racial tensions accruing from the police and vigilante killings of African Americans. The notable exception to this was Donald Trump, who—in contrast to Hillary Clinton, his Democratic Party opponent, who promised signif-icant and progressive criminal justice reform and campaigned with the support of African American mothers whose children were killed by the police—successfully ran on a highly racialized "law and order" platform, similar to that of Richard Nixon. Trump's call for a return to law and order was backed by assertions about what he characterized as a "war on our police," such as "the police are the most mistreated people in America" and "we need to give power back to the police." His campaign, which was strongly supported by police unions, also included accusations by Trump that the Black Lives Matter movement helped to instigate the killings of police officers, such as his assertion that the movement was a "threat" that was "essentially calling [for] death to the police." Trump also promised to target inner-city neighborhoods with more police and more stop-and-frisk actions, and said the federal government would make more military equipment available to local police departments. And those were not just empty campaign promises. After his election, President Trump made it clear through his appointments, statements, and policy proposals that he fully intended to move the nation in the exact opposite direction of progressive criminal justice reform.[44]

Such actions had many African Americans worried that during a Trump presidency, not only would their efforts at progressive police reform be stopped, but there would also be more police and vigilante repression of and violence against them. This sentiment was evident when—as the election returns came in and it became clear that Donald Trump would be elected president—Gwen Carr, the mother of Eric Garner, the father of six who was killed by the NYPD after a video showed him repeatedly shouting "I can't breathe," held hands and cried with other "Mothers of the Movement" who had placed their hopes for more police accountability in a Hillary Clinton presidency. In giving her take on what was to follow, Brittany Packnett, a member of President Obama's task force on policing, warned: "Donald Trump has proposed nothing short of a police state." She added that "this is backlash to a black president, a black movement and black people being self-determined, bold and unapologetic." And in expressing the need for opposition to Trump's proposals, Charlene Carruthers, the national director of the Black Youth Project 100, said: "We are now facing a presidential administration that not only does not value black people's lives, but will promote and support policies that will actively make our lives worse and kill more people."[45]

The police unions who supported Trump had a very different reaction, including the nation's largest police union, the Fraternal Order of Police (FOP), which has more than 330,000 members. They expected to get what they wanted from Trump. On the FOP's "first hundred days" wish list of Trump administration priorities was tossing out many of the reforms proposed by the Obama administration's President's Task Force on 21st Century Policing, such as encouraging the use of body cameras and the establishment of a national database on police use of force. It also called for a return to the use of racial profiling, banned in 2003 by the Bush II administration, and cutting off federal aid to "sanctuary cities" that have instituted policies deemed to be supportive of illegal immigrants. It should be noted that neither the FOP's endorsement of Trump nor its own regressive set of policy proposals represent the views of all police officers, or even all of its members. Today there is, as in the rest of the nation, a huge racial divide separating police officers who support and those who oppose progressive police reform. Many African American, Latino/a American, Muslim American, and progressive European American police officers strongly objected to the FOP's endorsement of Trump and to the policy proposals of Trump and their union. For example, Blacks in Law Enforcement of America publicly opposed FOP's endorsement of Trump, with Damon Jones, the organization's New York representative, calling it a "slap in the face of both black cops and the black community," while Lynn Hampton, president of the Black Shield union in Cleveland, warned that the FOP's endorsement of Trump, by "giving police more authority to operate on their biases," would "further polarize us and the community and cause more problems."[46]

In the *Wall Street Journal*, one of the nation's most influential voices for unbridled capitalism, Trump's victory was embraced in a commentary headlined "Trump Can End the War on Cops." The author did not take long to make it clear that she saw that "war" as nothing more than the whining and incompetence of people of color by beginning with the admonition: "stop treating police as racist and pushing lower hiring standards as a way to achieve 'diversity.'" In support of her anti-reform position she cited what she touted as the "successes" of the neoliberal policing policies initiated by Mayor Giuliani in New York City. Clearly, with the election of Donald Trump the nation's economic elite, who typically are in strong opposition to unions, have bridged their class differences by finding common ground with unionized police officers in the form of a common enemy: African American, and other, advocates of police reform. Time will tell if Trump-supporting police officers and neoliberal elites are able to work as well together today as plantation owners and their slave patrollers did under slavery.[47]

More Police Killings and Less Concern

In an article written just weeks after Donald Trump's inauguration, a *New York Daily News* columnist revealed two ominous trends in the police killings of African Americans since the country entered the Trump era of race relations: although the killings had not only continued but in fact increased since Trump was elected in early November of 2016, they had become nearly invisible. Shaun King reported that while January 2017 was the deadliest month for police killings since 2015, with at least 105 people killed by the police that month, there had been a profound shift in interest in the issue that had "gripped our nation, catalyzed a movement, and got the attention of the world for two straight years." In explaining that shift, King observed that

> the extended election cycle, from the primaries to the general, sucked the wind out of almost every important issue being discussed and debated across the country. Instead, like clockwork, our nation primarily obsessed over Donald Trump's latest tweets, the wide variety of white supremacists and neo-Nazis who professed their undying love for him, and the latest twist and turns into the investigation of Hillary Clinton's emails.

Since that time, the nation and the world have been riveted by various investigations into Russian connections to the Trump campaign and by his often bizarre words and actions, to the extent that it is difficult for any other news story to break through. I believe another reason that there has been relatively little national media coverage of police killings as of late is that the media and the nation have suffered a type of issue fatigue, which has been exacerbated by resignation that, under the extremely pro-police and law-and-order focused Trump administration, there can and will be no significant reform of the criminal justice system and its treatment of African Americans.[48]

An article written about six weeks after King's column documents seven incidents in which African Americans, specifically, were killed by the police during just the eight weeks of January 23 through March 19, 2017. One of them involved the fatal shooting of twenty-five-year-old Armond Brown in Kenner, Louisiana on January 23. Witnesses indicated that Brown, who had a history of mental illness, was armed with butter knives, was at least fifteen feet from the officer, and was separated by a brick wall, an iron gate, a mattress, and a parked car. Brown's father said the police promised him they would not use lethal force. Another incident occurred on February 8 when Chad Robertson, also aged twenty-five, was fatally shot as he ran away from the police in Chicago's Union Station with a small quantity of marijuana in his pocket. And there was the case of Alteria Woods, who was twenty-one years old and pregnant when she was killed as collateral damage in Gifford, Florida on March 19 by a SWAT team when her boyfriend, who used her as a human shield, fired at the police through a window."[49]

The Case of Jordan Edwards

A police killing that did manage to attract national attention by a media mesmerized by the strange antics of the new president was that of fifteen-year-old Jordan Edwards in late April 2017, in Balch Springs, a suburb of Dallas, Texas. Interest in that case was likely due to the young age of the boy killed, his popularity and reputation as a student and athlete, and the fact that, once again, a video recording revealed a huge discrepancy between what the police initially reported and what actually happened. Jordan, a freshman in high school, was shot in the head when police officer Roy Oliver fired multiple times with a rifle at the car Jordan and other teenagers were in, as they were leaving a party. The police chief, who initially reported that the officer was investigating a report of underage drinking and heard gun shots when the car reversed "aggressively towards the officer," recanted that statement and

fired Officer Oliver after a video camera showed that, in fact, the automobile had been moving away from him. There was no alcohol found in
the car or other evidence the young men had been drinking. Officer Oliver, who had previously been suspended and ordered to undergo anger
management training, was charged with murder. Even with those facts,
the Edwards killing did not receive nearly as much attention as previous outrageous killings. Moreover, it came at a time when the Trump
administration was intensifying its law and order policies. While federal prosecutors accepted the guilty plea of the police officer who killed
Walter Scott in North Charleston, South Carolina, the Justice Department declined to bring charges against the two police officers who fatally
shot Alton Sterling, in Baton Rouge, Louisiana. Not long afterwards,
Mayor Rahm Emanuel of Chicago used the Trump administration's
hostility to the use of consent decrees to reform police departments to
back away from the city's previous agreement with the Obama administration to have a federal judge oversee reforms to the city's police department. The local chapter of the Black Lives Matter Global Network and
five other community groups filed a federal lawsuit against the Emanuel
administration to force it to abide by the oversight agreement it made
with the Obama administration.[50]

A Warning to the Emerging "White Underclass": They Are Coming for You Next

In this chapter, I have added an important economic lens to my analysis
of the police and vigilante killings of African Americans. Examining
such fatal violence through that class lens is not only important analytically, but also provides both a warning of things to come and an
opportunity to build a broad class-based interracial coalition to fight
it. The urgency of organizing such a coalition is evident in the famous
quotation by the German minister and theologian Martin Niemoller,
who, after he found himself imprisoned in a Nazi concentration camp,
lamented the fact that he and so many others had done nothing as the
fascists came to take away members of various persecuted groups, only
to find that "then they came for me—and there was no one left to speak
for me." That same sentiment was echoed by the mother of Philando

Castile on June 16, 2017, who after hearing that the police officer who killed her son had been found not guilty, angrily cried out to a group of about two thousand protesters: "when they get done with us they coming for you."[51]

Where Does It Go from Here?

This chapter's analysis of the toxic mix of neoliberalism and Trumpism and its social consequences suggests that, consistent with the metaphor of African Americans as the canary in the mineshaft, the new victims of police and vigilante shootings may well be what both conservatives and liberals alike portray, in publications such as Charles Murray's *Coming Apart: The State of White America, 1960–2010* and Robert D. Putnam's *Our Kids: The American Dream in Crisis*—as an emerging hopeless and dangerous white underclass. Many African Americans are well aware that the same story of a pathological and hopelessly immobile underclass was applied to the "black underclass" as part of the ideological state apparatus used to justify the shifting of the U.S. federal racial state away from policies and programs to help inner cities and toward greater reliance on its repressive state apparatus of more oppressive police policies of mass incarceration, intimidation, and containment.[52]

The sentiments of some conservatives, who are not courting their votes, about such communities and the people who inhabit them was made clear in an article on "the white working class's dysfunction" published in the *National Review* by Keven D. Williamson:

> The truth about these dysfunctional, downscale communities is that they deserve to die. Economically, they are negative assets. Morally, they are indefensible. Forget all your cheap theatrical Bruce Springsteen crap. Forget your sanctimony about struggling Rust Belt factory towns and your conspiracy theories about the wily Orientals stealing our jobs ... The white American underclass is in thrall to a vicious, selfish culture whose main products are misery and used heroin needles. Donald Trump's speeches make them feel good. So, does OxyContin. What they need isn't analgesics, literal or political. They need real opportunity, which means that they need real change, which means that they need U-Haul.[53]

This emerging literature on the largely rural, so-called "white under-class," which used to be stereotyped as "poor white trash," can easily be used to justify not only political and economic policies that amount to forced relocation, but also harsh policing and other social policies targeted at this group as economic inequality increases and low-income European Americans, like their African American counterparts, are increasingly considered economically useless and socially dangerous. As you have seen, such criminalization can have deadly consequences by effectively justifying police and vigilante killings.

That does not mean, however, that the hardships experienced by many European Americans in economically abandoned areas are not real. Their secure economic lives and racial privileges are collapsing under the weight of the changing economy, the disappearance of well-paid jobs, and ever harsher neoliberal policies. Today, even lower-paid service jobs tend to be concentrated in urban areas, where people of color are most likely to reside. Consequently, since the recession of 2008, which has had devastating consequences for both groups, much of the new growth in jobs has benefited people of color rather than European Americans. The income and status lost has been particularly devastating for European American men in places such as the nation's rust belt, which have lost manufacturing jobs that pay well and do not require high levels of edu-cation. Those largely European American areas of "economic despair" such as the Midwest (where there has been manufacturing job loss over the past few decades), Appalachia, and rural New England, which have experienced little recent job growth and have endured a rise in vari-ous social pathologies such as drug addiction, alcoholism, and suicide, proved to be places whose residents voted overwhelmingly for Trump. Ironically, among European Americans at least, those Trump supporters may be the most likely to be caught in the crosshairs of cuts in social programs and health care, as well as increased police repression.[54]

It is important for me to note here that economically marginalized European and African Americans are not in a win/lose contest in which, under political and economic neoliberalism, one group gains as the other loses. In fact, it is more like a lose/lose game in which both groups, which are kept racially divided by highly racialized right-wing ideology and politics, are hurt sometimes in similar ways, and at other times in ways that may be unique to their own peculiar social, historical, and geographical circumstances.

What makes rural European Americans so susceptible to social pathologies such as alcoholism, drug addiction, and suicide, and such a potential threat to neoliberalism, is the fact that their economic marginalization is relatively new. Compared to many African Americans in inner cities, who are actually worse off economically due to unemployment or low-paying jobs, much of the depression, anger, and frustration-related social pathology of rural European Americans, especially men, has to do with the loss of the social and economic status and racial privilege they once enjoyed. In stark contrast, many inner-city African Americans have endured social and economic marginalization for so long that they have known nothing else and are therefore less likely to become depressed, frustrated, and angry due to their actual life circumstances not meeting their expectations. The irony of this fact is captured by a gallows humor-type joke among African Americans that begins with the question: given our social condition, "why is the suicide rate of African Americans so low?" The answer is another question. "How do you commit suicide by jumping out of a basement window?"

Because of their racial designation as "white" and its accompanying sense of entitlement, their insistence on being armed and boldly expressing other constitutional rights, and the possibility that they may align themselves politically with low-income people of color, economically marginalized European Americans could be seen by neoliberal economic and political elites as being especially dangerous. This is how Chris Hayes put it in his book *A Colony in a Nation*, using the metaphor of African Americans being treated as if they were an occupied colony within the nation with a completely different set of rights than European American citizens:

> Maintaining the division between the Colony and the Nation is treacherous precisely because the constant threat that the tools honed in the Colony will be wielded in the Nation; that tyranny and violence tolerated at the periphery will ultimately infiltrate the core. American police shoot an alarmingly high and

disproportionate number of black people. But they also shoot a shockingly large number of white people.[55]

Moreover, as African Americans push to make it clear to the police and government that killing African Americans will have serious social consequences, to the extent that they are not organized, economically marginalized European Americans might make easier targets.

These and other ominous trends suggest that because economically marginalized European Americans may be the next target of neoliberal and Trump-era police state repression, it may be in their best social, economic, and political interests to express solidarity with the Movement for Black Lives and its push for fundamental change, which goes way beyond the issue of police and vigilante shootings of African Americans. Again, such an interracial alliance can only work if the coalition of "white" factions that elected Donald Trump president and forged an alliance between Wall Street and white nationalism is broken and defeated.

Conclusion

As this chapter has demonstrated, to be fully understood, the police and vigilante killings of African Americans must be examined not only through the analytical lens of racial oppression, but within the context of a changing system of economic exploitation which is no longer dependent on low-skilled African American labor. Rather than being driven by *either* "race" or "class," as so many of today's social analysts simplistically mis-frame such issues, when racial and class-based oppression join forces the power of both can increase exponentially.

As you have seen, Donald Trump's white backlash-driven presidential campaign culminated in the election as president of what a preponderance of evidence suggests to be a racially bigoted, economically ruthless, unprincipled, mentally unstable, and authoritarian man. President Trump's powers are greatly amplified by the fact that he has strong support from Wall Street and business elites, leaders of other far-right nationalist nations, police unions, large numbers of angry and gun-toting right-wing extremists, and a Republican Party that controls all three branches of government. And even if the Trump presidency implodes due to a combination of his erratic behavior and the pressure of numerous investigations into Russian collusion, obstruction of justice, and corruption during and since the 2016 president campaign, his likely replacements—Vice-President Michael Pence or Speaker of the House Paul Ryan—tend to be even more conservative in their politics and policies. With these and other powerful forces aligned against them, African Americans, and poor people in general, have legitimate reason to be concerned that they may face an increase in state-sponsored or -sanctioned police and vigilante repression, as the powers of what may become a national police state increase. Moreover, when they attempt to fight against such oppression, which includes but is not limited to the police and vigilante killings of African Americans, powerful ideological state and repressive state apparatuses will be aligned against them. With few legitimate avenues of regress open to them, African Americans and other economically marginalized and oppressed people may either have to shut up and go along with the program of an unholy alliance of white nationalists and neoliberals, or place themselves at great physical risk by taking to the streets in protest.

Now that we have explored the macro-level factors behind the police and vigilante killings of African Americans, we are prepared to examine, in the next chapter, the meso- and micro- level factors that most immediately impact what happens on the ground during an actual fatal encounter between the police and vigilantes and the African Americans they kill.

Notes

1. Randolph Hohle, *Race and the Origins of American Neoliberalism* (New York: Routledge, 2015).
2. Paul Butler, *Chokehold: Policing Black Men* (New York, The New Press, 2017), 2, 14, 249.
3. Manfred B. Steger and Ravi K. Roy, *Neoliberalism: A Very Short Introduction* (New York: Oxford University Press, 2010), x.
4. Joseph Dillon Davey, *The New Social Contract: America's Journey from Welfare State to Police State* (Westport, CT: Praeger, 1995), xiv–xviii; Keeanga-Yamahtta Taylor, *From #BlackLivesMatter to Black Liberation* (Chicago, IL: Haymarket Books, 2016), 66–67.
5. Eduardo Bonilla-Silva, *Racism without Racists: Color-Blind Racism and the Persistence of Racial Inequality in America* (Lanham, MD: Rowman and Littlefield, 2014). For a critique of what I think are Bonilla-Silva's misconceptualizations of "race" and racism see

Noel A. Cazenave, *Conceptualizing Racism: Breaking the Chains of Racially Accommodative Language* (Lanham, MD: Rowman and Littlefield, 2016), 111–13, 122–26.

6. Nicholas Kristof, "Is Donald Trump a Racist?," *New York Times*, July 23, 2016, www nytimes.com/2016/07/24/opinion/sunday/is-donald-trump-a-racist.html?_r=0, Accessed December 13, 2016.

7. Kristof, "Is Donald Trump a Racist?"; Abbey White, "A Trump-Owned Casino Was Fined for Agreeing to Keep Black Employees Away from a Racist High Roller," *Paste*, March 10, 2016, https://www.pastemagazine.com/articles/2016/03/a-trump-owned-casino-was-fined-for-meeting-one-hig.html, Accessed March 7, 2017.

8. Kristof, "Is Donald Trump a Racist?"

9. Evan Osnos, "The Fearful and the Frustrated: Donald Trump's Nationalist Coalition Takes Shape—For Now," *The New Yorker*, August 31, 2015, www.newyorker.com/magazine/2015/08/31/the-fearful-and-the-frustrated, Accessed December 13, 2016; Kristof, "Is Donald Trump a Racist?" For other examples of Trump's racist words and actions see Lydia O'Connor and Daniel Marans, "Here are 15 Examples of Donald Trump Being Racist," *Huffington Post*, December 13, 2016, www.huffingtonpost.com/entry/president-donald-trump-racist-examples_us_584f2ccae4b0bd9c3dfe5566, Accessed December 14, 2016.

10. Peter Holley, "KKK's Official Newspaper Supports Donald Trump for President," *Washington Post*, November 2, 2016, www.washingtonpost.com/news/post-politics/wp/2016/11/01/the-kkks-official-newspaper-has-endorsed-donald-trump-for-president/?utm_term=.12490a0a4109, Accessed December 13, 2016.

11. Zack Beauchamp, "Donald Trump's Victory is Part of a Global White Backlash," *Vox*, November 9, 2016, www.vox.com/world/2016/11/9/13572174/president-elect-donald-trump-2016-victory-racism-xenophobia, Accessed December 14, 2016; German Lopez, "Study: Racism and Sexism Predict Support for Trump Much More than Economic Dissatisfaction," *Vox*, January 4, 2017, www.vox.com/identities/2017/1/4/14160956/trump-racism-sexism-economy-study, Accessed January 5, 2017; Thomas Wood, "Racism Motivated Trump Voters More than Authoritarianism," *Washington Post*, April 17, 2017, www.washingtonpost.com/news/monkey-cage/wp/2017/04/17/racism-motivated-trump-voters-more-than-authoritarianism-or-income-inequality/?utm_term=.0b0b-933d028e, Accessed May 16, 2017; Emma Green, "It Was Cultural Anxiety That Drove White, Working-Class Voters to Trump," *The Atlantic*, May 9, 2017, www.theatlantic.com/politics/archive/2017/05/white-working-class-trump-cultural-anxiety/525771/, Accessed May 16, 2017.

12. CNN Politics, Election 2016, Results, "Exit Polls," November 23, 2016, www.cnn.com/election/results/exit-polls, Accessed December 14, 2016.

13. Editorial, "Time to End the Electoral College," *New York Times*, December 20, 2016, A26.

14. Southern Poverty Law Center, "Ten Days After: Harassment and Intimidation in the Aftermath of the Election," November 29, 2016, www.splcenter.org/20161129/ten-days-after-harassment-and-intimidation-aftermath-election, Accessed December 15, 2016; Holly Yan, Kristina Sgueglia, and Kylie Walker, "'Make America White Again': Hate Speech and Crime Post-Election," CNN, November 29, 2016, www.cnn.com/2016/11/10/us/post-election-hate-crimes-and-fears-trnd/, Accessed on December 14, 2016.

15. O'Connor and Marans, "Here Are 15 Examples of Donald Trump Being Racist."

16. Cornel West, "Goodbye, American Neoliberalism. A New Era Is Here," *The Guardian*, November 17, 2016, www.theguardian.com/commentisfree/2016/nov/17/american-neoliberalism-cornel-west-2016-election, Accessed December 15, 2016; Wendy Brown, *Undoing the Demos: Neoliberalism's Stealth Revolution* (New York: Zone Books,

2015), 20–21; David Harvey, "Neoliberalism Is a Political Project," *Jacobin*, July 23, 2016, www.google.com/?gws_rd=ssl#q=David+Harvey%2C+%E2%80%9CNeoliberalism+Is+a+Political+Project%2C%E2%80%9D+Jacobin, Accessed December 15, 2016; Nancy Fraser, "The End of Progressive Neoliberalism," *Dissent*, January 2, 2017, www.dissent-magazine.org/online_articles/progressive-neoliberalism-reactionary-populism-nancy-fraser, Accessed January 7, 2017.

17. Hohle, *Race and the Origins of American Neoliberalism*, 1–4.

18. Michael Corcoran, "The Cabinet from Hell: Trumpism Meets Neoliberalism," *Truthout*, November 22, 2016, www.truth-out.org/news/item/38456-the-cabinet-from-hell-trumpism-meets-neoliberalism, Accessed November 23, 2016; Landon Thomas, Jr. and Alexandra Stevenson, "Trump's Economic Cabinet Picks Signal Embrace of Wall St. Elite," *New York Times*, November 30, 2016, www.nytimes.com/2016/11/30/business/dealbook/trumps-economic-cabinet-picks-signal-embrace-of-wall-st-elite.html?_r=0, Accessed December 15, 2016; David Jackson, "Trump Selects Cohn as Economic Adviser," *USA Today*, December 13, 2016, B4; Steve Peoples, Ricardo Alonso-Zaldivar, and Julie Pace, "Trump Picks from Wall Street, DC," *Hartford Courant*, November 30, 2016, A3; Peter Nicholas and Carol E. Lee, "Donald Trump Chooses Exxon Mobil CEO Rex Tillerson as Secretary of State," *Wall Street Journal*, December 13, 2016, www.wsj.com/articles/donald-trump-chooses-exxon-mobil-chief-rex-tillerson-as-secretary-of-state-1481600036, Accessed December 15, 2016.

19. Richard Quinney, *Class, State, and Crime: On the Theory and Practice of Criminal Justice* (New York: David McKay, 1977), v–vi.

20. Loic Wacquant, "The New 'Peculiar Institution': On the Prison as Surrogate Ghetto," *Theoretical Criminology*, 2000, 4 (3), 377; Loic Wacquant, *Punishing the Poor: The Neoliberal Government of Social Insecurity* (Durham, NC: Duke University Press, 2009), xi–xii.

21. Henry A. Giroux, "State Terrorism and Racist Violence in the Age of Disposability: Expanded Version," *Truthout*, July 10, 2016, www.truth-out.org/opinion/item/27832-state-terrorism-and-racist-violence-in-the-age-of-disposability-from-emmett-till-to-eric-garner, Accessed October 5, 2016.

22. Jeremy Kaplan-Lyman, "A Punitive Bind: Policing, Poverty, and Neoliberalism in New York City," *Yale Human Rights and Development Law Journal*, 2012, 15, 178–79.

23. Kaplan-Lyman. "A Punitive Bind," 192, 194, 202, 212–13.

24. Kaplan-Lyman. "A Punitive Bind," 195–97; Bruce Lambert, "Ex-Outreach Workers Say They Assaulted Homeless," *New York Times*, April 14, 1995, www.nytimes.com/1995/04/14/nyregion/ex-outreach-workers-say-they-assaulted-homeless.html?pagewanted=all, Accessed December 20, 2016.

25. Sidney M. Wilhelm, *Who Needs the Negro?* (Hampton, VA: U.B. and U.S. Books, 1993), xi–xii, xv; Samuel F. Yette, *The Choice: The Issue of Black Survival in America* (New York: Putnam's Sons, 1971), 19.

26. Manning Marable, *How Capitalism Underdeveloped Black America* (Boston, MA: South End Press, 1983), 106–7.

27. Sundiata K. Cha-Jua, "The New Nadir: The Contemporary Black Racial Formation," *The Black Scholar*, 2010, 40 (1), 38–39; Taylor, *From #BlackLivesMatter to Black Liberation*, 6, 7.

28. Cha-Jua, "The New Nadir," 38–39.

29. Taylor, *From #BlackLivesMatter to Black Liberation*, 108, 216.

30. Taylor, *From #BlackLivesMatter to Black Liberation*, 4–6.

31. Taylor, *From #BlackLivesMatter to Black Liberation*, 100–3. It should be noted that there was strong opposition to Clinton's crime bill from some of the dozen members of the Black Congressional Caucus who did not vote for it. Elizabeth Hinton, Julilly

Kohler-Hausmann, and Vesla M. Weaver, "Did Blacks Really Endorse the 1994 Crime Bill," *New York Times*, April 13, 2016, www.nytimes.com/2016/04/13/opinion/did-blacks-really-endorse-the-1994-crime-bill.html, Accessed July 12, 2017.

32. "About ALEC," American Legislative Exchange Council, no date, www.alec.org/about/, Accessed October 5, 2016; David Kidwell, "Pa. Judge Sentenced to 28 Years for Selling Black Teens to Prison," *U.S.A. Today*, August 11, 2011, usatoday30.usatoday.com/news/nation/2011-08-11-pa-courthouse-kickbacks-sentence_n.htm, Accessed October 5, 2016.

33. Evan Williams, "Death to Undesirables: Brazil's Murder Capital," *Independent*, May 14, 2009, www.independent.co.uk/news/world/americas/death-to-undesirables-brazils-murder-capital-1685214.html, Accessed October 5, 2016; Dionne Searcey and Jaime Yaya Barry, "Africans Turn a Video Lens on the Police," *New York Times*, September 17, 2016, A1, A3; Richard C. Paddock, "Philippines' Leader Says Obama 'Can Go to Hell,'" *New York Times*, October 5, 2016, A8; Joshua Berlinger and Elise Labott, "Trump Praises Duterte's Deadly Drug War in Leaked Transcript," CNN, May 24, 2017, www.cnn.com/2017/05/24/politics/donald-trump-rodrigo-duterte-phone-call-transcript/, Accessed May 26, 2017.

34. Noel A. Cazenave, *The Urban Racial State* (Lanham, MD: Rowman and Littlefield, 2011), 27, 30–31; The White House, President Donald J. Trump, "Standing Up for Our Law Enforcement Community," January 20, 2016, www.whitehouse.gov/law-enforcement-community, Accessed January 21, 2016.

35. Cazenave, *The Urban Racial State*, 24.

36. Cazenave, *The Urban Racial State*, 137–47.

37. Cazenave, *The Urban Racial State*, 26–27.

38. Cazenave, *The Urban Racial State*, 30–31.

39. Cazenave, *The Urban Racial State*, 140–42.

40. Herbert Blumer, "Race Prejudice as a Sense of Group Position," *Pacific Sociological Review*, 1958, 1 (1), 6; Cazenave, *The Urban Racial State*, 141–42.

41. Cazenave, *The Urban Racial State*, 142.

42. Cazenave, *The Urban Racial State*, 145–47.

43. Al Baker, J. David Goodman, and Benjamin Mueller, "Beyond the Chokehold: The Unexplored Path to Eric Garner's Death," *New York Times*, June 14, 2015, A26.

44. Yamiche Alcindor, "Minorities Worry What a 'Law and Order' Donald Trump Presidency Will Mean," *New York Times*, November 11, 2016, www.nytimes.com/2016/11/12/us/politics/minorities-worry-what-a-law-and-order-donald-trump-presidency-will-mean.html?_r=0, Accessed December 22, 2016; Alex Shephard, "Donald Trump Is Trying to Have it Both Ways on Police Brutality," *New Republic*, no date, newrepublic.com/minutes/134969/donald-trump-trying-ways-police-brutality, Accessed December 22, 2016; Jeremy Diamond, "Trump: Black Lives Matter Has Helped Instigate Police Killings," CNN, July 19, 2016, www.cnn.com/2016/07/18/politics/donald-trump-black-lives-matter/, Accessed December 22, 2016.

45. Alcindor, "Minorities Worry What a 'Law and Order' Donald Trump Presidency Will Mean."

46. Nathalie Baptiste, "Here's What the Biggest Police Union Wants from Trump," *Mother Jones*, December 13, 2016, www.motherjones.com/politics/2016/12/heres-what-biggest-police-union-wants-trump-his-first-100-days, Accessed December 22, 2016; Brandon Ellington Patterson, "Police Group Backs Trump, but These Cops Sure Don't," *Mother Jones*, September 22, 2016, www.motherjones.com/politics/2016/09/fraternal-order-police-trump-endorsement-minority-response, Accessed December 22, 2016; Alice Speri, "Police Unions Reject Charges of Bias, Find a Hero in Donald Trump," *The Intercept*,

October 9, 2016, theintercept.com/2016/10/09/police-unions-reject-charges-of-bias-find-a-hero-in-donald-trump/, Accessed December 22, 2016.

47 Heather Mac Donald, "Trump Can End the War on Cops," *Wall Street Journal*, December 16, 2016, www.wsj.com/articles/trump-can-end-the-war-on-cops-1481931231, Accessed December 22, 2016.

48. Shaun King, "King: Trump's 1st Month Is Deadliest Since 2015 for Cop Killings," *New York Daily News*, February 7, 2017, www.nydailynews.com/news/national/king-trump-1st-month-deadliest-2015-killings-article-1.2966610, Accessed May 16, 2017.

49. Michael Harriot, "In Case You Forgot, Cops Are Still Killing Black People," *The Root*, March 24, 2017, www.theroot.com/in-case-you-forgot-cops-are-still-killing-black-people-1793597703, Accessed May 16, 2017. The March 9th date in this story for the killing of Alteria Woods is an error. She was killed on March 19th. Meghan McRoberts, "Alteria Woods: Family of Woman Killed by Indian River County Deputies Demand More Answers at Meeting," WPTV, June 20, 2017, www.wptv.com/news/region-indian-river-county/alteria-woods-family-of-woman-killed-by-indian-river-county-deputies-demand-more-answers-at-meeting, Accessed July 25, 2017.

50. Alex Johnson, "Officer Who Killed Texas Teen Jordan Edwards Fired, Police Said," NBC News, May 3, 2017, www.nbcnews.com/news/us-news/officer-who-killed-texas-teen-jordan-edwards-fired-police-say-n754106, Accessed May 16, 2017; David A. Graham, "The Shooting of Jordan Edwards," *The Atlantic*, May 2, 2017, www.theatlantic.com/politics/archive/2017/05/the-shooting-of-jordan-edwards/525141/, Accessed May 16, 2017; Manny Fernandez and Matthew Haag, "Police Officer Who Fatally Shot 15-Year-Old Texas Boy is Charged with Murder," *New York Times*, May 5, 2017, www.nytimes.com/2017/05/05/us/roy-oliver-charged-murder-dallas-police-shooting-jordan-edwards.html?_r=0, Accessed May 16, 2017; Cleve R. Wootson, Jr., Peter Holley, Wesley Lowery, and William Wan, "Texas Police Officer Who Killed Black Teen Could Spend the Rest of His Life in Prison," *The Independent*, May 7, 2017, www.independent.co.uk/news/world/americas/texas-police-officer-killed-black-teen-spend-life-in-prison-a7722776.html, Accessed May 16, 2017; Alan Blinder, "Ex-Officer Who Shot Walter Scott Pleads Guilty in Charleston," *New York Times*, May 2, 2017, www.nytimes.com/2017/05/02/us/michael-slager-walter-scott-north-charleston-shooting.html, Accessed June 13, 2017; Matt Zapotosky and Wesley Lowery, "Justice Department Will Not Charge Baton Rouge Officers in Fatal Shooting of Alton Sterling," *Washington Post*, May 2, 2017, www.washingtonpost.com/world/national-security/justice-department-will-not-charge-baton-rouge-officers-in-fatal-shooting-of-alton-sterling/2017/05/02/ac962e66-2ea7-11e7-9534-00e4656c22aa_story.html?utm_term=.c816d98eab45, Accessed June 13, 2017; Rachel M. Cohen, "Crooked Chicago Cops May Get Off the Hook Thanks to Trump," *Vice*, June 8, 2017, www.vice.com/en_us/article/crooked-chicago-cops-may-get-off-the-hook-thanks-to-trump, Accessed June 9, 2017; Brandon Ellington Patterson, "As Feds Back Away from Police Oversight, Black Lives Matter Sues Chicago," *Mother Jones*, June 16, 2017, www.motherjones.com/crime-justice/2017/06/as-feds-back-away-from-police-oversight-black-lives-matter-sues-chicago/, Accessed June 17, 2017.

51. "Martin Niemoller," *Britannica Online Encyclopedia*, www.britannica.com/print/article/414633, Accessed December 22, 2016; Ryan W. Miller, "'Mad as Hell,' Philando Castile's Mother Reacts to Not Guilty Verdict," *USA Today*, June 16, 2017, www.usatoday.com/story/news/nation/2017/06/16/philando-castiles-mother-reacts-not-guilty-verdict/102936184/, Accessed June 17, 2017.

52. Nicholas Kristof, "The White Underclass," *New York Times*, February 8, 2012, www.nytimes.com/2012/02/09/opinion/kristof-the-decline-of-white-workers.html, Accessed December 23, 2016; Alec Macgillis and Propublica, "The Original Underclass," *The*

Atlantic, September 2016, www.theatlantic.com/magazine/archive/2016/09/the-original-underclass/492731/, Accessed December 23, 2016.

53. Kevin D. Williamson, "Chaos in the Family, Chaos in the State: The White Working Class's Dysfunction," *National Review*, March 17, 2016, www.nationalreview.com/article/432876/donald-trump-white-working-class-dysfunction-real-opportunity-needed-not-trump, Accessed December 23, 2016.

54. Binyamin Appelbaum, "The Vanishing Male Worker, Waiting it Out," *New York Times*, December 12, 2014, A1, B8; Eduardo Porter, "President-Elect Found Votes Where the Jobs Weren't," *New York Times*, December 14, 2016, B1, B 8; David Wenner, "High Drug Addiction Rates Correlate with Trump Votes: Penn State Study," *Penn Live*, December 9, 2016, www.pennlive.com/news/2016/12/high_drug_addiction_rates_corr.html, Accessed December 23, 2016.

55. Chris Hayes, *A Colony in a Nation* (New York: W.W. Norton, 2017), 39.

6

GROUND ZERO:
THE VICIOUS CYCLE OF FATAL
DOMINATIVE ENCOUNTERS

In previous chapters I examined macro-level factors such as systemic racism, politics, and economics that help to explain the pervasiveness, disproportionality, and persistence of police and vigilante killings of African Americans. The focus of this chapter is ground zero of those killings and the meso-level (i.e., group) and micro-level (i.e., interpersonal) antecedents that manifest themselves there. In addition to that emphasis on the immediate deadly encounters between the police and vigilantes and those they kill, and on their antecedents, I will also examine the aftermath of such encounters, as they impact not only future killings but also race relations in general.

By focusing on the actual fatal incidents, we can see what happens in the interactions between those who are killed and those who kill them. The widespread use of video cameras presents the view of the immediate situation most visible to the public—a perspective that is often followed by conjecture as to the attitudes, fears, and expectations that came to be embedded within a particular fatal encounter. However, when examining the interpersonal interactions immediately preceding a police or vigilante killing of an African American, it is important not to, as the proverb has it, miss the forest for the trees and lose sight of the larger social context in which it and other such killings occur. This is what *Washington Post* reporter Wesley Lowery has to say about the problem of the media's preoccupation with the victim and the police officer involved in such a killing.

> We fall into the fallacy of believing we can litigate the complicated story before us into a black-and-white binary of good guys and bad guys. There are no isolated incidents, yet the media's focus on the victim and the officer inadvertently erases the context of the nation's history as it relates to race, policing, and training for law enforcement. And by focusing on the character of the victim, we inadvertently take the focus off the powerful and instead train our eyes and judgement on the powerless.[1]

Lowery elaborates on this point with reference to the way in which the media's heavy attention to the character of Michael Brown, the teenager killed by a police officer in Ferguson, Missouri, helped to justify his killing by taking the focus off its larger social context: "The specifics of the shooting appeared to absolve the conscience of anyone who might have felt responsible for weighing whether Michael Brown's death, legally justified or not, fit a broader pattern and whether that pattern was one rooted in systemic injustice."[2]

Lowry's observation is sadly reminiscent of a tense racial encounter I had in a local gym shortly after Freddie Gray's death, which was all too representative of the tendency of many European Americans to justify such killings by engaging in yet a second sort of homicide: the destruction of the reputation of the deceased. One of the trainers, who was known as "a really nice guy," began his comments to a group of more than a half-dozen European Americans who were gathered around him by congratulating himself that he "had never seen the inside of a police car" and asserting that "the best thing that someone can do to avoid getting hurt in such a situation is not to get arrested in the first place." Engaging in a commonly used African American communication technique of speaking our truth to power known as "loud-capping," I looked at the person nearest to me and said, loud enough for the trainer and everyone else in the vicinity to hear, that in fact "the best thing that Freddie Gray could have done to avoid being killed was to have been born white."The woman to whom I had directed my remarks responded by assuring everyone, now as the conversation's voice of racial reason, that Gray was not "completely innocent"—a widely held belief later rejected by the prosecutor in that case.[3]

To overcome the type of myopic bias about which Lowery warns, it is essential to view analyses of such fatal encounters within the larger social context in which they are enveloped, one which can provide insights that go way beyond the intentions of the individual and group actors involved in particular incidents. That includes the various group-level factors both parties carry with them into that situation, which also impact how others, who were not present when the killing occurred, make sense of it.[4]

To that end, in this chapter I examine Proposition # 4 of this study: *the immediate interpersonal-level factors that are often associated with such violence include racial bias, displays of hypermasculinity, police and vigilante attitudes and culture, and the expression of negative emotions.* As Figure 6.1 illustrates, and consistent with its title and the proposition just stated, in this chapter I examine, with appropriate examples, those four sets of meso-level factors that set the micro-level stage for particular killings. Rarely, if ever, would a single factor be at play, and the factors' combined impact can be especially powerful. Next, using Lonnie Athens'

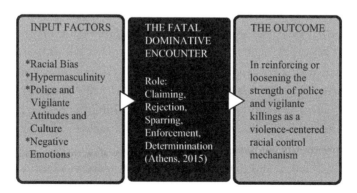

Figure 6.1 Group-Level Input Factors, the Role Stages of a Fatal Dominative Encounter, and Its Outcome in Either Reinforcing or Loosening the Strength of Police and Vigilante Killings as a Violence-Centered Racial Control Mechanism

radical interaction theory, I analyze the role-claiming, rejection, sparring, enforcement, and determination stages of the fatal dominative encounter that led to the death of Eric Garner. Finally, I examine the outcome effect of such killings in either enhancing or loosening the strength of police and vigilante killings as a violence-centered racial control mechanism.[5]

Group-Level Factors

Because the goal of this book is to examine the disproportionate police and vigilante killings of African Americans as a racial control mechanism, and because this chapter focuses on those killings at the interactional level of interpersonal relationships, I begin with a discussion of the impact of racial bias.

Racial Bias

You may recall that I take a systemic racism-theoretical approach in this study, which assumes that racism is a highly organized phenomenon that cannot be reduced to the prejudiced attitudes and behaviors of individuals. By viewing such killings from the macro level of systemic racism, we can better understand that it is not necessary for individual police officers or vigilantes to be either consciously or unconsciously biased for them to function as agents of racial control. A systemic racism perspective is especially important in understanding, as I noted earlier, the fact that African American police officers, who are more likely to work in largely African American neighborhoods, kill proportionately more African Americans than do European American police officers. Of course, the relatively small number of African American officers means that in absolute numbers, most such killings are done by European American officers. However, a systemic racism perspective does not imply that racial bias does not exist at the meso (group) and micro (individual) levels, and that it is not a motivating factor in some of those killings.[6]

There is a growing body of evidence about the implicit bias of police officers, which has reached such a wide audience of public policy makers and the general public that it was broached in a presidential campaign appearance by Hillary Clinton at an African American church in Philadelphia during the summer of 2016. Shortly after the police killings of two African American men—Alton Sterling in Baton Rouge, Louisiana and Philando Castile in a suburb of St. Paul, Minnesota—Clinton, who had previously acknowledged the problem of systemic racism and the need for criminal justice reform, stated that it was important for the nation to "acknowledge that implicit bias still exists across society and even in the best police departments." She then promised that if elected she would invest a billion dollars in research, training programs, and policies to address the problem. Let's take a closer look at the role of such group-supported racial bias in today's deadly encounters that culminate in police and vigilante killings of African Americans.[7]

As seen in previous chapters, there is nothing new about racial bias in American police departments. In his 1950 study of police violence in the police department of a small industrial city in the Midwest, William Westley found extensive evidence of group-reinforced racial bias. From interviews with and observations of those police officers he found, for example, that they tended to hold very racist attitudes toward African Americans, who were "considered inherently criminal both culturally and biologically," and that their attitudes toward African Americans generally were conflated with their negative views of slum dwellers and criminals. Despite the department having recently done a course on race relations and the fact that officers seemed uneasy about whether they could trust the interviewer, when fifty European American police officers from various ranks and positions were asked to express their views about "the Negro," 76 percent expressed "Anti-Negro" prejudice and 61 percent stated "that the Negro was somehow inherently (biologically) inferior and possessed characteristics that would lead to criminal activity." When thirty-six of the men in the department were asked why they thought the "Negro crime rate" was so high, their responses fit the following six categories, in order of frequency: "corrupted by living conditions" (39 percent); "naturally lazy and irresponsible" (25 percent); "still savages—just out of the jungle" (19 percent); "born criminals, they love crime" (8 percent); "naturally lacking in sense of morals" (6 percent); and "not fully developed mentally" (3 percent).[8]

While European American police officers' attitudes toward African Americans may not be expressed in as overtly racist a manner today as was the case in the 1950s, racial tension among police officers *within* departments is often intense, if for no other reason than the fact that there are now more police officers of color, and therefore more interracial interactions. In its survey of a random sample of police officers in 121 police jurisdictions in the United States in the late 1990s, the Police Foundation found a striking racial difference in views of whether European Americans were treated better by the police than African Americans and other people of color. While only 12 percent of European American police officers agreed or strongly agreed that "police officers often treat whites better than they treat blacks and other minorities," most (51%) of the African American officers responded that way. And while only 5 percent of the European American officers either agreed or strongly agreed that "police officers are more likely to use physical force against blacks and other minorities than against whites in similar situations," a sizeable majority (57 percent) of the African American officers did so.[9]

Much of the recent research, specifically on police shootings, has involved computerized simulations that reveal a greater tendency for police officers to shoot images of African Americans, regardless of their actual behavior. For example, E. Ashby Plant and B. Michelle Peruche found police officers were more inclined to shoot an image of an unarmed African American who was suspected of being a criminal than a European American suspect. In another study, they found that officers who saw African Americans as criminals were more inclined to shoot images of unarmed African American suspects.[10]

Unfortunately, implicit bias research is limited in what it can reveal about the total impact of racism on the disproportionate police and vigilante killings of African Americans. This is true because implicit bias accounts for only the metaphorical tip of the iceberg of such racism, in that it does not include either the explicit racial bias of police officers and vigilantes or the more macro-level systemic racism that requires neither implicit nor explicit bias on the part of individuals. Such research is also problematic in that, through its assumptions that such bias is unconscious, natural, and universal, it can remove both personal and social responsibility for racism. Within this very narrow view of racism as individual prejudice, the focus is taken off of dynamic racial structures and the functions they serve for members of the dominant racialized group and is instead placed on simple acknowledgment that the actions of individuals may be motivated by unconscious racial bias.[11]

As I noted earlier, as a phenomenon that operates at five levels of social organization, systemic racism cannot be reduced to the attitudes and behaviors of socially isolated individuals. There is of course the *individual* micro level covered by the research on implicit bias, which helps to explain why police and vigilantes seem to be especially trigger-happy when they encounter and confront African Americans whom they suspect to have engaged in criminal behavior. But then there is the *primary group* or meso level, at which individual racial attitudes and behaviors cannot be separated from those of the close-knit groups that routinely reinforce racist stereotypes and behavior. Then, as we move progressively toward the macro level, comes the *formal organizational* level, where such attitudes and behavior are encouraged by organizations such as police unions and white supremacist organizations. The disproportionate police and vigilante killings of African Americans are also encouraged and protected at the *institutional* level by, for example, laws, union contracts, pro-police district attorneys, judges, and courts. Finally, there is the *societal* level of systemic racism, which is composed of all of the interrelated institutions, organizations, culture, and ideologies that encourage police and vigilantes to target African Americans, and protect them when they do so.[12]

Of course, not all research on racial bias in police shootings is based on computer simulations and limited conceptually to implicit bias. In his study of nearly two thousand actual police shootings in the United States from 2011 to 2014, Cody Ross found that, when race-specific crime rates and other factors were controlled for, not only were unarmed African Americans three and a half times more likely to be shot by the police than European Americans, but *un*armed African Americans were as likely to be shot as *armed* European Americans. And, consistent with the racial threat hypothesis and the literature I reviewed on economic and political neoliberalism, Ross also found that "racial bias in police shootings is most common among police working in larger metropolitan counties with low median incomes and a sizable portion of black residents, especially when there is high financial inequality in that county." In another study mentioned earlier, Eric Hehman, Jessica K. Flake, and Jimmy Calanchini found that, controlling for all relevant demographic variables, police killings of African Americans are most likely to happen in those regions of the United States where European Americans are most racially prejudiced.[13]

Such racial differences in police shootings are not limited to civilians. A nationwide study focused on how racial bias impacts the phenomenon of police-on-police shootings, which typically entails the victim being an off-duty or undercover African American or Latino American. Such killings are powerful examples of the "black and blue" double bind faced by many African American police officers, who often endure both the resentment of fellow African American family members, friends, and neighbors who see the police as being racial oppressors who are licensed to kill African Americans with impunity, and the possibility that they themselves may fall victim to such violence. The study was commissioned by a governor's taskforce in New York in response to the May 2009 fatal shooting of off-duty police officer Omar J. Edwards in Harlem by a fellow, on-duty officer, who mistook Edwards for a criminal as the latter tried to make an arrest, and the killing of Christopher Ridley, also shot while he was off-duty, at the hands of three Westchester County police officers in White Plains, New York on January 2008. Through its examination of the nationwide killings of twenty-six police officers over the past thirty years by fellow officers who mistook them for criminals, it found that increasingly it was officers of color who were killed—this was the case in ten of fourteen killings since 1995. When the researchers focused specifically on off-duty police officers killed by so called "friendly fire," they found that nine of ten of those killed since 1982 were African American or Latino, with the last case of an off-duty European American police officer being mistakenly killed by on-duty officers happening that same year. Justifications for those shootings sometimes entailed little more than the victim's failure to comply with a verbal command to freeze, or to drop a weapon, associated with a "reflexive spin" or "the rapid turning of the head and body to determine the source of the verbal command."[14]

As I noted earlier in this chapter, recently both the unconscious bias and the systemic racism perspectives have received support from Democratic Party politicians, such as Hillary Clinton, seeking to win African American votes without alienating potential European American voters. Their appeal is derived in part from the fact that neither place blame on any individual or accuse any one individual of being racially bigoted. Unfortunately, there is now a backlash against the systemic racism perspective, as articulated by U.S. Attorney General Jeff Sessions at his confirmation hearings when he claimed that such a viewpoint indicts all police officers in a way that encourages not only public contempt for the police, but even their murder. At that hearing, Sessions also expressed reluctance to use the U.S. Justice Department to identify and monitor patterns of racial discrimination by local police departments, as it did in numerous cities during Obama's time in office.[15]

In this chapter, and elsewhere, I have stressed that to be fully understood, racial bigotry—conscious or not—must be placed within the larger context of systemic racism of which it is but one component. For example, as has been seen, many of the fatal encounters discussed began with the racial profiling of people who should not have been stopped in the first place. Through its investigation of high-profile killings in cases such as those of Michael Brown in Ferguson, Laquan McDonald in Chicago, Tamir Rice and others in Cleveland, and Freddie Gray in Baltimore, the U.S. Department of Justice found widespread patterns of racial profiling, harassment, and discrimination by the local police that went way beyond questions of whether those specific killings were justified or the individual officers involved were racially bigoted.[16]

In their own racial state capacities, other branches and levels of government have also issued very revealing reports. In Chicago, racism was also found to be prevalent in a report released by a task force established by the mayor in response to protests over the Laquan McDonald killing. State data revealed that the North Charleston police stopped African

Americans twice as often as they did European Americans in that city, where Walter Scott was killed after being pulled over for a broken tail light. And a state-commissioned study in Minnesota found that in the Minneapolis-St. Paul suburbs, where Philando Castile was killed during a traffic stop, African Americans were seven times more likely to be stopped than European Americans. While the focus of such investigations was on systemic racism, they also unearthed numerous examples of overt racial bias.[17]

Racial profiling and bias was certainly evident in the events that led up to the fatal shooting of Trayvon Martin by self-appointed Neighborhood Watchman George Zimmerman. The transcript of Zimmerman's conversation with a police dispatcher makes it clear that he saw much more in Martin than a teenager walking home from a local store with a can of ice tea, a bag of Skittles, and his hoodie up to protect him from the rain. As he pursued Martin, he stereotyped him as a "suspicious" criminal who "looks like he's up to no good, or he's on drugs or something," and disparaged him in group terms when he complained that "These assholes, they always get away." Similarly, the events leading up to Michael Dunn's killing of teenager Jordan Davis began when Dunn confronted Davis about playing his "thug" music too loud. Dunn crafted his failed defense around the highly racialized notion that Davis and his friends were not just teenagers playing music at too high a volume, as young people often do, but rather dangerous thugs who got what they had coming to them. Before he was killed by Officer Jeronimo Yanez during a traffic stop, Philando Castile had been stopped by the police forty-nine times over a thirteen-year period, with only six of those stops being for something the police officer could have observed prior to pulling him over. In an explanation as to why Castile was stopped that day, the police dispatcher was told that Castile looked like a robbery suspect "just because of the wide-set nose."[18]

Given the evidence just reviewed, it should not be surprising that 2014 survey results included in a presidential task force report on policing released the following year found that only 36 percent of African Americans (compared to 72 percent of European Americans) indicated they had a great deal or a fair amount of confidence that police officers in their communities treated "Blacks and Whites equally," and that the same percentage (36 percent) of African Americans (compared to 74 percent of European Americans) responded that they had a great deal or a fair amount of confidence that police officers in their communities would "not use excessive force on suspects."[19]

Hypermasculinity

Hypermasculinity entails "an exaggeration of traditionally masculine traits or behaviour" such as strength, toughness, and the ability to prevail in a physical confrontation with another male. Not surprisingly, therefore, what Jim Sidanius and Felicia Pratto refer to as "male dominance" is central to their social dominance theory of "intergroup relations." From their review of the evolutionary psychology literature, they conclude that because human males, like other primates, are predisposed to social dominance, "intergroup aggression is primarily a male enterprise." Such aggression includes defending their group boundaries and expanding the sphere of their dominance by, when necessary, the "stalking, attacking, and killing of outgroup males." This suggests that the primary responsibility for using violence to maintain the dominant racial order rests squarely on the shoulders of the "white" male. And because male behavior is not just biologically driven, an adequate explanation of male dominance must go beyond an analysis of testosterone levels to an examination of the social scripts that shape masculinity in ways that make men in different societies, and in different subgroups within the same society, more or less inclined toward social dominance-driven violence. For these reasons and more, hypermasculinity is a useful concept in analyzing male dominance behavior that includes not only violence in general but also, more specifically, homicide.[20]

Like racist ideologies and stereotypes, highly racialized masculine identities such as those which shape an individual's notion of what it means to be "a man" are not reinvented by each European American boy as he works his way into adolescence and manhood. Instead he is socialized into such heavily scripted roles by attitudes, emotions, and norms that existed within the larger society long before he was born. Moreover, because of the racially dominant role played by European

American men, notions of masculinity become especially intense when they encounter outgroup males whom they have learned to stereotype as dangerous black men. This is consistent with William Westley's finding, in his study of police violence, that the police he interviewed and observed were hypersensitive about being treated with respect and viewed African Americans as a group to which they gave, and from which they expected, little respect. Westley concludes that "the norms of the police (emphasizing secrecy, the use of violence for arrests, and the maintenance of respect for the police) represented a solution to the threats to their self-respect posed by the nature of their occupation." Such masculinity battles are also intensified by—as Michael Kimmel examines in his book *Angry White Men*—the fact that many working-class European American men, including police officers and vigilantes, are angry because they feel they are being left behind as a result of changes in the nation's racial, gender, and class structures. Many of them have also been hardened by numerous U.S. wars oversees, a War on Terror at home, their deployment as essentially occupying troops in a highly racialized domestic War on Drugs, changing racial demographics that have reduced their political clout, growing right-wing politics manifested in gun culture and, more recently, Trumpism. Finally, what I have referred to as the quest for masculine attainment is also especially difficult for men who, because they are racially oppressed, are systematically denied the resources—good jobs, respect, social status—through which men are normally able to demonstrate their manhood in socially acceptable ways. Consequently, many of those boys and men use alternative means to demonstrate their manhood, such as displaying physical toughness. Such males may be more easily provoked into hypermasculinity contests with police and vigilantes whom they perceive as trying to deny them their manhood, as is often the case when the police deploy stop-and-frisk tactics to engage in what amounts to the sexual assault and humiliation of the men and boys being frisked.[21]

When such hypermasculinity is combined with racial bias, its impact can be quite powerful. This is evident in Jessie Daniels' study of white supremacist thought, in which she makes two major points. First, white supremacists' racial, class, gender, and sexual attitudes differ from those of the general population of European Americans only in degree. Second, those four types of attitudes intersect in ways that significantly increase their potency way beyond what would be seen for any of them alone. As an example, Daniels refers to the highly gendered and racist notion of African American men as criminals:

> Whether in mainstream news reports or in white supremacist publications, Black men are represented as criminals. This construction rests fundamentally on a biological notion of Black masculinity as inherently volatile, explosive, and dangerous. In white supremacist literature, Black men are represented as a particular type of criminal: especially vicious thugs inclined toward rapacious, murderous attacks against whites.

This racist, hypermasculine stereotype of African American men helps to add a veneer of acceptability to many police and vigilante killings.[22]

In many police and vigilante killings of African American boys and men, not only is the impact of racial bias evident, but so is the role of hypermasculinity and masculinity contests. For example, as he pursued Trayvon Martin like a man hunting prey, with the backing of Florida's macho Stand Your Ground law, George Zimmerman, a Neighborhood Watch volunteer, expressed racial animus toward African American boys, whom he characterized as criminals. Zimmerman fatally shot Martin after the teenager seemed to get the better of him in the ensuing physical confrontation. Later that same year in the same state, with the same very masculine Stand Your Ground law used as defense, another seventeen-year-old African American boy, Jordan Davis, was killed by vigilante Michael Dunn, who confronted Davis and other boys he was with about playing their music too loud and later defended his action by suggesting that he was standing his ground against dangerous black thugs.[23]

The very same month Jordan Davis was killed, Cleveland police officers fatally shot an African American couple, Timothy Russell and Malissa Williams, after the couple's car backfired as it passed a patrol car and the police mistook the loud noise for gunfire. More than one hundred officers chased the couple into a school parking lot, where, after emptying two sixteen-round clips, officer Michael Brelo reloaded, jumped on the hood of the couple's car like he was the lead character in a Hollywood movie, and shot them through their car windshield. In a situation reminiscent of the killing of Amadou Diallo more than a dozen years earlier, 137 bullets were fired by thirteen officers.[24]

Two years later, Eric Garner, a large, middle-aged African American man was placed in a chokehold by a New York Police Department (NYPD) officer in a fatal contest of masculine wills as he attempted to stand his ground against what he saw as a pattern of police harassment. Pulling his hand back as the police attempted to handcuff him, Garner complained:

> Every time you see me, you want to mess with me. I'm tired of it. It stops today . . . Everyone standing here will tell you I didn't do nothing. I did not sell nothing. Because every time you see me, you want to harass me. You want to stop me (garbled) selling cigarettes. I'm minding my business, officer, I'm minding my business. Please just leave me alone. I told you the last time, please just leave me alone. Please, please don't touch me. Do not touch me.[25]

The Garner killing is but one of several by NYPD officers during the Giuliani administration that seem to have involved police with very high levels of testosterone. I have previously discussed the fatal shootings of Amadou Diallo and Patrick Dorismond, which fall into this frame, and later in this chapter, when I analyze the effect of negative emotions, I will examine another such killing; that of Anthony Baez. I have also described the macho actions of the NYPD officers involved in the non-fatal shooting of Antoine Reid and the savage sodomization of Abner Louima, and have stressed that such hypermasculinity did not just appear spontaneously on the part of individual police officers, but was instead highly institutionalized by harsh neoliberal policing policies that originated in the office of their racially abrasive and confrontational mayor.[26]

A few weeks after the killing of Eric Garner, teenager Michael Brown and a friend were confronted by a police officer for jay walking in Ferguson, Missouri, and Brown was shot from a distance of thirty feet in what many saw as an execution-style killing as he approached the officer with, as witnesses reported, his hands raised in the air. After an emotionally intense fight between the two large males, his body was left in the street for hours, as if a warning to others who might defy the authority of the Ferguson police. A couple years later, Terence Crutcher was fatally shot in Tulsa, Oklahoma by officer Betty Shelby as he walked, with his hands in the air, toward his stalled car, upon which he then placed his hands. Moments before the shooting, another officer, flying over the scene in a police helicopter, drew the following conclusion about the large African American man, whom he could see only from a considerable distance: "that looks like a bad dude." A jury found Shelby not guilty of manslaughter charges.[27]

It would be a mistake, however, to assume that the role of hypermasculinity in the police and vigilante killings of African Americans is limited to battles between African American men and boys and European American men. There are also African American and other police officers and vigilantes of color who act out hypermasculine scripts, and, as the Crutcher killing suggests, there is pressure for women who wish to be accepted in such masculine cultures to adopt such scripts as well. And while most of the African American victims of police and vigilante killings are men, women have also been killed or subjected to sexual or other forms of physical assault, as have gay, lesbian, and transgender people.

In brief, hypermasculinity also tends to be closely correlated with other forms of oppression, such as those based on gender and sexual orientation, which, when combined, may evoke negative emotions that are greatly enhanced in their impact. For example, what Philomena Essed refers to as "gendered racism" manifests itself in different ways for different groups of the disproportionately African American victims of police and vigilante killings. As noted earlier, in the fatal encounters between what are typically male European American police and vigilantes and straight African American males, it tends to take the form of highly racialized and testosterone-fueled masculinity games to establish or maintain social dominance. Another characteristic of hypermasculinity is sexism-fueled misogyny, which may be compounded into a form of triple jeopardy when the women they confront are also African American and from the working or lower classes. Such women may be seen as being both too unattractive, according to racist aesthetics of female beauty, and far too assertive, if they challenge the police or vigilantes in any way, to conform to racist and sexist notions of what it means to be feminine, and therefore valued. Moreover, men from socially dominant groups may assert their dominance by both protecting their own women and debasing women from groups they conquer, as has been done historically during times of war through rape and other forms of sexual assault. But more often, perhaps, there is simply a failure to see such women as meriting the type of "protection" associated with traditional male gender roles. This allows them to be treated both as unintended, but acceptable, causalities in group conflicts in which they were not the actual targets, and as appropriate targets for violence in situations where their behavior is deemed inappropriate. Whereas the protection of white womanhood has been a core principal of white supremacy, as Sojourner Truth made clear in 1851 in her famous "Ain't I a woman" speech, such womanhood has all too often been denied to African American women, whose lives seem simply not to matter.[28]

That lack of concern for the life of an African American woman was evident in the death of twenty-eight-year-old Sandra Bland, who was pulled over for a broken tail light by Texas state trooper Brian T. Encinia in Prairie View, Texas on July 10, 2015. Bland was arrested after refusing to put her cigarette out, and three days later was reported to have hung herself while in the county jail. Officer Encinia was later charged with perjury after a grand jury found his statement that he removed Bland from her car in order to maximize safety as he conducted a traffic investigation to be false. The grand jury drew that conclusion based on a video that captured actions by the officer that helped to escalate the situation, such as when he threatened to forcibly remove Bland from her car and to Taser her, warning "I will light you up."[29]

The same apparent lack of concern for the life of an African American woman was also evident a year later in the October 18, 2016 fatal shooting of Deborah Danner, a sixty-six-year-old woman who had suffered from mental illness for decades. Danner, who had had previous encounters with the police, was shot twice as she reportedly swung a bat at the head of a police office, Sergeant Hugh Barry, who was alone with her in her bedroom while other officers, who could have helped manage the situation, were outside of the room. In the midst of national outcries over police killings of African Americans, Barry was relieved of his gun and badge and placed on "modified duty" pending the outcome of an investigation. Both the mayor and the police commissioner criticized Barry for not following the protocol for dealing with emotionally disturbed people established more than three decades earlier after the killing of Eleanor Bumpurs, another mentally ill African American woman. Those guidelines called for efforts to de-escalate the situation until officers specialized in handling mental illness arrived, and, if necessary, for the use of a stun gun or other non-lethal force. What was especially eerie about the Danner killing were the prescient words she wrote in an essay titled "Living with Schizophrenia": "We are all aware of the all too frequent news stories about the mentally ill who come up against law enforcement instead of mental health professionals and end up dead."[30]

In an article published earlier that same year, Kate Abbey-Lambertz, a reporter for the *Huffington Post*, identified the following fifteen cases of African American women killed by the police from 2003 to 2014:

Kendra James, May 5, 2003, aged 21, Portland, Oregon
Alberta Spruill, May 16, 2003, aged 57, New York
Kathryn Johnston, November 21, 2006, aged 92, Atlanta
Tarika Wilson, January 4, 2008, aged 26, Lima, Ohio
Aiyana Stanley-Jones, May 16, 2010, aged 7, Detroit
Shereese Francis, March 15, 2012, aged 29, New York
Rekia Boyd, March 22, 2012, aged 22, Chicago
Shantel Davis, June 14, 2012, aged 23, New York
Alesia Thomas, July 22, 2012, aged 35, Los Angeles
Malissa Williams, November 29, 2012, aged 30, Cleveland
Darnisha Harris, December 2, 2012, aged 16, Breaux Bridge,
    Louisiana
Shelly Frey, December 6, 2012, aged 27, Houston
Miriam Carey, October 3, 2013, aged 34, Washington, D.C.
Yvette Smith, February 16, 2014, aged 47, Bastrop, Texas
Tanisha Anderson, November 13, 2014, aged 37, Cleveland.[31]

Like Deborah Danner and Eleanor Bumpurs, three of those women had mental health issues that impacted their thinking and actions. Four were shot while they were trying to resist arrest. One was killed engaging in reckless driving. Finally, supporting the view that to many officers the lives of low-income, African American women simply don't matter, the largest category of women killed (seven) died as what might best be described as "collateral damage," including incidents during which the police initially targeted someone else or when the women killed were passengers in an automobile into which the police fired. Most (four) of those collateral killings involved police raids, including the killing of seven-year-old Aiyana Stanley-Jones, who was shot during a no-knock police incursion as she slept on a couch with her grandmother, by Detroit police officers who said they were searching for a murder suspect who lived in the second-floor unit of their home. And there was ninety-two-year-old Kathryn Johnston, who was shot by officers who fired back at her thirty-nine times after she fired a pistol in self-defense during another "no-knock drug raid"—based on false information—of her Atlanta home. Three of the women had young children with them when they were shot. At the time of the article's publication, only seven of the killings had resulted in charges, and of those there was only one conviction.[32]

The fact that so many African American women are killed as collateral damage speaks volumes about their social invisibility; that is, many are killed simply because they don't matter. Unfortunately, the same invisibility is found when it comes to the failure to recognize that although African American males are most likely to be the victims of fatal violence by the police and vigilantes, as has just been seen, many African American women are also killed. To ensure that such women are not forgotten, when she speaks at various forums, including in her TED Talk, critical race theory scholar Kimberlé Crenshaw undertakes an exercise in which she asks audience members to stand up until they hear a name they don't recognize. She then says the names of African American men and boys who have been killed by the police or vigilantes—names such as Trayvon Martin, Eric Garner, Michael Brown, Tamir Rice, and Freddie Gray—and almost everyone remains standing.

However, this quickly changes when she calls out names such as Tanisha Anderson, Natasha McKenna, Michelle Cusseaux, Maya Hall, and Aura Rosser. That exercise has grown into the "#Say Her Name" campaign to force people to recognize the almost seventy African American women killed by the police and vigilantes—many over a period of just three years.[33]

In addition to being a driving force behind sexism, hypermasculinity also includes strong animus against lesbian, gay, bisexual, transgender, and queer (LGBTQ) people. Such hatred often manifests itself in violence, which is sometimes fatal, with many police officers not only being disinclined to show sympathy for the victims or to arrest the perpetrators, but also themselves engaging in such violence. Indeed, this nation's modern movement for gay rights had its origin in incidents like the civil unrest in 1969 after the NYPD raided The Stonewall Inn, a gay bar in New York City.[34]

The fact that LGBTQ people are still at risk of violence today even when they seek refuge in welcoming places was made evident in the summer of 2016 with the massacre of forty-nine people and the wounding of fifty-three others by a gunman at a gay nightclub in Orlando, Florida, only twenty miles from the spot where Trayvon Martin was fatally shot by George Zimmerman. The Orlando killings made clear that, despite the significant gains made in recent decades and years, it is still not safe to be a member of the LGBTQ community. As horrific as it was, that massacre represents only one, highly publicized example of the violence LGBTQ people face today in the United States. A 2014 national survey of LGBTQ people and people living with HIV found that of the 73 percent who had had encounters with the police within the preceding five years, 21 percent faced hostile attitudes and 14 percent reported encountering verbal assault by the police, 3 percent sexual harassment, and 2 percent actual physical assault. LGBTQ people of color are particular targets of police violence.[35]

Although in this study I have chosen to focus primarily on the disproportionate police and vigilante killings of African Americans as a racial control mechanism, as you have seen, there is often an intersectional overlap between racial, class-based, and gendered forms of social control

as violence that are used to protect the overlapping systems of oppression of racism, capitalism, and heteronormative masculinity and patri-
archy. Consequently, in some instances, such as when a police officer
violently attacks a low-income African American transgender person, it
would be difficult to isolate one primary source of oppression that has
more power than all three combined.

Since much of what men do in the way of learning and expressing
what they deem to be appropriate, heterosexual, masculine roles and
behavior is motivated by their desire for social acceptance by other men
whom they admire and respect, the hypermasculinity that is sometimes
fatal to African Americans of all genders and sexual orientations is
intensified by macho group membership like that of white supremacist
organizations, organized sports, the military, and of course police forces
and unions. For example, you may recall that "We own the night" was the
macho slogan of the cocky NYPD street crime unit to which the killers
of Amadou Diallo belonged, not something less intimidating like "To
protect and serve." Let's now take a closer look at the impact of police
and vigilante attitudes and culture on killings of African Americans.

Police and Vigilante Attitudes and Culture

As I have shown in this chapter's sections on racial bias and hypermasculinity, neither phenomenon occurs in a social vacuum. Both involve
socialization into norms that existed prior to the birth of the individuals
involved. Both are highly institutionalized in politics, policies, and other
social structures. And both are greatly enhanced by the membership
of individuals in groups where such attitudes are valued and rewarded.
For example, in my earlier review of literature on police and vigilante
attitudes and culture I mentioned a longitudinal study that found an
increase in the racial prejudice of European American police officers
during the study period, which began at the time they entered the academy and ended a year and a half later, when they were seasoned officers.
The same researcher found, in another study, that there was actually
a rise in anti-African American animus among European American
police officers who participated in a program designed to *increase* racial
understanding. He concluded that this white backlash was likely due

to their belief that the program was intended to benefit African Americans. Finally, I previously noted that yet another study, this time of college police officers, found that having negative racial attitudes was positively correlated with several measures of job performance and success. Clearly, the racist attitudes of police officers are fueled by their work-group culture.[36]

The militarization of the police also encourages the police and vigilantes to act as if they are an occupying force in African American communities, and that, in turn, increases both racial bias and hypermasculine aggression. That militarization has been driven by this nation's continuous involvement in foreign wars, with many police officers who are veterans of those conflicts, as well as its very macho "war" on drugs, "war" on gangs, and, most recently, "war" on terror. The extent of the militarization of the local police department in Missouri became obvious when, during the protests against the killing of Michael Brown, Ferguson and other areas' local police officers showed up with heavily armed military vehicles, camouflage gear, night goggles, and sniper rifles, made available to them by the U.S. Department of Defense. As the world watched, they trained their military-grade weapons on peaceful protestors who had their hands up, in a shocking image that resembled more an occupying army in a foreign land than the American ideal of the police at a largely peaceful protest. Lethal equipment, attitudes, and tactics are not the only things local police departments have received as a consequence of this nation's recent involvement in numerous wars. Americans have also been conditioned to accept as normal the fact that military missions entail "collateral damage"—that is, that it is to be expected and accepted that in the heat of battle, innocent people, like the women I discussed in an earlier section of this chapter, will be killed.[37]

While in his book *Rise of the Warrior Cop: The Militarization of America's Police Forces* libertarian journalist Radley Balko focuses on the militarization of the police in the United States over the past few decades, he notes that the phenomenon has a long history, extending back to the Roman Empire. In reference to the role of policing in American history, Balko notes, as other scholars have, that because the primary concern for European Americans in the agrarian South was slave revolts, "the first real organized policing systems in America arguably began in the South with *slave patrols*" whose chief functions were "to guard against rebellions and to look for escaped slaves." That fact, of course, supports my premise that from its very beginning, policing in the United States has served important racial control functions. Balko also sees race relations as the primary force behind the "dominant military culture within modern police agencies"—a trend which became particularly intense in the United States with "the social upheaval, civil unrest, and culture wars of the 1960s." Other factors he discusses are the War on Drugs of the 1970s and 1980s, the increasing use of SWAT teams, the deployment of military equipment by local police departments, "the federalization of policing in the 1990s," and the launch of the War on Terror in the early 2000s.[38]

It is not the job of troops to protect and serve their enemies in a war zone. They are there to kill. To that end they are provided everything they need, including training, equipment, and authorization to kill. And as Balko makes clear, like soldiers, today's police are also granted "greater protections from civil and criminal liability than normal citizens." They are, indeed, "a protected class" that politicians are reluctant to oppose in any way, including through the enactment of laws to make them more accountable, limit their powers, or make their actions more transparent. The power of the police was evident in Baltimore when the mayor complained that she and her city officials were unable to "fully engage" with the officers about the killing of Freddie Gray because they were protected by the state's "Law Enforcement Officers' Bill of Rights," a set of due process protections for officers under departmental investigation for misconduct. Those protections include a ten-day "cooling-off period" before an officer is required to give a statement about the incident—a provision that allows officers ample time to coordinate their accounts of what happened. Such laws exist in fourteen states and are additional to various other protections contained within union contracts.[39]

Like soldiers in tight-knit platoons, the police are, indeed, quite skilled at protecting their own; this includes shielding them from accountability for their actions. This is done through powerful police unions that deliver large amounts of money and votes to reward politicians who support them and that punish those who are depicted as being "anti-police." The police also have close relations with local district attorneys and judges, who are also usually elected officials and with whom they work on a daily basis. However, such protection is not always so obvious, or even legal. As I noted earlier, the criminal behavior of police officers is also protected by what has been called the "blue wall," "blue code," "blue shield," or "code of silence," which requires them to protect their own no matter what they do, and which resembles the norms of organized crime and less organized street gangs. As Balko puts it:

> There's a strict code of omerta that's enforced more ruthlessly and thoroughly than in any other non-criminal profession. Cops who rat out other cops tend not to remain cops for very long. Lying and exaggerating in police reports and on the witness stand isn't just common, its routine and expected. It's a part of the job.[40]

Balko's emphasis on the blue shield that protects and thereby encourages police misconduct is consistent with the findings of William Westley's study of police violence that I began discussing earlier, which entailed interviews and observations in a Midwestern police department to flesh out police attitudes, values, and norms that encourage their use of violence. Westley observed that because the police see themselves as beleaguered and besieged by a hostile public, they organize themselves into a "conflict group" bonded together with a "them-against-us" mentality—a bond that is made especially strong by external challenges such as the civil rights movement and, more recently, the Movement for Black Lives. For that reason, "the police are likely to be at the core of any 'backlash'" such as the successful "law and order" campaigns of Nixon and, later, Trump. The special bond of the police is cloaked in secrecy and confirmed in blood. As Westley puts it, "They insist that all policemen maintain strict secrecy about police affairs; act in a such a way as to maintain public respect for the police; and use whatever methods are necessary for the apprehension of the felon." When fifteen officers were asked whether they would report a fellow officer for stealing, eleven (73 percent) said no and when thirteen of those officers (two refused to answer) were asked if they would testify against a fellow officer, ten

(77 percent) said no. This is what one officer had to say in explaining why he would never testify against a fellow officer:

> You would get the name of a stool pigeon in the first place. In the second place if you did give testimony you would be putting yourself on the spot because you had to turn the man in in the first place. If you were a stool pigeon you are an outcast on the police force. Nobody wants to say anything to you. Nobody talks to you. Nobody wants to be around you and you never get to know what's going on in the department.[41]

The late-1990s Police Foundation survey of a representative sample of U.S. police officers in 121 police jurisdictions to which I referred earlier found that while officers ostensibly rejected the "code of silence" idea, 61 percent "indicated that police do not always report even serious criminal violations that involve the abuse of authority by fellow officers," 52 percent "agreed or strongly agreed that it is not unusual for police officers to 'turn a blind eye' to other officer's improper conduct," and 67 percent agreed or strongly agreed that "police officers who report incidents of misconduct are likely to be given a 'cold shoulder' by fellow officers." That survey also found that police culture was not shaped solely or even primarily by the attitudes and behavior of rank-and-file officers. The police officers surveyed indicated that it was leadership and administrative factors that kept police abuse of authority under control, with 85 percent of the officers either agreeing or strongly agreeing that "If a police chief takes a strong position against abuses of authority, he or she can make a big difference in preventing officers from abusing their authority." Further, 90 percent of the officers either agreed or strongly agreed that "Good first-line supervisors can help prevent police officers from abusing their authority." And 55 percent either agreed or strongly agreed that "Most police abuse of force could be stopped by more effective methods of supervision."[42]

Again, it is important to note that police attitudes, culture, leadership, administration, and other factors internal to police organizations are neither monolithic nor monochromatic. Instead, like the rest of American society they are highly racialized, with African Americans within policing tending to see issues of police misconduct quite differently than their European American colleagues. That huge racial divide is evident in the results of that Police Foundation survey of police officers, which found significant racial differences in the perception of police abuse of authority as a problem. As you may recall, African American police officers were much more likely to report that African Americans and other people of color were treated unfairly and suffered physical abuse by the police. They were also more likely to agree or strongly agree that the police are more likely to treat the poor unequally based on their socio-economic status.[43]

Such racial differences were also evident when it came to potential solutions for police abuse of power. African American police officers were more likely than their European American colleagues to agree or strongly agree that "Community-oriented policing ... decreases ... the number of incidents involving excessive force," with 65 percent of African Americans holding that view, compared with half (50 percent) "other minority" and about the same percentage (49 percent) of European Americans. In responding to the statement "Community-oriented policing ... decreases ... the seriousness of incidents involving excessive force," 63 percent of African Americans and 47 percent of "other minority" agreed or strongly agreed, compared to only 39 percent of European American officers. Finally, in response to the statement that "Citizen review boards are an effective means of preventing police misconduct," 70 percent of African American officers agreed or strongly agreed, compared to 41 percent "other minority" and only a third (33 percent) of European American officers. These huge racial differences on measures to reduce police abuse support this book's racial control argument, in that police who see the communities they patrol as hostile territory inhabited by dangerous black criminals are more likely to view their work as that of an occupying force. This stands in stark contrast to community-oriented policing and civilian review boards that are based on the assumption that community residents are fellow human beings and citizens who can be understood and worked with, not an alien race of beings to be patrolled and controlled.[44]

As you have seen, the blue code of police silence was evident after the killing of Laquan McDonald when numerous videos seemed to conveniently malfunction, and when a video of the incident that a judge eventually ordered released revealed a very different set of events than those described by the shooter and at least five other members of the Chicago Police Department. A video recording also proved false the account of the police officer who killed Walter Scott in North Charleston, South Carolina when it showed the officer picking up what seemed to be a Taser and dropping it near Scott's body, and exposed the falsehood of his fellow officers' claim that they had administered CPR. These examples are consistent with the findings of a team of *Washington Post* reporters that police shootings are rarely prosecuted, and when they are it is usually because there is video evidence that contradicts the accounts of the officers on the scene, or in those even rarer instances when there is conflicting testimony from other officers that does not support the claims of the shooter.[45]

Revealing insights into the power of police attitudes and culture as incubators of excessively violent police attitudes and behavior can be seen in the way officers who refuse to kill unnecessarily are treated by their superiors and colleagues. In May 2016 Officer Stephen Mader responded to a domestic disturbance call in Weirton, West Virginia from a woman who said that Ronald J. Williams was threatening to harm himself. Williams, who was apparently mentally ill, seemed to be trying to provoke the officer to ease his pain by engaging in what has come to be known as "police assisted suicide" or "suicide by cop." He pleaded with Office Mader to kill him, as he held an empty gun by his side—a gun a 911 operator had been told was not loaded. Mader concluded that the use of force was neither necessary nor appropriate. Unfortunately, another officer who arrived on the scene minutes later shot Williams in the head almost immediately. Instead of being commended for his restraint, it was Officer Mader who was fired. In a lawsuit Mader claimed he was also punished by the spread of misinformation and false allegations about his job performance.[46]

Negative Emotions

As has been seen, police and vigilante killings tend to be emotionally charged events. As I noted earlier, not only are the negative emotions driving such incidents often fueled by the racial bias, hypermasculinity, and police and vigilante attitudes and culture I have discussed, but when such killings occur they tend to reinforce those group-level factors, as well as related adverse feelings. Emotions are not only key, group-influenced components of the racial and gender attitudes that police and vigilantes bring with them to the encounters that too often prove fatal to African Americans; they also have their own direct impact on such killings. For example, in Chapter 2 I mentioned that Jonathan Turner et al placed emotional arousal at the core of their theory of racial oppression. Consistent with that view is neuroscience research based on functional magnetic resonance imaging which has found that the amygdala, the part of the brain most associated with the fear response, is activated more by images of African American, as compared to European American, faces. Such fear is, of course, rooted in and spread through widely held popular stereotypes and images of African Americans as dangerous black criminals.[47]

In line with the racial threat hypothesis discussed earlier, Turner et al argue that the greater the threat they experience, the more likely it is that people will react emotionally against members of a targeted group. And perhaps equally as important as the negative emotional arousal of the killers is their lack of emotional empathy for those they kill. For example, in a television interview after his acquittal, Darren Wilson, the police officer who shot and killed Michael Brown, showed no emotion or remorse for Brown or his family as he explained to reporters that he had no regrets about killing Brown and would do nothing differently if given the chance. All too often such emotional numbness toward African Americans who are killed is shared by members of the general dominant racial group population.[48]

The highly racialized emotions so often associated with police and vigilante killings of African Americans are, of course, inseparable from the racist culture which creates and provokes them. Racist ideologies, stereotypes, and images such as those that are embedded in the media and other cultural representations of the dangerous black criminal are easily mobilized by politicians as fuel for white racial backlashes in response to perceived threats to the established racial order. That is what happened with the strongly racialized "law and order" presidential

campaigns of the mid- and late 1960s in reaction to the successes of the
civil rights movement, and more recently with the election of Donald
Trump that followed the administrations of the United States' first African American president. Such racist culture has also been used as fuel
for the fear and hatred that motivated the passage of state-level Stand
Your Ground laws that encourage vigilante killings of African Americans while benefiting firearm manufacturers and retailers.

Theodore Kemper's power-status model of emotions suggests that we
should view many police and vigilante killings of African Americans
as fatal contests for status and respect which, if the loser had survived,
would have resulted in their experiencing the anxiety and fear that
accompanies loss of confidence. In addition to anxiety and fear, anger
at those who reject their authority and racism-driven hatred also appear
to be key emotions that can fuel the actions of police and vigilantes in
such conflict. As you have seen, fear is the reason police officers most
often give to justify such shootings. For example, in describing how he
feared for his life, the six-foot four-inch, 210-pound Darren Wilson
testified that struggling with Michael Brown, who was the same height
and weighed nearly 300 pounds, "was like a 5-year-old holding on to
Hulk Hogan"; and in reference to the foot chase after Brown turned
around and charged him, the teenager was described as being "like a
demon" who was "bulking up" as he attempted to run through Wilson's
volley of bullets.[49]

It is important to note here, however, the hazards of taking at face
value claims of "fear" as an explanation for such killings. Their actual
impact is likely to be greatly overstated, since police officers and vigilantes know they are more likely to escape prosecution and conviction
if they are able to make a convincing claim that they "feared for their
lives"—as did not only Officer Wilson, after he shot Michael Brown,
but also the NYPD officers who shot Amadou Diallo; the NYPD officer
who shot Patrick Dorismond; and vigilante George Zimmerman, who
killed Trayvon Martin, to cite just a few examples. Indeed, a Pro Publica
report on racial differences in police shootings notes that the amount
of cases of police officers citing "officer under attack" as the reason they
killed increased from a third (33 percent) of fatal shootings from 1980

to 1984, the year before the U.S. Supreme Court ruled that police could only use deadly force if the suspects were thought to pose a threat to the officer or to others, to nearly two-thirds (62 percent) from 2005 to 2009.[50]

Consistent with the sociology of emotions literature discussed earlier, anger also seems to be a potent negative emotion in police and vigilante shootings of people of color. A lethal combination of anger and hypermasculinity seemed to be at play in a number of those police and vigilante killings. In 1994 NYPD officer Frank Livoti, apparently angry that a football thrown by Anthony Baez hit his patrol car, placed Baez in a fatal chokehold that he refused to release despite Baez's father's warnings that his son was asthmatic. Just as George Zimmerman expressed his highly racialized anger that "These assholes, they always get away" before he killed Trayvon Martin, Michael Dunn expressed anger and contempt about Jordan Davis and his friends playing their "thug" music too loud before their fatal confrontation. And in Chicago, Laquan McDonald was shot by officer Jason Van Dyke after he slammed his hand against the windshield of a patrol car and punctured one of its tires with a knife. Of course, negative emotions such as anxiety, fear, anger, and hatred are not mutually exclusive, and their power is greatly enhanced when they are experienced simultaneously in very stressful, testosterone-fueled encounters.[51]

Now that we have examined the input factors of racial bias, hypermasculinity, police and vigilante attitudes and culture, and negative emotions, we are finally ready to analyze an actual fatal dominative encounter through the specific stages identified by Lonnie Athens in his radical interactionist theory of human subjugation.[52]

The Fatal Dominative Encounter

While not all the police and vigilante killings analyzed in this study entail an interpersonal struggle in which the person killed is an active participant (e.g., Amadou Diallo, Renisha McBride, Tamir Rice), there are many cases that do (e.g., Trayvon Martin, Michael Brown, Eric Garner). The basic premise of radical interactionist theory is that interpersonal violence results from "dominative encounters" over which an individual or group prevails, through the use of force, in asserting their will over another. I refer to situations in which there is such a struggle that results in the killing of at least one of the combatants as *fatal* dominative encounters. Such encounters require not only some individual or group imposing their authority over another, but also an act of rebellion during which that attempt to dominate is rejected. Lonnie Athens also stresses the fact that, because they challenge or strengthen the larger social hierarchy, the outcomes of such dominative encounters go well beyond the individuals and groups involved in that specific incident. Finally, he identifies eight stages that can be useful in analyzing the unfolding roles of key actors in dominative encounters. The first five of those role stages—what Athens refers to as the simple, as opposed to the later complex, dominative encounters—are most relevant to the subject matter of this study. In parentheses next to each, I have added my own descriptive terminology that I find useful specifically for the examination of those police and vigilante killings of African Americans that involve interpersonal struggles. They are: role claiming (the contact), role rejection (the rebellion), role sparring (the struggle), role enforcement (the use of force), and role determination (the killing). And because, as I have suggested, such encounters must be understood within their broader socio-historical context, I preface those five stages with a brief description, which I refer to as setting the stage.[53]

Because nearly all of it was captured on video recordings, and because there are also useful witness accounts, I will use the killing of Eric Garner as a case example to illustrate the unfolding of fatal dominative encounters during which African Americans are killed by the police or vigilantes. The unfolding actions and events that culminated in the death of Eric Garner were captured in a series of video-based photographs included in an investigative article published in the *New York Times* nearly a year later.[54]

Setting the Stage

The first photograph shows a picture of Garner with his hands pointed slightly downward as he seems to be trying to explain something to a police officer. The caption below it reads: "On July 17, a police lieutenant sees a group of men on a patch of sidewalk where illegal cigarettes are sold. Officers are dispatched to the scene. The officers confront Mr. Garner. Earlier that month, officers had a similar encounter with him, but backed off when he protested." As those words make clear, although this fatal dominative encounter seems to have begun with what appears to be initial contact between the key actors that day as they enter the scene in which the killing occurs, they brought a history of previous interactions with them that helped set the stage for that event and its outcome.[55]

Indeed, that caption suggests that the killing of Eric Garner was not just an unfortunate case of very personal masculine sparring gone awry. To the extent that it was driven by excessive police testosterone, the flow of that hormone was highly institutionalized—what might best be called *institutionalized hypermasculinity*. That is, such actions can best be understood as the on-the-ground articulation of the NYPD's very intense "broken windows" policy of crime reduction through the strict police enforcement of minor offenses, which was put into place in the mid-1990s under the administration of the very macho Mayor Rudolph Giuliani. As I noted earlier, such hypermasculinity was a driving force behind the cocky "We own the night" motto of the department's street crimes unit which we saw in play in the killing of Amadou Diallo. Such hyperaggressive policing feeds off the already existing macho police culture of the NYPD and pressures officers to shift their normally high level of masculine behavior into hyperdrive. Not only does it remove the discretion of individual officers who may have established some rapport with and understanding of people in the neighborhoods they patrol, but it also justifies police commanders' insistence that officers treat area residents not as people, but as a "condition" of social disorder that must be eradicated. Contributing to this dehumanization process in the killing of Eric Garner was the fact that Daniel Pantaleo, the plain-clothes officer who placed him in the fatal chokehold, was not a police officer who normally worked in that neighborhood, but was instead normally assigned to a violent crimes unit.[56]

As mentioned, the *New York Times* caption to which I referred noted, under its first photograph of the series of events that culminated in the killing of Eric Garner, that a previous encounter with the NYPD set the stage for what happened that day. Unfortunately for Garner, that earlier encounter—during which, according to witnesses, he shouted at police officers to back off and, instead of being detained, frisked, and arrested as he had been twice before in that same year, he was left alone with only a warning—may have convinced him that he had brokered an understanding with the police in which they would not continue to confront him. Also important in explaining how Garner saw himself that day was an incident that happened just prior to that fatal dominative encounter during which Garner, who sold loose cigarettes to help support his wife and their six children, had the opportunity to demonstrate his skills as a peacemaker and protector of wholesome community values. That positive view of himself was reinforced as he held two men apart and scolded them by saying "You can't keep doing this; there are kids out here." Garner, unlike the NYPD, saw himself not as a criminal to be arrested or condition to be eradicated, but as a responsible and esteemed neighborhood peacemaker: a man who had earned the right to be treated with dignity and respect.[57]

Role Claiming (The Contact)

Role claiming refers to the initial stage of a fatal dominative encounter during which one party makes clear their intention to assume the dominant position in the interaction—a role which requires that the other party willingly or unwillingly assumes the position of the subordinate. When Garner was approached by two officers that mid-July day, one of them issued the warning: "We can do this the easy way or the hard way."[58]

Role Rejection (The Rebellion)

The caption under the second photograph in the *New York Times* article shows Garner complaining to an officer that he is being harassed and asserting "It stops today," in apparent reference to previous such incidents.[59]

Role Sparring (The Struggle)

When officers tried to grab Garner's arms to handcuff him he pulled them away and told the officers: "Don't touch me please, do not touch me." It was then that officers moved in to force Garner to comply.[60]

Role Enforcement (The Use of Force)

After radioing for backup, Officer Pantalco placed one arm over Garner's shoulder and around his neck and the other under his arm and put him in a chokehold as the two men hit a plate-glass window. Other officers arrived on the scene and joined Pantaleo in pinning Garner to the ground.[61]

Role Determination (The Killing)

Two witnesses reported that the officers were instructed by a supervisor to let up on Garner. One stated that a sergeant who had arrived on the scene said "Let up, you got him already," and the other reported that a sergeant told the police officers "Let him go, let him go, he's done." An officer was reported to have looked up at that point, but not to have released his grip on Garner. After Pantaleo released Garner from his chokehold he pressed his head to the ground as other officers held Garner down to handcuff him. Garner was heard to say, eleven times, "I can't breathe." With the help of a video recording of the fatal encounter made by one of Garner's friends, the city's medical examiner concluded his death was caused by the chokehold and compression of his chest. However, Pantaleo's use of a department-outlawed chokehold—a fact not included in the initial police report of the incident; Garner's being pressed on his chest and elsewhere and held hard against the ground by numerous officers; and those officers' failure to heed the sergeant's instructions or Garner's pleas were not the only factors that led to Garner's death. When the officers called for an ambulance as Garner lay on the ground handcuffed and motionless they did so with the codeword "unknown," which indicated it was a low-priority request. In addition, when the emergency medical personnel did arrive about five minutes later, they failed to give oxygen to Garner, who had indicated he was having difficulty breathing. He only received oxygen once he was in the ambulance. The rescue effort was not only reported to be disorganized, with standard procedures not followed, but as a witness who videotaped the incident testified before a grand jury, the emergency medical personnel seemed to believe that Garner was, as she put it, "faking it." And in an interview for that same *New York Times* article, a union leader for the city's medical technicians stated: "I didn't see any real attempt initially to treat the patient." It was not until twelve minutes after they were called and Garner experienced cardiac arrest that his condition was upgraded to high priority. Less than an hour later, after he had been taken to a local hospital, Garner was declared dead.[62]

The Outcome of Police and Vigilante Killings as a Violence-Centered Racial Control Mechanism

In Chapter 2 of this book I concluded that, based on my review of more than a dozen police and vigilante killings, several conclusions could be drawn. There is a "blue code" of silence, lies, and other cover-up norms and tactics that protect police officers from prosecution in many such cases. Not only do the police tend to protect their own, no matter what they do, but they are rarely prosecuted for killing unarmed African Americans, and they are likely to be charged only when there is irrefutable video evidence combined with massive and extensive social protest. And even when the charges are severe and the evidence is strong, when the police do face criminal prosecution they are rarely convicted. As you have seen, this was the case in the killing of Eric Garner as well as in other high-profile police and vigilante killings such as those of Amadou Diallo, Timothy Thomas, Patrick Dorismond, Trayvon Martin, Tamir Rice, Michael Brown, and Freddie Gray.

Obtaining justice for African Americans has certainly been difficult in cities like Chicago, where the blue shield seems to operate quite effectively. A U.S. Department of Justice report on that city's police department, prompted by widespread protest over the discrepancy between what was revealed by the court-ordered release of the video of Laquan McDonald's killing and the reports of officers on the scene, documented "many circumstances in which officers' accounts of force incidents were later discredited, in whole or part, by video evidence." As I noted earlier, in addition to racial targeting, the most important reason for the pervasive, disproportionate, and persistent police and vigilante killings of African Americans is the fact they typically occur with impunity. That same Justice Department report—one of twenty-five investigations it carried out, under the Obama administration, into law-enforcement agencies regarding issues such as excessive force and racial bias—documents the fact that there was little accountability for police officers accused of mis-conduct. For example, of the more than thirty thousand complaints made five years prior to that investigation, "fewer than 2% were sustained, resulting in no discipline in 98% of these complaints." Such impunity, especially for killings that are very public and seem especially egregious, reinforce the stereotype that African Americans are a dangerous, crim-inal class of people, who not only can but should be killed. Each killing strengthens the cycle of violence connecting the output and input factors with actual fatal dominative encounters.[63]

This was certainly the case with the killing of Eric Garner, which, due to its video recordings, quickly spread his many "I can't breathe" pleas worldwide and sparked massive waves of protest throughout the United States. Through those rallies, protesters essentially echoed Eric Garner's words: "It stops today." Unfortunately, with the grand jury's refusal to bring charges against any of the officers involved, despite even more protests, the exact opposite message was sent: no matter how egregious their actions, when it comes to killing African Americans the police in the United States are a protected class. In this way, the fatal cycle of racial control perpetuates itself. Because the many unnecessary killings of African Americans are politically sanctioned, breaking that vicious cycle of violence will require political change—the type of change that can only come from a fundamental transformation of American race relations, and one which confirms that, indeed, "black" lives do matter as much as those of the nation's dominant racialized group.[64]

Conclusion

In this chapter I examined the disproportionate, pervasive, and per-sistent police and vigilante killings of African Americans at the inter-active (or interpersonal) level of those lethal encounters. We saw how the group-level input factors of racial bias, hypermasculinity, police and vigilante attitudes and culture, and negative emotions set the stage for such fatal dominative encounters, and how such killings are reinforced as a violence-centered mechanism of racial control when they happen with impunity, as that vicious cycle of stereotyping, killing, and the racial oppression maintained thereby intensifies as it repeats itself.

Chapter 7 concludes *Killing African Americans*. In that chapter I further explore the study's premise that the pervasive, disproportionate, and persistent police and vigilante killings of African Americans can best be understood as political violence by examining what political steps are being and should be taken to force the changes needed in race relations in the United States and elsewhere to truly make "black lives matter."

Notes

1. Wesley Lowery, *They Can't Kill Us All: Ferguson, Baltimore, and a New Era in America's Racial Justice Movement* (New York: Little Brown and Company, 2016), 36.
2. Lowery, *They Can't Kill Us All*, 37.
3. Sheryl Gay Stolberg, "Police Officers Charged in Freddie Gray's Death to Be Tried in Baltimore," *New York Times*, September 10, 2015, www.nytimes.com/2015/09/11/us/freddie-gray-trial-baltimore.html, Accessed January 13, 2017.
4. Lowery, *They Can't Kill Us All*, 37.
5. Lonnie Athens, *Domination and Subjugation in Everyday Life* (New Brunswick, NJ: Transaction Publishers, 2015), 175.
6. Paul Butler, *Chokehold: Policing Black Men* (New York: The New Press, 2017), 33–34.
7. Eugene Scott, M.J. Lee, and Dan Merica, "Clinton Says 'Implicit Bias' Still Exists in U.S.," CNN, July 8, 2016, www.cnn.com/2016/07/08/politics/hillary-clinton-joe-biden/index.html, Accessed July 26, 2017.
8. William A. Westley, *Violence and the Police: A Sociological Study of Law, Custom, and Morality* (Cambridge, MA: The MIT Press, 1970), 99–101.
9. David Weisburd, Rosann Greenspan, et al., "Police Attitudes Toward Abuse of Authority: Findings from a National Study," National Institute of Justice, Research in Brief, May 2000, 8–9, www.ncjrs.gov/pdffiles1/nij/181312.pdf, Accessed February 20, 2017.
10. E. Ashby Plant and B. Michelle Peruche, "The Consequences of Race for Police Officers' Response to Criminal Suspects," *Psychological Science*, 2005, 16 (3), 180; B. Michelle Peruche and E. Ashby Plant, "The Correlates of Law Enforcement Officers' Automatic and Controlled Race-Based Responses to Criminal Suspects," *Basic and Applied Social Psychology*, 2006, 28 (2), 193.
11. Noel A. Cazenave, *Conceptualizing Racism: Breaking the Chains of Racially Accommodative Language* (Lanham, MD: Rowman and Littlefield, 2016), 209–10.
12. Cazenave, *Conceptualizing Racism*, 172–74.
13. Cody T. Ross, "A Multi-Level Bayesian Analysis of Racial Bias in Police Shootings at the County-Level in the Unites States, 2011–2014," *Plos One*, 2015, 10 (11), 1, 6, 12; Eric Hehman, Jessica K. Flake, and Jimmy Calanchini, "Disproportionate Use of Lethal Force in Policing is Associated with Regional Racial Biases of Residents," *Social Psychological and Personality Science*, released online, 2017 (July 27), 1.
14. Al Baker, "Bias Seen in 'Police-on-Police' Shootings," *New York Times*, May 27, 2010, www.nytimes.com/2010/05/27/nyregion/27shoot.html, Accessed October 17, 2016.
15. Domenico Montanaro, "Watch Live: Jeff Sessions' Attorney General Confirmation Hearing," *NPR*, January 10, 2017, www.npr.org/2017/01/10/509039636/watch-live-jeff-sessions-attorney-general-confirmation-hearing, Accessed January 10, 2017.
16. Eric Tucker, "Officials: Justice Dept. Finds Patterns of Racial Bias in Ferguson Police, Court and Jail," *U.S. News and World Report*, March 3, 2015, www.usnews.com/news/us/articles/2015/03/03/ferguson-officials-to-meet-with-justice-department, Accessed

January 10, 2017; United States Department of Justice Civil Rights Division and United States Attorney's Office Northern District of Illinois, "Investigation of the Chicago Police Department," January 13, 2017, 1, www.justice.gov/opa/file/925846/download, Accessed January 14, 2017; Lowery, *They Can't Kill Us All*, 76–77; U.S. Department of Justice, Civil Rights Division, "Investigation of the Baltimore City Police Department," April 10, 2016, www.justice.gov/opa/file/883366/download, Accessed January 10, 2017.

17. Police Accountability Task Force, "Recommendations for Reform: Restoring Trust between the Chicago Police and the Communities They Serve," Executive Summary, April 2016, chicagopatf.org/, Accessed May 9, 2015; Lowery, *They Can't Kill Us All*, 120; Eyder Peralta and Cheryl Corley, "The Driving Life and Death of Philando Castile," NPR, Morning Edition, July 15, 2016, www.npr.org/sections/thetwo-way/2016/07/15/485835272/the-driving-life-and-death-of-philando-castile, Accessed January 11, 2017; Sharon LaFraniere and Mitch Smith, "Philando Castile Was Pulled Over 49 Times in 13 Years, Often for Minor Infractions," *New York Times*, July 16, 2016, www.nytimes.com/2016/07/17/us/before-philando-castiles-fatal-encounter-a-costly-trail-of-minor-traffic-stops.html, Accessed January 11, 2016.

18. Lowery, *They Can't Kill Us All*, 82; Lizette Alvarez, "Florida Man Is Convicted of Murdering Teenager in Dispute Over Loud Music," *New York Times*, October 1, 2014, www.nytimes.com/2014/10/02/us/verdict-reached-in-death-of-florida-youth-in-loud-music-dispute.html?_r=0, Accessed January 11, 2017; LaFraniere and Smith, "Philando Castile Was Pulled Over 49 Times in 13 Years, Often for Minor Infractions"; Peralta and Corley, "The Driving Life and Death of Philando Castile."

19. President's Task Force on 21st Century Policing, *Final Report of the President's Task Force on 21st Century Policing* (Washington, DC: Office of Community Oriented Policing Services, 2015), 13.

20. "Hypermasculine," *Collins Dictionary*, no date, www.collinsdictionary.com/dictionary/english/hypermasculine, Accessed January 11, 2017; Linnea R. Burk, Barry R. Burkhart, and Jason F. Sikorski, "Construction and Preliminary Validation of the Auburn Differential Masculinity Inventory," *Psychology of Men and Masculinity*, 2004, 5, (1), 4; Jim Sidanius and Felicia Pratto, *Social Dominance: An Intergroup Theory of Social Hierarchy and Oppression* (Cambridge: Cambridge University Press, 1999), 49, 55.

21. Westley, *Violence and the Police*, xiv–xv, 96; Michael Kimmel, *Angry White Men: American Masculinity at the End of an Era* (New York: Nation Books, 2013), xii, xiv, 16; James William Gibson, *Warrior Dreams: Violence and Manhood in Post-Vietnam America* (New York: Hill and Wang, 1994), 9, 11, 17, 33; Radley Balko, *Rise of the Warrior Cop: The Militarization of America's Police Forces* (New York: Public Affairs, 2013), xii, xvi; Noel A. Cazenave, "Black Men in America: The Quest for 'Manhood'," in Harriette McAdoo, ed., *Black Families* (Beverly Hills, CA: Sage, 1981, 1st ed.), 177–78, 181; Butler, *Chokehold*, 98–103.

22. Jessie Daniels, *White Lies: Race, Class, Gender, and Sexuality in White Supremacist Discourse* (New York: Routledge, 1997), 83.

23. Lowery, *They Can't Kill Us All*, 81–82, 175–76; Alvarez, "Florida Man Is Convicted of Murdering Teenager in Dispute over Loud Music."

24. Lowery, *They Can't Kill Us All*, 95.

25. Susanna Capelouto, "Eric Garner: The Haunting Last Words of a Dying Man," CNN, December 8, 2014, www.cnn.com/2014/12/04/us/garner-last-words/, Accessed October 26, 2016.

26. Noel A. Cazenave, *The Urban Racial State: Managing Race Relations in American Cities* (Lanham, MD: Rowman and Littlefield, 2011), 137–47.

27. Lowery states that the police investigation suggested that Brown did not have his hands up when he was shot. Lowery, *They Can't Kill Us All*, 24; Tobias Salinger, "Video

Released in Fatal Shooting of Unarmed Oklahoma Man," *New York Daily News*, September 19, 2016, www.nydailynews.com/news/crime/video-released-fatal-police-shooting-unarmed-oklahoma-man-article-1.2798435, Accessed November 3, 2016; Erik Ortiz and Phil Helsel, "Jury Acquits Tulsa Officer Betty Shelby in Shooting Death of Terence Crutcher," NBC News, May 18, 2017, www.nbcnews.com/news/us-news/jury-acquits-tulsa-officer-shooting-death-terence-crutcher-n761206?cid=par-xfinity_20170518, Accessed May 18, 2017.

28. Philomena Essed, *Understanding Everyday Racism: An Interdisciplinary Theory* (Newbury Park, CA: Sage, 1991), 31; Paul Halsall, "Modern History Sourcebook: Sojourner Truth: 'Ain't I A Woman?' December 1851," Fordham University, August 1997, sourcebooks.fordham.edu/mod/sojtruth-woman.asp, Accessed October 20, 2016.

29. David Montgomery, "Texas Trooper Who Arrested Sandra Bland is Charged with Perjury," *New York Times*, January 6, 2016, www.nytimes.com/2016/01/07/us/texas-grand-jury-sandra-bland.html?_r=0, Accessed May 1, 2017.

30. Eli Rosenberg and Ashley Southall, "DeBlasio Calls Police Shooting 'Unacceptable,'" *New York Times*, October 20, 2016, A1, A21.

31. Kate Abbey-Lambertz, "These 15 Black Women Were Killed During Police Encounters. Their Lives Matter, Too," *Huffington Post*, May 26, 2016, www.huffingtonpost.com/2015/02/13/black-womens-lives-matter-police-shootings_n_6644276.html, Accessed October 21, 2016. The dates refer to the days they actually died.

32. Abbey-Lambertz, "These 15 Black Women Were Killed During Police Encounters."

33. Homa Khaleeli, "#SayHerName: Why Kimberle Crenshaw is Fighting for Forgotten Women," *The Guardian*, May 30, 2016, www.theguardian.com/lifeandstyle/2016/may/30/sayhername-why-kimberle-crenshaw-is-fighting-for-forgotten-women, Accessed March 20, 2017.

34. Liam Stack, "A Brief History of Attacks at Gay and Lesbian Bars," *New York Times*, June 13, 2016, www.nytimes.com/2016/06/14/us/a-brief-history-of-attacks-at-gay-and-lesbian-bars.html, Accessed October 24, 2016.

35. Lizette Alvarez, Richard Perez-Pena, and Christine Hauser, "Orlando Gunman Was 'Cool and Calm' After Massacre, Police Say," *New York Times*, June 13, 2016, www.nytimes.com/2016/06/14/us/orlando-shooting.html, Accessed October 24, 2016; Dan Barry, "Realizing It's a Small, Terrifying World After All," *New York Times*, June 20, 2016, www.nytimes.com/2016/06/21/us/orlando-shooting-america.html, Accessed October 24, 2016; Christy Mallory, Amira Hasenbush, and Brad Sears, *Discrimination and Harassment by Law Enforcement Officers in the LGBT Community*, The Williams Institute, UCLA School of Law, March 2015, 1, 6–7, williamsinstitute.law.ucla.edu/wp-content/uploads/LGBT-Discrimination-and-Harassment-in-Law-Enforcement-March-2015.pdf, Accessed October 26, 2016; National Coalition of Anti-Violence Programs, "A Report from the National Coalition of Anti-Violence Programs, Lesbian, Gay, Bisexual, Transgender, Queer, and HIV Affected Hate Violence in 2014," 2015 Release Edition, 5, www.avp.org/storage/documents/2014_IPV_Report_Final_w-Bookmarks_10_28.pdf, Accessed October 25, 2016.

36. John E. Teahan, "A Longitudinal Study of Attitude Shifts among Black and White Police Officers," *Journal of Social Issues*, 1975, 31 (1), 47; John E. Teahan, "Role Playing and Group Experience to Facilitate Attitude and Value Changes among Black and White Police Officers," *Journal of Social Issues*, 1975, 31 (1), 35; Dennis W. Leltner and William E. Sedlacek, "Characteristics of Successful Campus Police Officers," *Journal of College Student Personnel*, 1976, 17 (July), 304, 307.

37. Paul D. Shinkman, "Ferguson and the Militarization of Police," *U.S. News and World Report*, August 14, 2014, www.usnews.com/news/articles/2014/08/14/ferguson-and-the-shocking-nature-of-us-police-militarization, Accessed October 31, 2016;

Mike King, "The Cancer of Police Violence," in Kevin Alexander Gray, Jeffrey St. Clair, and JoAnn Wypijewski, eds., *Killing Trayvons: An Anthology of American Violence* (Petrolia, CA: CounterPunch Books, 2014), 118.

38. Balko, *Rise of the Warrior Cop*, vii, ix, xii, xvi, 28, 52, 58, 64, 67.

39. Balko, *Rise of the Warrior Cop*, 334–35; Eli Hager, "Blue Shield: Did You Know Police Have Their Own Bill of Rights?," The Marshall Project, April 27, 2015, www.themarshallproject.org/2015/04/27/blue-shield#.P5tl3k8Oy, Accessed October 31, 2016.

40. Balko, *Rise of the Warrior Cop*, 334.

41. Westley, *Violence and the Police*, xii–xiii, 110, 113–14.

42. Weisburd et al., "Police Attitudes Toward Abuse of Authority: Findings from a National Study," 1, 3, 7.

43. James J. Fyfe, "Blind Justice: Police Shootings in Memphis," *Journal of Criminal Law and Criminology*, 1982, 73 (2), 708–9; Weisburd et al., "Police Attitudes Toward Abuse of Authority," 8–9.

44. Weisburd et al., "Police Attitudes Toward Abuse of Authority," 10.

45. Michael S. Schmidt and Matt Apuzzo, "South Carolina Officer is Charged with Murder of Walter Scott," *New York Times*, April 7, 2015, www.nytimes.com/2015/04/08/us/south-carolina-officer-is-charged-with-murder-in-black-mans-death.html?_r=0, Accessed May 10, 2016; Lowery, *They Can't Kill Us All*, 113.

46. Trymaine Lee, "West Virginia Cop Fired after Not Shooting Suicidal Man Sues City," NBC News, May 10, 2017, www.nbcnews.com/news/us-news/west-virginia-cop-fired-after-not-shooting-suicidal-man-sues-n756976, Accessed May 16, 2017; "Police Assisted Suicide Law and Legal Definition," U.S. Legal, no date, definitions.uslegal.com/p/police-assisted-suicide/, Accessed May 16, 2017.

47. Jonathan H. Turner, Royce Singleton, Jr., and David Musick, *Oppression: A Socio-History of Black-White Relations in America* (Chicago, IL: Nelson-Hall, 1984), 4; Matthew D. Lieberman, Ahmad Hariri, Johanna M. Jarcho, Naomi I. Eisenberger, and Susan Y. Bookheimer, "An fMRI Investigation of Race-Related Amygdala Activity in African-American and Caucasian-American Individuals," *Nature Neuroscience*, 2005, 8 (6), 720, www.nature.com/neuro/journal/v8/n6/abs/nn1465.html, Accessed July 12, 2017; Jaclyn Ronquillo, Thomas F. Denson, Brian Lickel, Zhong-Lin Lu, Anirvan Nandy, and Keith B. Maddox, "The Effects of Skin Tone on Race-Related Amygdala Activity: An fMRI Investigation," *Social Cognitive and Affective Neuroscience*, 2007, 2 (1), 39, www.ncbi.nlm.nih.gov/pmc/articles/PMC2555431/, Accessed July 12, 2017.

48. Turner, Singleton, Jr., and Musick, *Oppression*, 4; Matt Pearce and Maria L. La Ganga, "Officer Darren Wilson: No Regrets about Shooting, Says Brown Made Him Fear for His Life," *Hartford Courant*, A3, November 26, 2014.

49. Jonathan H. Turner and Jan E. Stets, *The Sociology of Emotions* (Cambridge: Cambridge University Press, 2005), 216; Pearce and La Ganga, "Officer Darren Wilson: No Regrets about Shooting, Says Brown Made Him Fear for His Life," A3.

50. Cazenave, *The Urban Racial State*, 142, 145; Lowery, *They Can't Kill Us All*, 82; Pearce and LaGanga, "Officer Darren Wilson: No Regrets about Shooting, Says Brown Made Him Fear for His Life," A3; Ryan Gabrielson, Ryann Grochowski Jones, and Eric Sagara, "Deadly Force, in Black and White: A ProPublica Analysis of Killings by Police Shows Outsize Risk for Young Black Males," *ProPublica*, October 10, 2014, www.propublica.org/article/deadly-force-in-black-and-white, Accessed February 1, 2017.

51. Cazenave, *The Urban Racial State*, 139; Lowery, *They Can't Kill Us All*, 82; Alvarez, "Florida Man is Convicted of Murdering Teenager in Dispute over Loud Music"; Monica Davey and Mitch Smith, "Video of Chicago Police Shooting a Teenager is Ordered

Released," *New York Times*, November 19, 2015, www.nytimes.com/2015/11/20/us/laquan-mcdonald-chicago-police-shooting.html?_r=0, Accessed January 12, 2017.

52. Athens, Domination and Subjugation in Everyday Life, 175–76.
53. Athens, Domination and Subjugation in Everyday Life, 175–76.
54. Al Baker, J. David Goodman, and Benjamin Mueller, "Beyond the Chokehold: The Unexplored Path to Eric Garner's Death," *New York Times*, AI, A26–27, June 14, 2015.
55. Baker, Goodman, and Mueller, "Beyond the Chokehold," A26.
56. Baker, Goodman, and Mueller, "Beyond the Chokehold," A1, A26.
57. Baker, Goodman, and Mueller, "Beyond the Chokehold," A1, A26.
58. Baker, Goodman, and Mueller, "Beyond the Chokehold," A26.
59. Baker, Goodman, and Mueller, "Beyond the Chokehold," A26.
60. Baker, Goodman, and Mueller, "Beyond the Chokehold," A26.
61. Baker, Goodman, and Mueller, "Beyond the Chokehold," A26–27.
62. Baker, Goodman, and Mueller, "Beyond the Chokehold," A1, A26–27.
63. United States Department of Justice Civil Rights Division and United States Attorney's Office Northern District of Illinois, Investigation of the Chicago Police Department, 6–7; Sari Horwitz, Mark Berman, and Wesley Lowery, "Sessions Orders Justice Department to Review All Police Reform Agreements," *Washington Post*, April 3, 2017, www.washingtonpost.com/world/national-security/sessions-orders-justice-department-to-review-all-police-reform-agreements/2017/04/03/ba934058-18bd-11e7-9887-1a5314b56a08_story.html?utm_term=.7a3fc18d2996, Accessed September 20, 2017.
64. Baker, Goodman, and Mueller, "Beyond the Chokehold," A27.

7

MAKING BLACK LIVES MATTER: LESSONS LEARNED AND UNFINISHED BUSINESS

A key assumption of this book is that, as *political* violence, the pervasive, disproportionate, and persistent police and vigilante killings of African Americans can only be stopped through collective *political* action.

Unfortunately, the desperation and urgency African Americans have asserted about making "black lives matter" are increasingly being tested today, now that we have entered what is for many a frightening Trump era of American politics and race relations. Today many, if not most, European Americans dismiss the arguments of the Movement for Black Lives as the mere rantings of African American malcontents, who are too quick to play the "race card" of bogus accusations. Too many European Americans cannot bear to hear the words "Black Lives Matter" without attempting to shout them down with a rebuttal of "*All* Lives Matter," "*Blue* Lives Matter," or "*White* Lives Matter."[1]

In stark contrast, and as powerful evidence of this nation's huge racial divide, that same movement is not only mainstream within the collective consciousness of most African Americans, but is a unifying force that is bridging barriers of age, class, gender, sexual orientation, and politics. Here is television actor, filmmaker, and Movement for Black Lives activist Jesse Williams in June 2016:

> We know that police somehow manage to deescalate, disarm and not kill white people everyday. So what's going to happen is we are

going to have equal rights and justice in our own country or we will restructure their function and ours.[2]

And these are the words of pop music superstar Beyoncé Knowles in July of that same year.

> We are sick and tired of the killings of young men and women in our communities. It is up to us to take a stand and demand that they "stop killing us"... We're going to stand up as a community and fight against anyone who believes that murder or any violent action by those who are sworn to protect us should consistently go unpunished.

Williams, who had recently released his "Stay Woke: The Black Lives Matter Movement" documentary, made his remarks to millions of African Americans who watched his acceptance speech after he was given the Black Entertainment Television Humanitarian Award, during which he made mention specifically of the killings of Tamir Rice, Rekia Boyd, Eric Garner, Sandra Bland, and Darrien Hunt. Knowles has supported the movement financially and embedded militant movement images in her "Lemonade" music video DVD, which presents the mothers of Trayvon Martin, Michael Brown, and Eric Garner with photographs of their sons. The words quoted above were posted on her website, and she held a moment of silence at her concert in Glasgow, Scotland to express her outrage over the killing of Alton Sterling in Baton Rouge, Louisiana and of Philando Castile in a suburb of Minneapolis, Minnesota a day later. At that concert, their names were displayed on a large video screen, along with those of others killed by the police. For Williams, Knowles, and many other African Americans, the civil rights movement is back.[3]

In keeping with this book's assumption that both the causes of and the solutions to disproportionate police and vigilante killings of African Americans are political, in this chapter I examine Proposition # 5: *Because, as actions of oppression, power and politics best explain why such killings are so pervasive and target African Americans so disproportionately, it is only by African Americans and other people of goodwill organizing in movements to change race relations and politics that they can be significantly reduced.* To that end, I begin by examining what we know about African

American insurgency both from the relevant social science literature and from history. Then I take a closer look at the origins, organization, strategies, tactics, demands, and successes of the Movement for Black Lives, as well as the challenges it faces, and its future. Next, I discuss ameliorative political remedies to the problem and what is needed for fundamental political change. Finally, I conclude the chapter, and the book, with a brief summation of the lessons learned and a statement as to where we must go from here.

Understanding African American Insurgency

Given this study's assumption that the pervasive, disproportionate, and persistent police and vigilante killings of African Americans are ultimately *political* acts that can only be stopped by *collective* action that *forces* changes in existing racial *power* relations, it makes sense to briefly review a social movement theory that views African American insurgency through a political lens.

Theoretical Insights

In his political process model of African American insurgency, sociologist Doug McAdam identifies the following four factors as the necessary and sufficient conditions for its occurrence: expanding political opportunities, indigenous organizational resources, cognitive liberation, and a favorable social control response to insurgency. In McAdam's model, cognitive liberation is further divided into its two components: (1) a collective awareness of injustice (i.e., grievances) and (2) the belief that that such grievances can be addressed through collective action. In brief, McAdam argues that there is African American insurgency when those four conditions exist, whereas when they do not, there is a relative quiescence.[4]

Not only does McAdam view the emergence, and the decline, of African can American insurgency as political processes, but he also argues that to understand the development of movements such as the modern civil rights movement, one must recognize that they do not arise spontaneously, but instead emerge slowly and cumulatively over decades. For example, the arrival of the modern civil rights movement required not only macro-level societal changes in the economy and the political systems that made racial insurgency feasible, but also: strong indigenous organizational resources, such as NAACP chapters, African American colleges, and African American churches; the belief on the part of African Americans that their cause was just and winnable; and confidence that it could survive the repressive measures its opponents would surely take to suppress it.[5]

McAdam's political process model stresses, therefore, the importance of placing the origin, evolution, and future of movements such as the Movement for Black Lives within a historical perspective that extends back long before the vigilante killing of Trayvon Martin or the extensive protests about the often fatal police violence against African Americans in New York, Los Angeles, and other American cities in the 1990s. It also suggests we can expect that movement to change as socio-historical conditions such as the economy, politics, and race relations do. For example, McAdam's theory raises questions as to the movement's sustainability during the Trump era and its contracting political opportunity structure, challenges to the belief that the problem can be addressed through collective action, and unfavorable social control response. However, as I will argue later, the real question is not *if* the movement will survive, but *how*, and *in what form*.

Movements for Black Lives

Let's take a closer look at the challenges such change presents by examining the origins and evolution of the latest manifestation of that long struggle: the Movement for Black Lives. As you will see, neither the notion that black lives matter nor the need to boldly proclaim it in one way or another began in 2013, when, in response to the killing of Trayvon Martin, three young African American women created the #BlackLivesMatter hashtag to expressed their outrage, pain, and love. Indeed, in its various manifestations, making black lives matter has been the dominant challenge and struggle throughout the history of African Americans. So, just as it is important to place the killings of African Americans in their proper socio-historical context as racial violence, as I did in Chapter 3, this section begins with an examination of the history of the African American responses to such violence.[6]

The Deep Historical Roots of the African American Struggle to Make Their Lives Matter

In his intellectual history of the Black Lives Matter idea, Christopher J. Lebron traces the roots of the current Movement for Black Lives to the words and actions of African American public intellectuals such as the abolitionist Frederick Douglass; the anti-lynching crusader Ida B. Wells-Barnett; the poet Langston Hughes; writers such as Zora Neale Hurston, James Baldwin, and Audre Lorde; and, of course, the charismatic civil rights leader Martin Luther King, Jr. And as will be seen, it was not only African American elites who gave voice to the challenge of making black lives matter in a racially oppressive society; the African American grassroots had much to say about that issue, and sometimes their own way of saying it.[7] The deep historical roots of the African American struggle against racial violence were illustrated in Chapter 3 when we examined the need for struggles against the racial control systems of slavery, peonage, and Jim Crow and their violence-centered and criminalization-justified racial control mechanisms of vigilantism and lynching, the death penalty, and mass incarceration.

African American Challenges to Racial Control Systems

Contrary to popular racist stereotypes of happy and docile slaves, the people whose offspring were to become African Americans did not just accept their bondage. Many did everything they could to resist, escape, and abolish slavery. That included various individual and organized actions intended to provide their "masters" with as little work as possible, such as breaking tools and other equipment, engaging in organized work slowdowns, making costly work-related "mistakes," overworking field animals, burning crops, mutilating their own bodies, and conspiring to get their overseers fired by making them appear incompetent. Other actions included theft, helping runaways, escaping themselves, and causing harm to plantation owners' family members. Slaves also engaged in various forms of cultural resistance through religion, songs, and folktales. Other acts of resistance included suicides, homicides, slave rebellions, participation in the abolition movement and the underground railroad, fighting on both sides during the American

Revolution and the War of 1812, and serving the North in the Civil War as laborers, spies, and troops.[8]

As has been seen, peonage flourished in largely rural areas where there was little exposure of its corruption and the illegal atrocities often committed by large business entities with national reputations to protect. Although peonage was challenged in the courts and elsewhere by African Americans throughout its history, it lingered into the 1940s and beyond, when it eventually collapsed as the modern civil rights movement began to take shape, with increasing media coverage. Like bacteria that dies when exposed to light, as the media became increasingly national and the civil rights movement intensified, there was little chance that American peonage could continue to operate unexposed.

In their fight against Jim Crow, African Americans used migration out of the South; court challenges; their growing national strength in electoral politics, civil rights, and other organizations; economic boycotts; and various social protest strategies and tactics, including civil disobedience, as well-orchestrated components of a large, highly organized, and ultimately successful civil rights movement.

African American Challenges to Violence-Centered Racial Control Mechanisms

African Americans challenged vigilantism and lynching in many ways, not the least of which was their physical movement out of those areas where they were most common. They also organized to fight them, with African American newspapers and anti-lynching journalists such as Ida B. Wells-Barnett working tirelessly to keep the issue in the national spotlight. Those anti-lynching campaigns led to the formation of a number of important civil rights organizations, including the NAACP. There were also more grassroots actions taken, such as economic boycotts against owners of businesses who were involved in lynchings, hiding fugitives from mobs, and self-defense. And, at the national level, African American leaders and organizations unsuccessfully pressured members of Congress and presidents for federal anti-lynching legislation.[9]

Because the death penalty is largely a legal issue, it is not surprising that the major African American challenges to it have been in the courts, especially before the U.S. Supreme Court. Much of that litigation work has been led by the Legal Defense Fund, an organization that began as the legal branch of the NAACP. It was the Legal Defense Fund that was the driving force behind the Furman decision, which, for a while (1967–77) at least, abolished capital punishment. Today the struggle of African Americans against the highly racialized death penalty continues. For example, its abolition is one of forty policy priorities included in a statement released in August 2016 by the Black Lives Matter Global Network and scores of other organizations of African Americans under the "Movement for Black Lives" banner.[10]

As has been seen, African Americans have not been quiet about the phenomenon of mass incarceration which has decimated their communities. Although mainstream, essentially middle-class civil rights organizations, obsessed with "the politics of respectability," were slow to address that highly stigmatized issue, community activists at the grassroots level have not been so timid. Unfortunately, in the absence of an effective national movement, such earlier efforts did not have much clout. Moreover, mass incarceration has grown to such a scale, and has become so well integrated into the racial and economic fabric of American life, that, as Michelle Alexander concludes, the notion that it "can ever be dismantled through traditional litigation and policy-reform strategies that are wholly disconnected from a major social movement seems fundamentally misguided." Fortunately, that movement's moment may have arrived, at least for African Americans, as mass incarceration is now a central concern of the Movement for Black Lives. Mass incarceration, an issue frequently mentioned at Movement for Black Lives rallies, has been addressed in the "End the War Against Black People" platform demands released by the Black Lives Matter Network and numerous other activist organizations. The Movement for Black Lives was successful in placing the issue of mass incarceration front and center of the 2016 presidential election, with most candidates, both Democrat and Republican, acknowledging the need for significant criminal justice reform. Of course, that movement faces many additional challenges since the election of Donald Trump and his administration's efforts to return to the anti-drug and other racially targeted policing policies and practices that made mass incarceration such a problem in the United States. However, efforts at reforms to address the problem of mass incarceration continue, which may also reduce the number of police and vigilante killings of African Americans.[11]

There have of course also been more direct efforts by African Americans to challenge police and vigilante violence. African American historian Manning Marable notes that police use of "excessive force and violence" was a key component of the major civil rights issue facing African Americans in the 1990s—"racism within all aspects of the U.S. criminal justice system"—and they have confronted the issue of unwarranted police and vigilante killings throughout American history. In New York, the nation's largest city, for example, African Americans have protested against police violence not only recently and in the 1990s, but in the 1960s and the 1940s as well.[12]

Meeting Violence with Violence: Race Riots and Urban Rebellions

Of course, African Americans' response to white racial violence prior to today's Movement for Black Lives was not limited to the work of their elite intellectuals and leaders and the largely non-violent movements which they and idealistic young activists have led. The African American masses have also engaged in their own struggles, and their actions have not been limited to non-violent strategies and tactics.

Confronting white race riots. Let's take a look at the African American response to another violence-centered racial control mechanism that entails group vigilantism: race riots and other anti-African American mob violence. Each of the four major phases of such violence have emerged in reaction to African Americans attempting to break free of racial controls by asserting their civil rights. First there was the period following the emancipation of African American slaves in the North after the revolutionary war, which became especially intense in the mob violence of the 1830s and 1840s that targeted African American homes and churches. Next was the period after the emancipation of African American slaves in the South after the Civil War, which included violent raids by white supremacist organizations such as the Ku Klux Klan that were established to keep newly freed slaves in line, as well as what amounted to political pogroms in which large numbers of African Americans were massacred—for example, perhaps two hundred were killed in Opelousas, Louisiana in 1868. Then there was the white racist reaction to the migration and urbanization of African Americans, which involved race riots against African Americans in northern cities such as East St. Louis in 1917 and Chicago in 1919. Finally, there was mob violence against civil rights activists in the 1950s and 1960s, such as that which targeted the activists who participated in the sit-ins and freedom rides.[13]

Unlike the civil rights movement leaders and activists who were committed to non-violence, many African Americans saw no alternative but to defend themselves and their communities by, as Malcolm X would later put it, "any means necessary." This was the case during what African American intellectual and civil rights leader James Weldon Johnson called the "Red Summer" of 1919, so named because of the blood that flowed in the streets of more than two dozen cities and towns over a six-month period. African Americans, and some of their European American attackers, were killed not only in large and medium-sized cities such as Chicago, Washington, D.C., and Knoxville, Tennessee, but also in small towns and rural areas such as Longview, Texas and Phillips County, Arkansas, where as many as 120 African Americans were massacred as they tried to organize a sharecroppers' union. Those riots climaxed two years later in Tulsa, Oklahoma, when angry European American mobs slaughtered more than 200 African Americans and destroyed a prosperous business district and a thousand homes.[14]

African American urban rebellions. In this book's first chapter I noted that the main cause of the scores of major violent civil disturbances in U.S. cities since the 1960s—including Harlem and Philadelphia in 1964, Watts in 1965, Newark and Detroit in 1967, Miami in 1980, Los Angeles in 1992, Cincinnati in 2001, Ferguson in 2014, and Baltimore in 2015—has been African Americans' unaddressed grievances about their treatment by the police.

In a study released at the peak of the violent unrest of the late 1960s, Robert Fogelson found that "with a few exceptions ... the nineteen-sixties riots were precipitated by police actions." That assertion was consistent with the findings of a study whose results were released that same year, 1968, as part of a report by the National Advisory Commission on Civil Disorders, in which African Americans ranked police misconduct as first among their various grievances. Consistent with the view that such violence results from a long-running series of grievances against the police rather than a single incident, Robert Fogelman found that while most of the precipitating incidents involved minor police actions such as traffic stops, police efforts to break up a fight, or turning off a fire hydrant, it was the police who were the main target of area residents' hostility. The police were of course prime targets not only because it was their actions that most likely sparked the disturbance, as well as due to resentment over their long history of transgressions in African American communities, but also because, during those disruptions, they were the main racial control agents whose job it was to protect the racial status quo from African American insurrection. Consequently, as Fogelman put it, "once full-scale rioting was underway the Negroes directed a great deal of violence at the police. During the day, they glared at them with loathing and contempt; and at night they threw bricks and stones and, on occasion, fired rifles at them." He also noted that African American leaders who spoke out on the issue stressed three major causes: African Americans were routinely harassed and brutalized by the police, they saw the police as being corrupt, and they felt that there was no other way to have their grievances taken seriously. Finally, in explaining why African Americans were more likely to respond violently than previous ethnic groups who had lived in such neighborhoods, Fogelman cited the growing militancy of African Americans in the 1960s and, consistent with my racial control argument, the fact that African Americans faced more and more persistent racial discrimination, were more likely to be subjected to involuntary segregation, and had heavier patrols in their neighborhoods than was the case for previous ethnic groups.[15]

Fogelson's research helps us break through some of the common misunderstandings about the goal and nature of that violent unrest. First, it was neither random nor purposeless. Rather, it was a series of articulate, selective, targeted, and restrained acts of protests against legitimate grievances such as police harassment and violence. In their study of what they refer to as "ghetto revolts," Joe R. Feagin and Harlan Hanh came to the same conclusion, which they encapsulated in their concept of the "politics of violence." That is, contrary to the usual connotation of a "riot," such violence cannot be dismissed as "random and senseless destruction"; instead, "the ghetto rioting that erupted in hundreds of cities represented a concerted attempt to achieve political objectives that had not been gained through other means." Fogelson also challenges the rigid and false dichotomy between violent and non-violent protest. He argues that the conceptualization of "a political continuum ranging from apathy, at one end, to insurrectionary activity at the other" is more analytically useful.[16]

Those and other studies of violent urban rebellions offer clues as to what we might expect if peaceful efforts at stopping the disproportionate police and vigilante killings of African Americans fail. There are, of course, other lessons of history that seem to point in the same direction. It was out of that same frustration with being harassed, brutalized, and killed with impunity by the police and other European American men with guns that, in the mid- and late 1960s, African American self-defense groups such as the Deacons for Defense, the Nation of Islam, and the Black Panther Party arose, to confront what they characterized as the white racist "pigs" they saw as terrorizing African American communities and attempting to destroy them and their movement. For some, such as the two African American military veterans who, in the wake of the Alton Sterling and Philando Castile shootings, killed five police officers in Dallas and three in Baton Rouge, Louisiana, respectively, during the summer of 2016, the only solution may come not from non-violent social protests, violent civil disturbances, or the organization of self-defense militias, but through sniper bullets.[17]

As Paul Butler concludes in his study of the police oppression of his fellow African Americans, violence and lawbreaking have had such a long and valued history as a force for change in America that serious Movement for Black Lives activists must revisit the question: "at what point is violence acceptable as a tactic for achieving racial justice?" While, for now, Butler—a Georgetown University law professor and former federal prosecutor—rejects violence for both moral and strategic reasons, he concludes that lawbreaking in the form of social protest and civil disobedience may be as appropriate today as it was at the height of the civil rights movement.[18]

The More Immediate Origins of #Black Lives Matter and the Movement for Black Lives

With the socio-historical context just provided, we are now ready to examine the more recent origins of what was originally referred to as the Black Lives Matter movement and today is known by activists as the Movement for Black Lives. A good place to begin is a brief article published in *The Feminist Wire* by Alicia Garza, one of its co-founders. Its title, "A Herstory of the #BlackLivesMatter Movement by Garza," is as revealing as the name of the online publication in which it was published. Garza notes that the use of "Black Lives Matter" as a rallying cry for the movement began with the hashtag #BlackLivesMatter, which she launched with Patrisse Cullors and Opal Tometi in response to the killing of Trayvon Martin. Elsewhere, Garza described the terror she felt and what she did in Oakland, California on the day she heard that George Zimmerman had been found not guilty of all charges related to his killing of Trayvon Martin.

> The one thing I remember from that evening, other than crying myself to sleep that night, was the way in which as a black person, I felt incredibly vulnerable, incredibly exposed and incredibly enraged. Seeing these black people leaving the bar, and it was like we couldn't look at each other. We were carrying this burden around with us every day: of racism and white supremacy. It was a verdict that said: black people are not safe in America. [19]

Later, she expressed that feeling in a "love note to black people" post to Facebook which ended with the words: "Black people. I love you. I love us. Our lives matter." After Patrisse Cullors, a close friend and fellow community organizer, read that post from some three hundred miles away, she reposted Garza's comments under the hashtag #blacklivesmatter, and the next day the two women discussed how to transform that hashtag into "a call to action" to ensure that "we are creating a world where black lives actually do matter." That campaign went viral when, along with Opal Tometi, an immigration rights activist they knew, they set up Twitter and Tumblr accounts that encouraged others to share their own #blacklivesmatter stories. The leaders of the emergent movement took another huge step forward a year later when, in response to the killing of Michael Brown, they organized a "freedom ride" to Ferguson of more than five hundred people from eighteen cities in the U.S. and Canada as part of the year-long protests and rallies that came to be known as the Ferguson movement.[20]

Today the words Black Lives Matter, and more recently the Movement for Black Lives, are general phrases for the scores of organizations and millions of people who in one way or another express concern about the police and vigilante killings of African Americans. An interesting fact about what is now known as the Movement for Black Lives is that, although most of the highly publicized police and vigilante killings of African Americans involve men and boys as victims, the three co-founders of the movement are women. In addition—and this should not be surprising, based on how some police officers treat people whose sexual orientation is anything other than heterosexual—as what Garza refers to as "queer Black women," its founders are all either members of the LGBTQ community or supportive of it.[21]

Garza defines Black Lives Matter as "an ideological and political intervention in a world where Black lives are systematically and intentionally targeted for demise" as well as "an affirmation of Black folks' contributions to this society, our humanity, and our resilience in the face of deadly oppression." Through the organizational work of Garza, Cullors, and Tometi in Ferguson arose the social movement organization now called the Black Lives Matter Global Network.[22]

The important role that both social and conventional media played in the birth and growth of the Black Lives Matter movement is evident in the fact that it began with a Twitter hashtag that carried images caught on smartphones, as well as other on-the-scene reporting and commentary, that were distributed across the internet and through extensive newspaper, magazine, radio, and television coverage. For example, at the height of the Ferguson protests in December 2014 there were more than a hundred thousand #BlackLivesMatter tweets on some days. And while in 2014, beginning August 20—eleven days after Michael Brown was killed—the *New York Times* ran eighteen news stories or other articles or segments with the words "black lives matter" in them, it published 162 such stories in 2015, and 422 in 2016.[23]

Movement Organization, Strategies, and Tactics

Organization

As noted, what is now called the Movement for Black Lives is not limited to one organization. Today it consists of not only the Black Lives Matter Global Network, comprising dozens of city and state chapters throughout the United States and elsewhere, but also many other organizations, such as the Dream Defenders organization of mostly college students, who, after the killing of Trayvon Martin, occupied the governor's office in Florida for thirty-one days, and the Chicago-based Black Youth Project 100. Aside from being a movement slogan, the phrase "black lives matter" is now used to refer specifically to one organization within the movement, the Black Lives Matter Global Network, while Movement for Black Lives is the umbrella term used to refer to the movement that emerged from a 2015 meeting in Cleveland of more than two thousand activists representing more than fifty organizations. That movement is also supported in one form or another (e.g., emotionally, ideologically, financially) by millions of African Americans and other individuals who, although not members of any of those social movement organizations, share its grievances and goals.[24]

Strategies and Tactics

In reference to the generational clashes between the established civil rights leadership and the new Movement for Black Lives activists that surfaced during the Ferguson movement, hip-hop artist Tef Poe proclaimed: "This ain't your grandparents' civil rights movement." Let's take a closer look at the roots of that generational divide by examining the similarities of and differences between those two movements. Today's Movement for Black Lives and the non-violent, direct-action

civil rights movement of the 1950s and 1960s share two important similarities. Neither was, or is, monolithic organizationally; both have been
composed of many social movement organizations that have often held
not only different but sometimes conflicting organizational goals, strategies, tactics, leadership styles, and types of members. Consequently,
both have experienced sometimes intense conflict, some of which has
manifested itself in intergenerational skirmishes.[25]

While the Movement for Black Lives and the old civil rights movement of the 1950s and 1960s also share other similarities (e.g., their
reliance largely on the strategy of non-violent direct action and the
Movement for Black Lives' use of tactics such as the busing of people
from across the United States and Canada to Ferguson, Missouri, which
seemed like a reincarnation of the freedom rides of the early 1960s), the
two movements also differ in significant ways, at least based on what
most people think of as the old civil rights movement. Key differences
include the Movement for Black Lives' rejection of all the following:
exclusive reliance on a strategy of non-violence; charismatic, top-down
(rather than grassroots) leadership; a single-issue reform strategy; and
respectability politics which prescribes that African Americans should
engage in exemplary behavior as a testimony to the fact that they have
earned equal treatment. Another important difference is a greatly
diminished role for the African American church, and its and other
largely male and heteronormative leadership.[26]

Despite these and other differences, the mostly young leaders of the
Movement for Black Lives insist that they do respect their movement
elders and have learned valuable lessons from the civil rights movement.
They are especially indebted to the guidance Ella Baker gave the young
people who started the Student Nonviolent Coordinating Committee
(SNCC). Following that advice, the leaders of the Movement for Black
Lives made sure that it was a movement controlled by young people and
not just an appendage of the old, and what many consider to be largely
discredited, civil rights leadership. They also made certain that, like the
SNCC, it is a radical movement that encompasses multiple overlapping
issues that impact the lives of African American people, and which calls
for a fundamental transformation of the entire social structure rather

than a narrower reform focus such as civil or human rights or criminal justice reform. Building on the SNCC's example, movement leader Alicia Garza states that the movement can be viewed as "a tactic to (re)build the Black liberation movement" as one that includes many issues, transcends black nationalism, and allows a central role for women and LGBTQ people. Moreover, she stresses that, because our fates are intertwined, only through the liberation of African Americans can all people be free, and those who organize under the slogan Black Lives Matter are indeed committed to the liberation of all oppressed peoples. And just as was the case during the Black Power stage of the civil rights movement, when it was a key goal of organizations such as the SNCC and Black Panthers that was not pursued by the more mainstream civil rights establishment that embraced respectability politics, a major aim of today's Movement for Black Lives is the liberation of African Americans from repression by the police, and the criminal justice system more broadly.[27]

An examination of the Movement for Black Lives' strategies and tactics makes clear the influence of the more militant and youth-centered civil rights social movement organizations such as the Student Nonviolent Coordinating Committee. However, when its leaders seek to distinguish themselves from what they consider to be mainstream civil rights leadership they stress that their movement is not the movement of the charismatic Martin Luther King, Jr. and the more traditional and reform-oriented civil rights organizations like his Southern Christian Leadership Council (SCLC) and the NAACP.[28]

In explaining how the Movement for Black Lives activists differ from the leaders of traditional civil rights organizations such as the SCLC and NAACP in their approach to organizing, Jelani Cobb states that the founders of Black Lives Matter "advocate a horizontal ethic of organizing, which favors democratic inclusion at the grassroots level." And, in reference to the then "more than thirty Black Lives Matter chapters in the United States, and one in Toronto," Cobb notes that while they all adhere to "the organization's guiding principles," "they vary in structure and emphasis, and operate with a great deal of latitude, particularly when it comes to choosing what 'actions' to stage."[29]

In one of the first books published about the movement, *From #BlackLivesMatter to Black Liberation,* Keeanga-Yamahtta Taylor notes that an important factor that led to the rise of what is now called the Movement for Black Lives was the failure of the old civil rights movement's leadership and organizations. That generational clash became evident during the Ferguson movement following the police killing of Michael Brown. The young activists in Ferguson rejected both the efforts of members of the civil rights establishment such as the Congressional Black Caucus, the NAACP, Al Sharpton, and Attorney General Eric Holder to pressure them to focus on making relatively minor reforms within the existing criminal justice system and what they saw as the paternalism involved in that. Taylor quotes a young Ferguson activist as saying that the established civil rights leadership had failed them and was no longer relevant to their lives. Another local activist even went as far as to confront civil rights icon Jesse Jackson with "When you going to stop selling us out, Jesse? We don't *want* you here in St. Louis!" And still another activist stated that "the youth leading this movement is important because it is our time. For so long the elders have told us our generation doesn't fight for anything, or that we don't care about what goes on in the world. We have proved them wrong." It was within this climate of distrust that activists turned their backs on NAACP president Cornell William Brooks as he gave a speech despite not actually having been involved in the Ferguson protests, and, as mentioned earlier, hip-hop activist Tef Poe told the audience: "This ain't your grandparents' civil rights movement."[30]

The movement's women and queer leaders have also made sure that, much more so than the traditional civil rights movement, it is intersectional in its focus. As Taylor puts it:

> Placing police brutality into a wider web of inequality has largely been missing from the more narrowly crafted agendas of the liberal establishment organizations, like Sharpton's National Action Network (NAN), which have focused more on resolving the details of particular cases than on generalizing about the systemic nature of police violence. This has meant that mainstream civil rights

organizations tend to focus on legalistic approaches to resolve police brutality, compared to activists who connect police oppression to other social crises in Black communities.[31]

In reference to what she sees as the limitations of the Movement for Black Lives' "decentralized and 'leaderless'," but presumably more democratic, approach, Taylor cautions that "at a time when many people are trying to find an entry point into anti-police activism and desire to be involved, this particular method of organizing can be difficult to penetrate." Consequently, it "can actually narrow opportunities for democratic involvement of many in favor of the tightly knit workings of those already in the know." While Taylor stresses the importance of the movement resolving this issue so that it can provide an example of how to effectively organize at many levels, some of the leaders of the Movement for Black Lives see the leadership issue differently.[32]

Consistent with their SNCC roots, today many Movement for Black Lives leaders do not see their movement as leaderless. Instead, they stress that one of its goals is to develop leadership at the grassroots level. Therefore, they characterize their leadership strategy as being leader*ful* rather than leader*less*. This is what historian, activist, and Ella Baker biographer Barbara Ransby has to say about Baker's conceptualization of what sociologist Charles Payne has dubbed "group-centered leadership":

> Rather than someone with a fancy title standing at a podium speaking for or to the people, group-centered leaders are at the center of many concentric circles. They strengthen the group, forge consensus and negotiate a way forward. That kind of leadership is impactful, democratic, and, I would argue, more radical and sustainable, than the alternatives.

Indeed, it can be argued that it is its leaderful or group-centered leadership style that has allowed the Movement for Black Lives both to survive as long as it has and to remain relevant to the needs and aspirations of the people who are most likely to be targets of police and vigilante violence, while facing an intense and well-organized white backlash that has included political and police repression. Unlike what has proven to be true for traditional, charismatic civil rights leadership, it is difficult to stop a movement built from the grassroots with a few well-aimed bullets, or by discrediting or co-opting its leadership.[33]

Movement Demands, Successes, and Challenges

Demands

As has been seen, the Movement for Black Lives is not a single-issue reform movement. It is, instead, a multi-issue movement for the fundamental transformation of oppressive social structures, whether that oppression is based on racial designations, gender, sexual orientation, class, or a combination of those factors. On August 1, 2016, a few days after the 2016 Democratic National Convention, the Movement for Black Lives coalition of more than fifty organizations released its platform, with thirty-eight demands in six platform areas: "end the war on black people," "reparations," what the nation should "invest-divest" in and from, "economic justice," "community control," and "political power." Included within the ten demands under the category "end the war on black people" are the following, which are most relevant to this study's focus on the police and vigilante killings of African Americans: "an immediate end to the criminalization and dehumanization of Black youth," "an end to the war on Black trans, queer and gender nonconforming people," and "the demilitarization of law enforcement."[34]

The demands of the Movement for Black Lives are built on a wide-ranging vision and set of demands that came out of the Ferguson movement, which included the previously mentioned "De-militarization of Local Law Enforcement across the country." It also included demands for "a Comprehensive Review of systemic abuses by local police departments, including the public development of best practices," and "repurposing of law enforcement funds to support community based alternatives to incarceration and the conditioning of DOJ funding on non-discriminatory policing and the adoption of DOJ best practices." Other demands included "a Congressional Hearing investigating the criminalization of communities of color, racial profiling, police abuses and torture by law enforcement," support for "the Passage of the End

Racial Profiling Act," and that "the Obama Administration develops, legislates and enacts a National Plan of Action for Racial Justice."[35]

Another group, Campaign Zero, developed the following list of ten demands for the 2016 presidential campaign, with a focus specifically and exclusively on police violence: "end broken windows policing," "community oversight," "limit use of force," "independently investigate and prosecute;" "community representation," "body cameras/film the police," "training," "end for- profit policing," "demilitarization," and "fair police union contracts." By this last demand, Campaign Zero means contracts that do not shield the police from accountability for their actions.[36]

Successes

A movement's success can be measured in different ways. One is its ability to bring the issue it champions to public attention. A second is its capacity to mobilize the power needed to have that issue identified as a social problem that should be addressed. Third is the extent to which actual changes are made to address those concerns in ways that make a measurable difference.

When it comes to bringing the issue of the pervasive, disproportionate, and persistent police and vigilante killings of African Americans to national attention, the Movement for Black Lives has, through extensive social and conventional media coverage, made significant inroads in convincing many Americans that such killings are a social problem that should be addressed. Those gains in support for the movement have been especially noteworthy among America's youth. This should not be surprising since so many of those killed are young, and the young people who lead the movement—like young people generally—are especially adept in the use of social media. A poll of eighteen- to thirty-year-olds conducted in August 2016 found that 85 percent of African Americans, 67 percent of Asian Americans, and 62 percent of Latino Americans either somewhat supported or strongly supported the movement. But what was most surprising was that since June of that year there had been a ten-point increase—creating a slight majority (51 percent)—in the number of European Americans in that age group who responded that they either somewhat supported or strongly supported it. And because the movement has received extensive international coverage through both social and conventional media, its appeal is not limited to the United States. Inspired by Movement for Black Lives activism in the United States, movements against police repression have spread to countries throughout the world, including Canada, Britain, France, Palestine, Germany, Brazil, South Africa, and Senegal.[37]

The Movement for Black Lives has had such success in shining both a national and an international spotlight on the issue of disproportionate police and vigilante killings of African Americans that it was named as a runner-up for the 2015 *Time* Magazine "Person of the Year" award. In an article about its accomplishments, the magazine shed light on how the movement was making the difficult transition from bringing the issue to national attention to making it a national priority; or, as the author of that essay put it, turning "a protest cry into a genuine political force." As a case in point as to how the movement was doing that, *Time* took the reader inside a very tense meeting between movement activists and Hillary Clinton during the Democratic Party primary campaign—a "confrontation" that "turned out to be a catalyst." Days later, during a debate, Clinton railed against mass incarceration and called for the police to wear body cameras, and weeks after that—just as her main opponent, Bernie Sanders, was forced to do in response to disruptive protests at his campaign rallies—Clinton announced a campaign platform on criminal justice that, among other things, called for the demilitarization of the police and stronger federal investigations into police misconduct. Other successes include police chiefs and prosecutors deemed as unresponsive to demands for change being forced from their jobs and well-publicized prosecutions of police who had killed African Americans. As Brittany Packnett, a movement activist who served as a member of President Obama's task force on police reform, put it: "In 2015, we know we can both tell the story and change the story."[38]

Let's now take a closer look at what the Movement for Black Lives, then commonly known as Black Lives Matter, was able to pressure Barack Obama, Hillary Clinton, and Bernie Sanders into proposing, and many states into doing, to help make the lives of African Americans matter.

Task Force Recommendations, Campaign Promises, and State and Local Level Reforms

President Obama's December 18, 2014 signing of the executive order that established his Task Force on 21st Century Policing did not happen in a racial or political vacuum. That summer and fall, a wave of high-profile police killings of African Americans, which sparked massive nationwide protests and extensive media coverage, forced the Obama administration to abandon its usual policy of steering clear of what it had previously characterized as local matters. In July, Eric Garner was killed on Staten Island, NY; in August, it was Michael Brown in Ferguson, Missouri; in October, it was Laquan McDonald in Chicago; and in November, less than a month before President Obama signed that executive order, it was twelve-year-old Tamir Rice in Cleveland. Racial tensions were at boiling point and African Americans, President Obama's most loyal constituents, demanded action.[39]

The assignment for the task force was to identify police practices that could best reduce crime "while building public trust." To that end, it proposed numerous recommendations under the umbrella of the following two "overarching recommendations." First, the President should establish a National Crime and Justice Task Force to make recommendations for "comprehensive criminal justice reform." Second, he should initiate community-based programs to address poverty and related social issues. The task force report contained sixty-two specific recommendations and even more "action item" suggestions for the implementation of specific recommendations. Here I include only a sampling of some of those that are most directly relevant to this study.[40]

The Obama task force concluded that law enforcement agencies could achieve the goal of trust-building and legitimacy by: acknowledging "the role of policing in past and present injustice and discrimination"; establishing "a culture of transparency and accountability"; considering "the potential damage to public trust when implementing crime fighting strategies"; tracking "the level of trust in police by their communities just as they measure changes in crime"; and striving "to create a workforce that contains a broad range of diversity."[41]

The recommendations and action items most relevant to this study and its focus on making the police more accountable fall under the category of policy and oversight. One such recommendation calls for collaborating "with community members to develop policies and strategies." Another policy and oversight recommendation is having "comprehensive policies on the use of force that include training, investigations, prosecutions, data collection, and information sharing." As I noted earlier, specific recommendations in the report are followed by action items. There were six action items for the policies on the use of force recommendation. The first three are: "training on use of force should emphasize de-escalation and alternatives to arrest or summons in situations where appropriate"; policies that "mandate external and independent criminal investigations in cases of police use of force resulting in death, officer-involved shootings resulting in injury or death, or in-custody deaths;" and "policies that mandate the use of external and independent prosecutors in cases of police use of force resulting in death, officer-involved shootings resulting in injury or death, or in-custody deaths." Those were followed by policies that "require agencies to collect, maintain, and report data to the Federal Government on all officer-involved shootings, whether fatal or non-fatal, as well as any in-custody death" and "clearly state what types of information will be released, when, and in what situation, to maintain transparency," and the establishment of "a Serious Incident Review Board comprising sworn staff and community members to review cases involving officer-involved shootings and other serious incidents that have the potential to damage community trust or confidence in the agency." Two other use-of-force policy recommendations included in the taskforce report are the establishment of "some form of civilian oversight of law enforcement" and the adoption and enforcement of "policies prohibiting profiling and discrimination."[42]

As has been seen, few of the Obama police task force's recommendations entailed the federal government spending much money, changing power relationships, or making officers more accountable. Most seemed unrealistic in that they relied totally on the willingness of police departments to change and on relevant federal agencies providing them with the information and other resources with which to do so. The task force's basic assumption seemed to be that all that was needed for meaningful change was for the police departments to be told what the best policing practices were and to be given some encouragement to implement them.

As I mentioned earlier, in response to disruption by Movement for Black Lives activists, Hillary Clinton—whose success as a candidate was heavily dependent on African American voters—made criminal justice reform a centerpiece of her campaign. Clinton seemed to echo those demands in a statement made on July 8, 2016 that serves as a preface to the criminal justice reform section of her campaign website:

> People are crying out for criminal justice reform. Families are being torn apart by excessive incarceration. Young people are being threatened and humiliated by racial profiling. Children are growing up in homes shattered by prison and poverty. They're trying to tell us. We need to listen.[43]

The nine Clinton campaign promises most relevant to this study were placed under the category-heading "strengthen bonds of trust between communities and police." The first five of those were: "bringing law enforcement and communities together to develop national guidelines on the use of force by police officers"; "acknowledging that implicit bias still exists across society—even in the best police departments—and [tackling] it together"; "making new investments to support state-of-the-art law enforcement training programs at every level"; "supporting legislation to end racial profiling by federal, state, and local law enforcement officials"; and "strengthening the U.S. Department of Justice's pattern or practice unit—the unit that monitors civil rights violations—by increasing the department's resources, working to secure subpoena power, and improving data collection for pattern or practice investigations." The remaining four Clinton campaign promises were: "doubling funding for the U.S. Department of Justice 'Collaborative Reform' program" that encourages departments to innovate new policing strategies; "providing federal matching funds to make body cameras available to every police department in America"; "promoting oversight and accountability in use of controlled equipment, including by limiting the transfer of military equipment to local law enforcement from the federal government"; and "collecting and reporting national data to inform policing strategies and provide greater transparency and accountability when it comes to crime, officer-involved shootings, and deaths in custody." Other campaign promises that were aimed at reducing mass incarceration and helping to reintegrate those who had been incarcerated back into society would also make deadly encounters between the police and African Americans less likely.[44]

Although there is overlap between the Obama task force recommendations and Clinton's campaign promises, the Clinton proposals committed much more in the way of federal expenditures and clout to make the suggested changes happen. For example, as mentioned in an earlier chapter, Clinton promised that her administration would spend a billion dollars on research and training just to address her concern about implicit bias, and said she would push for new legislation to combat racial profiling at every level of government.[45]

Like Hillary Clinton, Bernie Sanders, who also courted the African American vote, also responded to disruption to his campaign on the part of Movement for Black Lives activists. He did so by hiring a Movement for Black Lives activist as part of his staff and adding an entire racial justice section to his campaign website. Its section on physical violence perpetrated by the state section began by listing the following names of people of color killed by the police or while in police custody: "Sandra Bland, Michael Brown, Rekia Boyd, Eric Garner, Walter Scott, Freddie Gray, Jessica Hernandez, Tamir Rice, Jonathan Ferrell, Oscar Grant, Antonio Zambrano-Montes, Samuel DuBose and Anastacio Hernandez-Rojas." And, as was for true for both the Obama task force and the Clinton campaign, it was clear that the Movement for Black Lives was a moving force behind those promises as Sanders' website continued: "Each of them died unarmed at the hands of police officers or in police custody. The chants are growing louder. People are angry and they have a right to be angry."[46]

Sanders made nine campaign promises that specifically targeted state-sponsored physical violence that disproportionately impacts African Americans. The first five were: "demilitarize our police forces so they don't look and act like invading armies"; "invest in community policing," including "increasing civilian oversight of police departments"; "create a police culture that allows for good officers to report the actions of bad officers without fear of retaliation and allows for a department to follow through on such reports"; have "police forces that reflect the diversity of our communities, including in the training academies and leadership"; and "establish a new model police training program ... with input from a broad segment of the community including activists and leaders from civil rights organizations."[47]

The remaining four of Sanders' campaign promises aimed at reducing police violence were: "federally fund and require body cameras for law enforcement officers to make it easier to hold them accountable"; "require police departments and states to collect data on all police shootings and deaths that take place while in police custody and make that data public"; establish "new rules on the allowable use of force" and training to de-escalate conflict, especially involving people with mental illness; and provide "more federal justice grant money" for states and local governments that make progress in carrying through on those reforms, while slashing such funds for those that do not.[48]

Like the Clinton campaign promises, more federal funds and clout would be used to bring about reforms than was the case with the Obama police task force recommendations. Of the three political sets of recommendations and promises discussed it was Sanders' website that came the closest in articulating the need, not just for such ameliorative reforms, but for fundamental change. As that website put it: "We need a societal transformation to make it clear that black lives matter and racism will not be accepted in a civilized country."[49]

There were also attempts at police reform at the state and local levels. Within a year of the nationwide protests of the killing of Michael Brown, twenty-four states passed at least forty new laws, including laws requiring police officers to wear body cameras, stipulating that they receive training to address racial bias, mandating independent investigations of police use of force, and placing limitations on the police use of military equipment. Unfortunately, a review of state initiatives by the Associated

Press concluded that "despite all that action, far more proposals have stalled or failed . and few states have done anything to change laws on when police are justified to use deadly force." That failure led NAACP president Cornell William Brooks to lament that "What we have right now in the country is an emerging consensus as to the need to act. What we don't have is a consensus as to how to act, what to act on and how to do this in some kind of priority order."[50]

Of course, not all the recommendations for police reform have come in the form of demands from Movement for Black Lives activists or as political platforms or other actions from the politicians they have pressured. Not only are movement activists and politics not monolithic, but the same is true of police officers. There are police officers who, due to factors such as their own experiences as racially oppressed people, the challenges they face in trying to administer large urban police departments, their progressive worldview and politics, their concerns about increasing racial tensions over policing, and of course pressure from movement activists, genuinely don't want things to continue as they have been. For example, in the aftermath of the Eric Garner killing, Blacks in Law Enforcement of America recommended that there should be legislation at the state level that defines what police actions are criminal, the creation of a state-wide special prosecutor to handle cases involving possible police criminal actions, and a requirement that police live in the communities they serve. The Law Enforcement Leaders to Reduce Crime and Incarceration, an organization comprising more than 175 police administrators and prosecutors, and leaders of other organizations that think reforms such as better training for the police in the use of force are needed, has expressed its apprehension about what will happen as a result of the Trump administration's shift from a civil rights to a law enforcement focus.[51]

As has been seen, bringing an issue to public attention is not the same as forcing those in power to make it a national, state, or local priority. Although the Movement for Black Lives made significant inroads toward the former end, it lost much of the ground it had gained within the halls of power as the "emerging consensus on the need to act" touted by NAACP head Cornell William Brooks dissipated after running into the "law and order"-focused political wall of a white racial backlash upon which Donald Trump successfully built his presidential campaign. For example, a poll of registered voters conducted six months after Trump took office found that 83 percent of African Americans had a favorable view of the movement, compared to only 35 percent of European Americans. With that—now institutionalized—white backlash, the movement was not able, at that point, to force the federal racial state to treat the disproportionate police and vigilante killings of African Americans as a problem the nation must mobilize its resources to address. But that was not for lack of effort or viable leadership, strategies, and tactics. However, as has been seen, there have been some concrete changes, including extremely pro-police prosecutors who have been voted out of office, police chiefs who have been fired or forced to implement various reform measures such as the use of body cameras, and police officers who are now well aware that their actions are being continuously monitored.[52]

More work is needed, however, to transform the disproportionate police and vigilante killings of African Americans from an issue largely of concern to African Americans and other people of color to a national priority. Until that happens, the actual changes that are possible will continue to be ameliorative and piecemeal, and we should not expect to see evidence of a significant decline in such killings. Indeed, with the Trump-election backlash it is unlikely that the federal government will even be willing to collect such statistics in the foreseeable future— which, as indicated earlier, is itself a political choice. But this should not be taken as a criticism of the movement. By definition, those who are oppressed have less power than their oppressors. Indeed, what makes the story of David and Goliath so compelling is the fact that it doesn't usually happen that way. Typically, when David goes against Goliath, no matter how determined or good of a rock slinger he is, if Goliath is big enough David will get smacked down to the ground, and it is Goliath who will be victorious. A sad lesson of U.S. history is that African Americans can have great leaders, brilliant strategies and tactics, fierce determination, and exceptional unity, and still remain oppressed. In the next section, I take a closer look at some of the challenges faced by the Movement for Black Lives.

Challenges

The most important challenge faced by the Movement for Black Lives is, of course, the white backlash it has provoked by challenging the racial status quo. That racial backlash has often cloaked itself in colorblind camouflage such as the attempts to drown out the words "Black Lives Matter" with shouts of "*All* Lives Matter." The FBI and local police departments have engaged in surveillance of movement activists, and a police officer has even brought a lawsuit against movement leaders whom he claimed were responsible for deaths of fellow officers.[53]

Other challenges are not so obvious. As a social and conventional media-driven movement, the Movement for Black Lives is having difficulty competing for the nation's attention with President Trump, who is quite skillful at keeping the nation's attention on himself and the outrageous things he says and does, often through early morning tweets. With so much attention on Trump and his often unusual antics there is now less national focus on social issues, including the police and vigilante killings of African Americans. Because the movement is so heavily dependent on media, a major challenge it faces is keeping the issue alive both in the national news and within African American communities when there is no "big event" spectacle that can capture national media attention, and when many movement supporters may experience a type of issue burnout that leads them to accept most killings as being so normal as not to merit even a tweet or Facebook posting.

Another major issue the movement faces today is where it receives its funding from, and how that impacts its activities. In a section of her book on the Black Lives Matter movement aptly titled "The Revolution Will Not Be Funded," Keeanga-Yamahtta Taylor warns of the co-opting influence of foundation funding from wealthy individuals and foundations such as the Soros and Ford foundations and Resource Generation. After noting that some organizations try to maintain their independence through membership dues and soliciting donations from the public at rallies, Taylor argues that the potential chilling impact of private funding "makes fully independent movement groups all the more necessary." As an example, she notes that, due to its dependence on funding from the American Fund for Public Service, the NAACP has shifted its focus from racial violence to education. As she puts it: "Ultimately, funders and other philanthropic organizations help to narrow the scope of organizing to changing 'policy' and other measures within the existing system." Taylor also expresses her concern that "foundation money also 'professionalizes' movements in a way that promotes careerism and the expectation that activism will be externally funded."[54]

That funding issue is a part of the larger challenge regarding how such a movement manages to retain its militancy and ambition for fundamental change as many of its most talented leaders trade autonomy for influence, pursuing careers that enable them to walk the halls of power through relatively high-paying jobs in politics and non-profit advocacy groups. In brief, the question is: how will careerism and the desire to have access to power impact the movement?

Finally, there is a challenge for the movement in the need to ensure it can retain a sharp and clear focus on the police and vigilante killings of African Americans and keep these under the microscope as it broadens its scope and engages in coalition-building. Will it be able to do that, or will it become a movement that, by focusing on multiple issues—or one issue that is assumed to be larger and encompassing, such as hypercapitalism—loses sight of what, for many, was its original concern? In brief, the challenge here is to avoid zooming in so closely that the larger socio-historical context of the killings is not seen, or out so broadly that clear sight of the killings themselves is lost.

The Necropolitics of Making All Lives Matter

As you have seen in this and previous chapters, there is no shortage of well-researched suggestions as to how to address the disproportionate police and vigilante killings of Africans Americans. And, of course, there are still other things that could be done. As the expression goes, "where there's a will, there's a way." However, the quick and dramatic change of momentum on an issue that was in the process of being transformed into a national priority prior to the election of Donald Trump reminds us that ultimately those killings are a political phenomenon, which can only be addressed politically.

Put differently, such violence can best be viewed through the lens of necropolitics—that is, the state's "power and capacity to dictate who may live and who must die." Viewed in this way, the key question becomes: what can African Americans and their supporters do during this repressive Trump era of American politics and race relations, and whatever may follow, to *make* their lives matter? As McAdam put it in explaining why the generation and sustainability of African American insurgency is dependent on having a political environment that is vulnerable to its pressures:

> the survival of a social movement requires that insurgents be able to maintain and successfully utilize their newly acquired political leverage to advance collective interests. If they are able to do so, the movement is likely to survive. If, on the other hand, insurgent groups fail to maintain a favorable bargaining position vis-à-vis other groups in the political arena, the movement faces extinction. In short, the ongoing exercise of significant political leverage remains the key to the successful development of the movement.[55]

In brief, the continued effectiveness of the Movement for Black Lives as a national movement is likely to depend on its ability to identify and exploit the vulnerabilities of the various branches and levels of the racial state, as well as the other key institutions that comprise American society. This might entail African Americans and other concerned citizens mobilizing to target, through disruption and non-cooperation, specific government and private entities which they see as being hostile or insensitive to their interests. That could include, but certainly not be limited to, refusal to co-operate with police and investigative bodies; the jury nullification practice of not convicting African American criminal defendants; refusal to pay taxes, to serve in the military, or to respond to census surveys; work slowdowns; economic boycotts of businesses that support repressive politicians and policies; and international exposure of U.S. human rights abuses. Given the size and power of the African American community, it should not be difficult to imagine numerous ways in which the Movement for Black Lives could collectively bring the normal workings of American society to a halt until its concerns are taken seriously.

Political Solutions: Big and Small

In brief, what I am again stressing is that the pervasive, disproportionate, and persistent police and vigilante killings of African Americans are

ultimately a *political* issue that can only be seriously addressed by changing *power relations.* Here, in discussing both ameliorative and radical
solutions to the problem, I will limit my focus to political solutions—
solutions that either stop the targeting of African Americans or ensure
that there is sufficient accountability to prevent such killings from happening with impunity when they do. I begin with ameliorative solutions.

Making Things Better

Here is a list of some things I believe can be done to help reduce the
number of police and vigilante killings of African Americans by making
those responsible more accountable.

1. Establish a Movement for Black Lives Foundation to raise and
    distribute funding to finance law enforcement accountability ini-
    tiatives. The tax-deductible funding could come from celebrities,
    fundraising concerts and shows, and ordinary individuals.
2. Establish local, state, and national data centers and archives for all
    police and vigilante killings.
3. Establish a legal defense hotline of pro bono lawyers to advise peo-
    ple of their rights before and, when possible, during and after their
    encounters with law enforcement officers and vigilantes.
4. Encourage "whistleblowing" by police officers and others employed
    within the criminal justice system by providing them with the
    financial, legal, media, and other support they need.
5. Monitor the policies and pay-outs of companies that provide local
    governments with insurance that covers police misconduct.
6. Monitor and, when possible, become involved in the negotiation of
    police union contracts to ensure that they don't provide unreason-
    able protection for officers who use lethal force.
7. Monitor and make public the records of the handling of local
    police and vigilante killings by mayors, police chiefs, prosecutors,
    and judges.
8. Develop police and vigilante accountability political platforms to
    be endorsed by candidates for elected office at every branch and
    level of government.

9. Distribute smartphone apps to advise those confronted by the police and vigilantes and to record those encounters on cloud-based servers.
10. Pressure local police departments to establish civilian review boards.
11. Pressure state and local governments to appoint special prosecutors to handle all police killings.
12. Bring lawsuits that challenge existing laws and court rulings regarding when the police may use lethal force.
13. Organize neighborhood "Copwatch" groups to monitor police and vigilante activity.
14. Make appeals to the United Nations to investigate and monitor the persistence of the disproportionate police and vigilante killings of African Americans as a violation of their human rights and its anti-genocide pact.

Forcing Fundamental Change

Ultimately significant changes will come only with major changes in U.S. racial and economic relations. As Paul Butler puts it in his explanation of why piecemeal liberal reforms of the system to make it fairer will not work, "The system is now working the way it is supposed to, and that makes black lives matter less. That system must be dismantled and the United States of American must . . . be 'remade.'" The following actions are radical not only in that their goal is to bring about fundamental change but also in terms of the commitment they require based on the harsh, and possibly violent, reactions they are likely to provoke from those intent on preserving the racial status quo.[56]

1. *Massive and sustained protests* that disrupt every aspect of American life (e.g., work, politics, transportation, religious services, and sporting events).
2. *Economic boycotts* that target all economic activity in communities that tolerate the lack of police and vigilante accountability.
3. *Programs of non-cooperation* including jury nullification, refusal to pay taxes, and refusal to serve in the military.

4. *General strikes and slowdowns* in which African Americans and their supporters refrain from making their normal contributions to society (e.g., work and school).
5. When necessary, *the establishment of armed militias for self-defense.*

Conclusion

Lessons Learned and Unfinished Business

In this study, I provided socio-historical evidence that the police and vigilante killings of African Americans can best be understood as political violence deployed as a violence-centered racial control mechanism. The historical evidence presented suggests that as long as oppressive racial and economic conditions persist there will be some forms of racial control systems and mechanisms. That is, escape from the vicious cycle of partial victories followed by new and often more intractable forms of oppression is possible only with fundamental changes in this nation's race relations and its economic system that make such racial control systems and mechanisms both unnecessary and intolerable. In brief, the main lesson learned from this study is that the unfinished business, for those truly committed to making this a nation where all lives do indeed matter, is not the crafting of dozens more recommendations as to how to ameliorate the disproportionate police and vigilante killings of African Americans and other forms of oppression we face, but, a radical transformation of America's racial and economic orders. As Martin Luther King, Jr. concluded decades ago: "'Where do we go from here?'. . . we must honestly face the fact that the movement must address itself to the question of restructuring the whole of American society."[57]

So, Where Do We Go from Here?

Early in this chapter I discussed the socio-historical conditions that led to the rise and demise of African American insurgency. That examination raised the sobering question of the extent to which the Movement for Black Lives can be sustained when the conditions that spurred its emergence have changed significantly. For example, with a less inviting and more repressive social and political climate for such protests and the reforms they seek under the current racially repressive Trump era of U.S. history, will large numbers of African Americans continue to believe that change is possible through their collective action? As I noted earlier, such keeping of the faith is especially difficult at a time when there is a president who is skilled at keeping the media focused on himself and his often outrageous actions such that there is little space for the coverage of social issues, especially those that seem, to many, so intractable that they are increasingly accepted as just a normal fact of American life.

The good news regarding the Movement for Black Lives during the rise of Trumpism is, of course, that this movement, so sorely needed at this time, is already in place. While it is not likely to die, the movement will be challenged to make changes as it adjusts to its new racial and political environment. The reason why the Movement for Black Lives is unlikely to die despite these and other major challenges goes way beyond issues of its adaptability, leadership, strategies, and tactics. It is difficult to imagine that if the killings continue, African Americans will simply accept what many of us see as open season on what we value most: our children. So the real question, as I see it, is not *if* the movement will survive, but *what it will look like* in this more repressive environment. For example, until the national political climate is changed, the Movement for Black Lives may continue with less national news coverage, less support from European Americans, and even greater attention placed on change at the local level. Its focus may be on making states, cities, and other places where African Americans have more political clout, more responsible.[58]

And while most supporters continue to engage in peaceful protests, others may become so frustrated that they no longer see this as viable. As happened in 2016 in Dallas and Baton Rouge, after the killings of Alton Sterling and Philando Castile, some African Americans may resort to killing police officers and vigilantes. Others may engage in the type of militia-styled, gun-brandishing self-defense and community patrolling conducted by the Black Panthers and other organizations during the Black Power stage of the civil rights movement. The lessons of American history suggest that either, or both, are likely to provoke a huge white backlash and the wrath of an angry and powerful racial state repressive apparatus as still more violence is unleashed to control a criminalized African American insurgency. But, given the violent history of this nation and its treatment of the racially oppressed, it would be foolish for African Americans to take the option of self-defense off the table.

Again, assuming that it will survive, we are left with important questions regarding the future of the Movement for Black Lives. Will the movement continue to grow and develop increasingly more effective strategies and tactics? Did it reach its peak in 2016, just as the civil rights movement did in 1963, more than a half century earlier, with its successful Birmingham movement and the March on Washington? Or will historians a hundred years from now see the movement as a permanent feature of American race relations, with many peaks and valleys? Finally, no matter what its duration, trajectory, form, and name, will the movement be an effective force in making black lives matter?

While I don't know the answers to these questions, my faith in humanity, and more specifically African Americans as a people, impels me to conclude that the movement, which includes at its center the basic human right to live, must continue, and that it will prevail. I conclude this book, therefore, with the following challenge, originally made in an essay I wrote shortly after the killing of Michael Brown in Ferguson, Missouri as I began to formulate my ideas for this book:

> Ultimately, it is power that explains oppression and it is only by changing power relations that people can end it. No oppressor is going to take his or her foot off of someone's neck because it is the right, the rational, and the reasonable thing to do as made clear by some wonderful sociological study. That foot can only be removed by us, and only if we muster the courage and the power to remove it.[59]

I ended that essay, as I conclude this book, with a quotation from Frederick Douglass that I think best articulates what African Americans and others fighting for social justice have learned from centuries of struggle: "power concedes nothing without a demand. It never did and it never will."

Notes

1. Noel A. Cazenave, "'Black Lives Matter' Versus 'All Lives Matter': Latest Racial Battle over Language," *Racism Review*, September 15, 2015, www.racismreview.com/blog/2015/09/15/black-lives-matter-versus-all-lives-matter-latest-racial-battle-over-language/, Accessed March 30, 2017; Sarah Viets, "Meet White Lives Matter: The Racist Response to the Black Lives Matter Movement," Southern Poverty Law Center, Hatewatch, March 18, 2016, www.splcenter.org/hatewatch/2016/03/18/meet-white-lives-matter-racist-response-black-lives-matter-movement, Accessed March 30, 2017.

2. Megan Lasher, "Read the Full Transcript of Jesse Williams' Powerful Speech on Race at the Bet Awards," *Time.com*, June 27, 2016, time.com/4383516/jesse-williams-bet-speech-transcript/, Accessed March 16, 2017; Donie O'Sullivan and Megan Thomas, "Beyoncé Pays Tribute to Alton Sterling and Philando Castile at Concert," CNN, July 7, 2016, www.cnn.com/2016/07/07/entertainment/beyonces-open-letter-on-police-shootings/, Accessed March 16, 2017.

3. Lasher, "Read the Full Transcript of Jesse Williams' Powerful Speech on Race at the BET Awards"; "Beyoncé, Freedom Lyrics," *Genius,* no date, genius.com/beyonce-freedom-lyrics, Accessed March 16, 2017; O'Sullivan and Thomas, "Beyoncé Pays Tribute to Alton Sterling and Philando Castile at Concert."

4. Doug McAdam, *Political Process and the Development of Black Insurgency: 1930–1970* (Chicago, IL: University of Chicago Press, 1999), 51–53, 59.

5. McAdam, *Political Process and the Development of Black Insurgency: 1930–1970*, 65–66, 132.

6. Alicia Garza, "A Herstory of the #BlackLivesMatterMovement by Garza," *The Feminist Wire*, October 7, 2014, www.thefeministwire.com/2014/10/blacklivesmatter-2/, Accessed November 12, 2016; Christopher J. Lebron, *The Making of Black Lives Matter: A Brief History of an Idea* (New York: Oxford University Press, 2017), xi.

7. Lebron, *The Making of Black Lives Matter*, xv–xxi.

8. John Hope Franklin and Alfred A. Moss, Jr., *From Slavery to Freedom: A History of African Americans* (New York: Alfred A. Knopf, 1994), 140, 142; Leslie Howard Owens, *This Species of Property: Slave Life and Culture in the Old South* (New York: Oxford University Press, 1977), 74, 79–80, 82–83, 93, 104; "Slavery, the American Revolution, and the Constitution," Digital History, no date, www.digitalhistory.uh.edu/active_learning/explorations/revolution/revolution_slavery.cfm, Accessed September 5, 2016; "The War of 1812," PBS, www.pbs.org/wned/war-of-1812/essays/black-soldier-and-sailors-war/, Accessed September 5, 2016; W.E.B. DuBois, *Black Reconstruction in America, 1860–1880* (New York: Touchstone, 1992), 65, 104, 121.

9. Equal Justice Initiative, *Lynching in America: Confronting the Legacy of Racial Terror, Report Summary* (Montgomery, AL: Equal Justice Initiative, 2016, 2nd ed.), 18–19, eji.org/sites/default/files/lynching-in-america-second-edition-summary.pdf, Accessed June 14, 2017; Lerone Bennett, Jr., *Before the Mayflower: A History of Black America* (New York: Penguin Books, 1984), 271–72.

10. David Garland, *Peculiar Institution: America's Death Penalty in an Age of Abolition* (Cambridge, MA: Belknap Press, 2010), 218–19; The Movement for Black Lives, "Our Platform," "End the War on Black People," no date, https://policy.m4bl.org, Accessed August 23, 2016.

11. Evelyn Brooks Higginbotham, *Righteous Discontent: The Women's Movement in the Black Baptist Church, 1880–1920* (Cambridge, MA: Harvard University Press, 1994), 14, 185–87; Michelle Alexander, *The New Jim Crow: Mass Incarceration in the Age of Colorblindness* (New York: The New Press, 2012), 15, 212; The Movement for Black Lives, "Our Platform," "End the War on Black People," 1–2; Peter Baker, "2016 Candidates are United in Call to Alter Justice System," *New York Times*, April 27, 2015,

www.nytimes.com/2015/04/28/us/politics/being-less-tough-on-crime-is-2016-consensus.html, Accessed June 14, 2017; Joseph Tanfani and Evan Halper, "Sessions Restores Tough Drug War Policies that Trigger Mandatory Minimum Sentences," *Los Angeles Times,* May 12, 2017, www.latimes.com/politics/la-na-politics-sessions-drugwar-20170511-story.html, Accessed May 12, 2017.

12. Manning Marable, *Race, Reform, and Rebellion: The Second Reconstruction and Beyond in Black Americas, 1945–2006* (Jackson, MS: University Press of Mississippi, 2007), 221; Marilynn Johnson, *Street Justice: A History of Police Violence in New York City* (Boston, MA: Beacon Press, 2003), 1, 8.

13. Paul A. Gilje, "Racial Disturbances against Blacks," in Waldo F. Martin, Jr. and Patricia Sullivan, eds., *Civil Rights in the United States, Volume 2* (New York: Macmillan Reference USA, 2000), 627–28.

14. William M. Tuttle, Jr., *Race Riot: Chicago in the Red Summer of 1919* (New York: Atheneum, 1970), 14; William M. Tuttle, "Red Summers of 1917–1921," in Waldo F. Martin, Jr. and Patricia Sullivan, eds., *Civil Rights in the United States, Volume 2* (New York: Macmillan Reference USA, 2000), 643; Scott Ellsworth, *Death in a Promised Land: The Tulsa Race Riot of 1921* (Baton Rouge, LA: Louisiana State University Press, 1982), 6–7, 17.

15. Robert M. Fogelson, "The Police, the Negroes, and the Outbreak of the Nineteen-Sixties Riots," *Political Science Quarterly*, 1968, 83 (2), 217, 219–20, 243; The National Advisory Commission on Civil Disorders, *Report of the National Advisory Commission on Civil Disorders* (New York: Bantam Books, 1968), 143; Robert M. Fogelson, *Violence as Protest: A Study of Riots and Ghettos* (Garden City, NY: Doubleday, 1971), 100.

16. Fogelson, *Violence as Protest*, 31, 102, 189; Joe R. Feagin and Harlan Hahn, *Ghetto Revolts: The Politics of Violence in American Cities* (New York: Macmillan, 1973), 43.

17. Manny Fernandez, Richard Perez-Pena, and Jonah Engel Bromwich, "Five Dallas Officers Were Killed as Payback, Police Chief Says," *New York Times*, July 8, 2016, www.nytimes.com/2016/07/09/us/dallas-police-shooting.html, Accessed May 15, 2017; Alan Blinder, "The 3 Officers Killed in Baton Rouge," *New York Times*, July 18, 2016, www.nytimes.com/2016/07/19/us/the-3-officers-killed-in-baton-rouge.html, Accessed May 15, 2017.

18. Paul Butler, *Chokehold: Policing Black Men* (New York: The New Press, 2017), 246–47.

19. Garza, "A Herstory of the #BlackLivesMatterMovement by Garza"; Elizabeth Day, "#BlackLivesMatter: The Birth of a New Civil Rights Movement," *The Guardian*, July 19, 2015, www.theguardian.com/world/2015/jul/19/blacklivesmatter-birth-civil-rights-movement, Accessed March 18, 2017.

20. Day, "#BlackLivesMatter."

21. Garza, "A Herstory of the #BlackLivesMatterMovement by Garza."

22. Garza, "A Herstory of the #BlackLivesMatterMovement by Garza."

23. Michael McLaughlin, "The Dynamic History of #BlackLivesMatter Explained: This Is How a Hashtag Transformed into a Movement," *Huffington Post*, February 29, 2016, www.huffingtonpost.com/entry/history-black-lives-matter_us_56d0a3b0e4b0871f60e-b4af5, Accessed November 15, 2016; *New York Times* word search by year using Proquest database. Results are for the newspaper only. They do not include blogs, podcasts, websites, or magazines. Accessed August 4, 2017.

24. Keeanga-Yamahtta Taylor, *From #BlackLivesMatter to Black Liberation* (Chicago, IL: Haymarket Books, 2016), 151; The Movement for Black Lives, "About Us," no date, https://policy.m4bl.org/about/, Accessed March 23, 2017.

25. Taylor, *From #BlackLivesMatter to Black Liberation*, 161.

26. Higginbotham, *Righteous Discontent*, 14, 185–87.

27. Black Lives Matter, "11 Major Misconceptions about the Black Lives Matter Movement," no date, blacklivesmatter.com/11-major-misconceptions-about-the-black-lives-matter-

movement/, Accessed March 22, 2017; Garza, "A Herstory of the #BlackLivesMatter-Movement by Garza;" Carl C. Chancellor, "How #BlackLivesMatter Deeply Connects to Black Power Movement," *USA Today*, February 1, 2016, www.usatoday.com/story/news/nation-now/2016/02/01/black-lives-matter-black-power-movement/78991894/, Accessed March 22, 2017.

28. Taylor, *From #BlackLivesMatter to Black Liberation*, 159–63.

29. Jelani Cobb, "The Matter of Black Lives: A New Kind of Movement Found Its Moment. What Will Its Future Be?," *The New Yorker*, March 14, 2016, www.newyorker.com/magazine/2016/03/14/where-is-black-lives-matter-headed, Accessed November 15, 2016.

30. Taylor, *From #BlackLivesMatter to Black Liberation*, 158–63.

31. Taylor, *From #BlackLivesMatter to Black Liberation*, 167–68.

32. Taylor, *From #BlackLivesMatter to Black Liberation*, 176.

33. Danielle C. Belton, "Leaderless or Leader-ful?," *The Root*, August 10, 2015, www.theroot.com/leaderless-or-leader-ful-1790860733, Accessed March 22, 2017; Barbara Ransby, "Ella Taught Me: Shattering the Myth of the Leaderless Movement," *Colorlines*, June 12, 2015, www.colorlines.com/articles/ella-taught-me-shattering-myth-leaderless-movement, Accessed March 22, 2017.

34. Robin D.G. Kelley, "What Does Black Lives Matter Want?," *Boston Review*, August 17, 2016, bostonreview.net/books-ideas/robin-d-g-kelley-movement-black-lives-vision, Accessed March 23, 2017; Trymaine Lee, "Black Lives Matter Releases Policy Agenda," NBC News, August 1, 2016, www.nbcnews.com/news/us-news/black-lives-matter-releases-policy-agenda-n620966, Accessed March 23, 2017; The Movement for Black Lives, "Our Platform." Underlining in the original.

35. Ferguson Action, "Ferguson Action Demands," April 25, 2016, www.uucsj.org/wp-content/uploads/2016/05/Ferguson-Action-Demands.pdf, Accessed March 23, 2017. Capitalizations as in original.

36. Campaign Zero, "We Can End Police Violence in America," no date, www.joincampaignzero.org/#campaign, Accessed March 23, 2017.

37. Krista Gray, "Here Is Proof that Hashtag Activism Can Drive Real World Change," Brit & Co, March 25, 2016, www.brit.co/hashtag-activism/, Accessed March 20, 2017; Jesse J. Holland and Emily Swanson, Associated Press, "Poll: Support for Black Lives Matter Grows among White Youth," PBS Newshour, September 5, 2016, www.pbs.org/newshour/rundown/poll-support-black-lives-matter-grows-among-white-youth/, Accessed March 20, 2017; Haweya Fadal, "#BlackLivesMatter Goes Global," NBC News, August 11, 2016, www.nbcnews.com/news/nbcblk/blacklivesmatter-goes-global-n618156, Accessed March 21, 2017; Thales Carneiro, "Black Lives Matter Protest Rio Police Violence Ahead of Olympics," Reuters, World News, www.reuters.com/article/us-olympics-rio-race-idUSKCN1030XU, Accessed March 21, 2017.

38. Alex Altman, "Person of the Year, The Short List, No. 4, Black Lives Matter," *Time*, December 21, 2015, www.time.com/time-person-of-the-year-2015-runner-up-black-lives-matter/, Accessed March 24, 2017.

39. President's Task Force on 21st Century Policing, *Final Report of the President's Task Force on 21st Century Policing* (Washington, DC: Office of Community Oriented Policing Services, 2015), 1.

40. President's Task Force on 21st Century Policing, *Final Report of the President's Task Force on 21st Century Policing*, 1, 7–8, 85–99.

41. President's Task Force on 21st Century Policing, *Final Report of the President's Task Force on 21st Century Policing*, 85–86. The quotations cited are not of the full recommendations or action items; but are, instead, presented to capture their essential points.

42. President's Task Force on 21st Century Policing, *Final Report of the President's Task Force on 21st Century Policing*, 2, 87–90.

43. Hillary for America: Hillary Clinton 2016, Issues, Criminal Justice Reform, no date, www.hillaryclinton.com/issues/criminal-justice-reform/, Accessed March 29, 2017.

44. Hillary for America: Hillary Clinton 2016, Issues, Criminal Justice Reform. Bold print in the original removed. Some of these recommendations quotations have been abbreviated.

45. Hillary for America: Hillary Clinton 2016, Issues, Criminal Justice Reform.

46. Bernie Sanders for President, Bernie Sanders on the Issues, Racial Justice, Physical Violence, no date, www.berniesanders.com/issues/racial-justice/, Accessed March 29, 2017.

47. Bernie Sanders for President, Bernie Sanders on the Issues, Racial Justice, Physical Violence.

48. Bernie Sanders for President, Bernie Sanders on the Issues, Racial Justice, Physical Violence.

49. Bernie Sanders for President, Bernie Sanders on the Issues, Racial Justice, Physical Violence.

50. David A. Lieb, "Ferguson: Killing Spurs 40 New Laws," *Hartford Courant*, August 3, 2015, A1, A8.

51. Damon K. Jones, "Blacks in Law Enforcement of America Recommendations," *Impact New York*, February 15, 2016, www.impacny.tumblr.com/, Accessed March 23, 2017; Timothy Williams and Richard A. Oppel, Jr., "Police Chiefs Contend Trump's Law Enforcement Priorities are Out of Step," *New York Times*, February 13, 2017, A8.

52. Jonathan Easley, "Poll: 57 Percent Have Negative View of Black Lives Matter Movement," *The Hill*, August 2, 2017, www.thehill.com/homenews/campaign/344985-poll-57-percent-have-negative-view-of-black-lives-matter-movement, Accessed August 4, 2017.

53. Cazenave, "'Black Lives Matter' Versus 'All Lives Matter'"; Ben Norton, "FBI, Homeland Security Sued for Records on Surveillance of Black Lives Matter Activists," *Salon*, October 20, 2016, www.salon.com/2016/10/20/fbi-homeland-security-sued-for-records-on-surveillance-of-black-lives-matter-activists/, Accessed March 30, 2017; Travis M. Andrews, "Black Dallas Police Officer Sues Black Lives Matter on Behalf of 'Christians, Jews and Caucasians,' Others," *Washington Post*, September 21, 2016, www.washingtonpost.com/news/morning-mix/wp/2016/09/21/black-dallas-police-officer-sues-black-lives-matter-on-behalf-of-christians-jews-and-caucasians-others/?utm_term=.7341d5ded744, Accessed March 30, 2017.

54. Taylor, *From #BlackLivesMatter to Black Liberation*, 177–80.

55. Achille Mbembe, "Necropolitics," *Public Culture*, 2003, 15 (1), 11; McAdam, *Political Process and the Development of Black Insurgency: 1930–1970*, 51–52.

56. Butler, *Chokehold*, 200.

57. Martin Luther King, Jr. with Cornel West, ed., *The Radical King: Martin Luther King, Jr.* (Boston, MA: Beacon Press, 2015), 176.

58. Associated Press, "Black Lives Matter Activists Turn Attention to Statehouses," NBC News, April 2, 2017, www.nbcnews.com/news/nbcblk/black-lives-matter-activists-turn-attention-statehouses-n741741, Accessed April 3, 2017.

59. Noel A. Cazenave, "Understanding Our Many Fergusons: Kill Lines—The Will, the Right and the Need to Kill," *Truthout*, September 29, 2014, www.truth-out.org/opinion/item/26484-understanding-our-many-fergusons-kill-lines-the-will-the-right-and-the-need-to-kill, Accessed March 1, 2017; Frederick Douglass, "West Indian Emancipation," Speech Delivered at Canandaigua, New York, August 3, 1857," in Philip S. Foner, ed., *Frederick Douglass: Selected Speeches and Writings* (Chicago, IL: Lawrence Hill, 1999), 367.

INDEX

ABOUT THE AUTHOR

Noel A. Cazenave is Professor of Sociology at the University of Connecticut (UConn). He is also on the faculty of the Urban and Community Studies program of UConn's Hartford campus and is a faculty affiliate with UConn's Africana Studies Institute and its American Studies Program. His recent and current work is in the areas of: racism theory, U.S. poverty policy, political sociology, urban sociology, criminal justice, and the sociology of emotions. In addition to numerous journal articles, book chapters, and other publications, Professor Cazenave co-authored *Welfare Racism: Playing the Race Card against America's Poor*, which won five book awards, and has since then published *Impossible Democracy: The Unlikely Success of the War on Poverty Community Action Programs*, *The Urban Racial State: Managing Race Relations in American Cities*, and *Conceptualizing Racism: Breaking the Chains of Racially Accommodative Language*. His current book project is tentatively titled *The Courage to Be Kind*.